The Noetic Effects
of Sin

The Noetic Effects
of Sin

*A Historical and Contemporary
Exploration of
How Sin Affects Our Thinking*

Stephen K. Moroney

LEXINGTON BOOKS
Lanham • Boulder • New York • Oxford

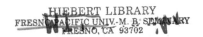

LEXINGTON BOOKS

Published in the United States of America
by Lexington Books
4720 Boston Way, Lanham, Maryland 20706

12 Hid's Copse Road
Cumnor Hill, Oxford OX2 9JJ, England

British Library Cataloguing in Publication Information Available

Library of Congress Cataloging-in-Publication Data

Moroney, Stephen K., 1962–
    The noetic effects of sin : a historical and contemporary exploration of how sin
affects our thinking / Stephen K. Moroney.
        p.   cm.
    Includes bibliographical references and index.
    ISBN 0-7391-0018-1 (hardcover : alk. paper)
    1. Sin—Psychology. I. Title.

BT715 M75   2000
241′.3—dc21   99-048063
                                                                CIP

Printed in the United States of America

♾™ The paper used in this publication meets the minimum requirements of American
National Standard for Information Sciences—Permanence of Paper for Printed Library
Materials, ANSI/NISO Z39.48–1992.

Contents

Preface

This book examines the frequently neglected topic of how sin distorts human thinking, a phenomenon known as the noetic effects of sin. Many Christian thinkers have acknowledged, in passing, that sin influences our thinking (see appendix two), but few have delved into the subject in great depth. The first two chapters of this book focus on John Calvin, Abraham Kuyper, and Emil Brunner because they have formulated especially detailed models of the ways in which sin affects our reasoning. Useful insights can be gleaned from each of these three theologians, though problems in their models indicate the need for a more adequate contemporary treatment of the subject. The final section of chapter two sets forth a new model which extends beyond all previous views by relating the noetic effects of sin to the complex and unpredictable interaction between the object of knowledge and the knowing subject. The new model is further distinguished from preceding views by examining the noetic effects of corporate (not just individual) sin.

The last three chapters discuss some of the implications of the noetic effects of sin for modern currents of thought. Chapter three investigates the rationalist theology of Wolfhart Pannenberg, and chapter four focuses on the reformed epistemology of Alvin Plantinga and Nicholas Wolterstorff. The argument in both cases is that these influential scholars have not yet accounted sufficiently for the ways in which sin distorts our thinking. Chapter five undertakes a cross-disciplinary study of what social psychology and Christian theology contribute to our understanding of one particular manifestation of the noetic effects of sin, namely the fact that we humans consistently engage in self-serving cognitive distortion, thinking of ourselves more highly than we ought.

In brief, the book attempts to answer two main questions. (1) What can be learned from past Christian thinkers as their thoughts are criticized and modified in the process of developing a new model of how sin affects our thinking? (2) What are the interdisciplinary implications of the noetic effects of sin for some prominent ideas in the fields of theology, philosophy, and psychology? Though sin's influence on our thinking has long been recognized, to my knowledge there are no lengthy, concentrated studies on the subject. This book attempts to fill this lacuna. The primary audience for the book is scholars, advanced students, and pastors, though the text is written so as to be accessible to interested lay persons as well.

This book includes reworked material from two essays: "How Sin Affects Scholarship: A New Model," *Christian Scholar's Review* 28:3 (spring 1999): 432-451; and "Thinking of Ourselves More Highly Than We Ought: A Psychological and Theological Analysis," from a forthcoming InterVarsity Press book edited by Timothy Phillips and Mark McMinn. Used by permission of InterVarsity Press, P.O. Box 1400, Downer's Grove, IL 60515.

I would like to thank several colleagues and relatives for their suggestions and encouragement during the production of this book. Special thanks go to Janice Anderson, Stephanie Fair, Doug Henry, John Moroney, Margaret Moroney, Teresa Pittinger, Bruce Swaffield, Geoffrey Wainwright, Duane Watson, and Helen Williams. Above all I thank my wife, Sue, whose ideas helped to shape the book and whose support made its completion possible.

Chapter 1

Calvin's Teachings on Reason and the Noetic Effects of Sin

I. Introduction

John Calvin (1509-1564) had much to say about the ways in which sin distorts our thinking, though his pronouncements on this topic have received very little direct scholarly attention. There is much literature devoted to Calvin's views concerning the natural knowledge of God, natural theology, natural law, common grace, and other related topics, and this literature addresses tangentially Calvin's view of the noetic effects of sin. There is, however, only one major study which focuses on Calvin's view of human reason, and there are no major studies on Calvin's account of the noetic effects of sin.[1]

The one extensive study on Calvin's view of human reason is a doctoral dissertation by Leroy Nixon, later published, with some revisions, as a book.[2] The major problem with Nixon's book is that he anachronistically uses mainly twentieth-century writings in the philosophy of religion to construct the categories which serve as a grid through which he reads Calvin. A few of the works which Nixon uses to determine "the basic questions about human reason which are raised in any philosophy of religion" are H. J. Blackham's *Six Existentialist Thinkers* (1952), William James's *The Varieties of Religious Experience* (1902), Karl Jasper's *Reason and Anti-Reason in Our Time* (1952), E. C. Massner's *Bishop Butler and the Age of Reason* (1936), D. L. Scudder's *Tennant's Philosophical Theology* (1936), and H. N. Wieman's *American Philosophies of Religion* (1936).[3]

Obviously, when twentieth-century existential and American philosophies are used to establish the categories for analyzing sixteenth-century theology, some problems may arise in producing a historically responsible exposition. Nixon himself notes (with apparent surprise) the fact that Calvin's teachings do not fit neatly into his prefabricated grid.[4] This methodological flaw causes Nixon's analysis to pay inadequate attention to the crucial distinctions which Calvin made between human reason at creation, fallen human reason, and redeemed human reason. So, there are some serious shortcomings in what, to my knowledge, is the only lengthy publication on Calvin's view of reason.

Like everyone else, I too read Calvin through a particular set of interpretive lenses, but the creation-fall-redemption schema which I use in my exposition is implicit throughout Calvin's thought, and indeed is explicit in some of his remarks about human reason.[5] Thus, I contend that creation, fall, and redemption are not alien categories which I impose on Calvin's view of human reason, but are categories which were integral to his understanding of human reason.

It can be argued that Calvin's understanding of human reason also included a fourth category—that of consummation or glorification—because he included this category in his discussion of the *imago dei*.[6] But I have omitted consummation or glorification as a fourth category in my exposition because I was unable to find any discussion by Calvin of "glorified human reason," or how our reason might function in heaven.

My primary goal in the expositional part of this chapter is to fill an important gap in present Calvin scholarship by providing a historically responsible exposition of Calvin's understanding of human reason, with a special focus on his teachings on the noetic effects of sin.[7] My main sources are Calvin's *Institutes* and *Commentaries*, though I also occasionally use his sermons and other treatises as these bear directly on the topic.

My research focuses primarily on the *Institutes* and on Calvin's comments on key biblical passages (Genesis 1-11; Isaiah 6:8-13, 19:11-15, 29:9-16, 40:12-17; Ezekiel 11:17-21; Matthew 6:22-24, 11:25-30, 13:1-17; John 1:1-13, 8:12-14; Acts 17:16-34, 28:21-31; Romans 1:18-2:2, 8:5-8, 11:33-12:2; 1 Corinthians 1:14-3:4; 2 Corinthians 3:4-4:6; and Ephesians 4:17-24). An exhaustive examination of Calvin's writings or even just Calvin's *Commentaries* is beyond the scope of the present study. For general readers I have provided references which can be located in nearly all translations, citing the *Institutes* by book, chapter, and section, and citing the *Commentaries* by biblical book and verse. For specialists I have provided references to the originals, with *CO* and *OS* used in the customary way.

In the first part of this chapter (section II) I make every effort to allow Calvin to speak for himself.[8] The reader who simply wants to hear Calvin's voice may read the text without distracting excursions to the endnotes, wherein my interactions with modern Calvin scholarship are found. For those with an interest in the secondary literature on Calvin, special attention should be given to notes 1, 25, 35, 47, 105, 112, and 119.

In the brief final part of the chapter (section III) I critically evaluate Calvin's teachings to ascertain what he might contribute to current theological discourse. I argue that Calvin can serve as an important source for contemporary reflections on how sin affects thinking, as his ideas on the subject are critically appropriated by theologians today. To summarize, this chapter attempts to answer two main questions. (1) What did John Calvin teach about human reason and the noetic effects of sin? (2) Are there useful insights which can be drawn from a critical engagement with Calvin's thoughts on the noetic effects of sin? For a discussion of Calvin's use of psychological terms, with special attention given to his understanding of the relationship between body, soul, and spirit and the relationship between reason and will, see appendix one on Calvin's psychology.

II. An Exposition of Calvin's Teachings

A. Human Reason at Creation and at the Fall

In Calvin's understanding, human reason is that faculty by which humanity "distinguishes between good and evil, and by which [it] understands and judges."[9] Calvin believed that in the original creation (of Adam and Eve), humanity was endowed with "an inborn gift of reason, to discern between vice and virtue."[10] In brief, Calvin held that "God provided man's soul with a mind, by which to distinguish good from evil, right from wrong; and, with the light of reason as guide, to distinguish what should be followed from what should be avoided."[11]

The faculty of reason, according to Calvin, was God's (nearly) universal gift to humanity, so that all humans are "partakers of the same reason."[12] Calvin further believed that reason was God's gift to humans alone, not shared with the "brute beasts."[13] In Calvin's schema, it was reason and intelligence which marked human life as superior to other forms of animal life.[14]

More specifically, Calvin believed that humans were "endowed with reason and understanding so that by leading a holy and upright life, we may press on to the appointed goal of blessed immortality."[15] That is, humans were "created so as to be endued with reason and understanding for contemplating the works of God."[16] Furthermore, this "true knowledge of God by observation of his works" which could be attained through proper use of our reason was to be "a saving knowledge of God."[17] Calvin followed Augustine in teaching that Adam was able not to sin (*posse non peccare*),[18] and Calvin believed that if Adam had remained upright, the very order of nature would have led humanity to a primal and simple knowledge of God.[19] Adam did not remain upright, however, and through pride and unbelief he fell, disobeying God and introducing sin into the world.[20]

According to Calvin the results of the fall were disastrous, as "all parts of the soul were possessed by sin after Adam deserted the fountain of righteousness."[21] He was highly critical of the late medieval teaching of Peter Lombard, followed by "the Papal theologians" of Calvin's own day, according to which, "man was commonly thought to be corrupted only in his sensual part and to have a perfectly unblemished reason and a will also largely unimpaired."[22] Calvin was doggedly insistent that in fallen humans, "no part is free from the infection of sin."[23] Within his doctrine of the pervasiveness of human depravity, Calvin especially stressed the point that "the reason of man is not less blind than his affections are perverse."[24]

After the fall, Calvin insisted, humanity's original faculty of reason was seriously impaired. Calvin employed a variety of metaphors to describe the dulling of human reason at the fall. Although Calvin's language is rich and multifaceted, scholars have tended to perceive his dominant metaphors as either auditory (deafness) or visual (blindness).[25] To encompass both of these metaphors (as well as the others such as intoxication, insanity, and hardening), I have chosen the broad term "serious impairment" to describe Calvin's teaching on the way in which human reason was tarnished, injured, and, for some particular purposes, rendered completely ineffective at the fall.

Calvin believed that this impairment of human reason is due, at least in part, to our fall in Adam.[26] He argued that "the first blindness, therefore, which occupies the minds of men, is the punishment of original sin, because Adam, after his rebellion, was deprived of the true light of God, in the absence of which there is nothing but fearful darkness."[27] Moreover, beyond the dullness which we inherit as Adam's descendants, Calvin taught that each of us further impairs our reason by committing actual sins. He observed that people "choose to obey their fancies rather than God, and so stifle the light of reason. . . . Men choose to corrupt and spoil that gift of a sane mind which they had received."[28] We are key players in the impairment of our own reason but, according to Calvin, we are not the only players.

Satan also has an important role. Calvin maintained that all unbelievers' "minds have been darkened by Satan that they may not see the glory of Christ shining in the gospel without an intervening veil."[29] So, a second explanation that Calvin offered for the impairment of humanity's reason was that "Satan has so prepossessed the minds of men with wicked affections that although the light may shine ever so bright, they still remain blind, and see nothing at all."[30]

Yet a third explanation Calvin suggested was that the impairment of humanity's reason was the work of God. In this vein, Calvin asserted that God "gives up to a *reprobate mind* (Rom. 1:28) those whom he has appointed to destruction."[31] Calvin understood Paul to teach that "the reprobate are so driven out of their mind by the secret judgment of God, that they are lost in amazement and are incapable of forming any judgment at all."[32] In fact, Calvin postulated that blinding people's thinking was one of God's characteristic ways of punishing sinful humans,[33] though Calvin was always quick to add the reminder that God always acts for good and just reasons, even if those reasons are not immediately evident to us.[34]

Calvin believed in the ultimate compatibility of humanity impairing its own reason, Satan impairing humanity's reason, and God impairing humanity's reason.[35] Calvin was convinced that (1) humanity's original and actual sin, (2) Satan's work of deception, and (3) God's secret purposes of judgment all worked together in some harmonious way to impair the reasoning capacities of fallen humans.[36] In assigning responsibility for the noetic effects of sin, however, Calvin stressed that fallen humanity is without excuse because its failure to attain a true and saving knowledge of God is self-caused.[37] In Calvin's diagnosis of sinners, "the error by which they were deceived was self-chosen."[38] According to Calvin, we are responsible for not using our reason to know God rightly, since "we are ignorant through our own fault," and our "ignorance is closely connected with pride and indolence, and is therefore voluntary."[39] First and foremost, Calvin maintained, we fallen sinners are self-blinded.[40]

Calvin's belief in the disastrous effects of the fall led him to insist that we not judge God's prelapsarian gift of reason by its postlapsarian manifestation in fallen humans. He insisted that "the light given to men in the beginning must not be assessed by their present state, since in this marred and degenerate nature light has been turned to darkness."[41] At creation God gave the faculty of reason to people with the intention that they use this gift to know God through contemplating God's magnificent works. By their sinful disobedience, however, humans fell and experienced extensive depravity, which included the impairment of their reason, brought about by the harmonious "workings" of humanity, Satan, and God. After the fall, human reason was so self-impaired as to become ineffective in reaching its intended goal of true and saving knowledge of God.[42] Fallen human reason can arrive at only a partial and feckless knowledge of God.[43] In our postlapsarian state, Calvin believed "our reason is overwhelmed by so many forms of deceptions, is subject to so many errors, dashes against so many obstacles, is caught in so many difficulties, that it is far from directing us aright."[44] In short, Calvin held that after the fall, "natural reason will never direct men to Christ."[45]

B. The Variable Abilities of Fallen Human Reason

The fact that true and saving knowledge of God could not be attained by fallen human reason, unaided by God's grace, did not lead Calvin to despair over the possibility of fallen humans attaining any true knowledge at all. Rather, Calvin, just as Luther before him, made a distinction between the capacity of fallen human reason in "earthly matters" and "heavenly matters."[46] This sub-section of the chapter shows that this distinction between reason's prowess in earthly matters and its impotence in heavenly matters is a distinction that is important to Calvin. However, it is a distinction that has received proportionately little attention in most of the secondary works on Calvin, at times leading to misunderstandings of Calvin.[47] Calvin was critical of those "who have confused earthly things with heavenly," and he argued that it was important to differentiate the two.[48]

> Therefore, to perceive more clearly how far the mind can proceed in any matter according to the degree of its ability, we must here set forth a distinction. This, then, is the distinction: that there is one kind of understanding of earthly things, another of heavenly. I call 'earthly things' those which do not pertain to God or his kingdom, to true justice, or to the blessedness of the future life; but which have their significance and relationship with regard to the present life and are, in a sense, confined within its bounds. I call 'heavenly things' the pure knowledge of God, the nature of true righteousness, and the mysteries of the

heavenly kingdom. The first class includes government, household management, all mechanical skills, and the liberal arts. In the second are the knowledge of God and of his will, and the rule by which we conform our lives to it.[49]

Calvin's writings generally reflect a greater interest in "heavenly things" than in "earthly things." Nevertheless, Calvin did occasionally address himself to "earthly things," and herein he lauded the ingenuity of human reason. Calvin repeatedly expressed admiration and gratitude for the true insights granted to us by the fallen reason of unbelievers. In Calvin's view, all truth has its source in God, and so truth ought not to be rejected, wherever it is found, whether in believers or in unbelievers.[50] This conviction is plain in the three following statements from Calvin:

> Let us then know, that the sons of Cain, though deprived of the Spirit of regeneration, were yet endued with gifts of no despicable kind; just as the experience of all ages teaches us how widely the rays of divine light have shone on unbelieving nations, for the benefit of the present life; and we see, at the present time, that the excellent gifts of the Spirit are diffused through the whole human race. Moreover, the liberal arts and sciences have descended to us from the heathen. We are, indeed, compelled to acknowledge that we have received astronomy, and the other parts of philosophy, medicine, and the order of civil government, from them.[51]

> What then? Shall we deny that the truth shone upon the ancient jurists who established civic order and discipline with such equity? Shall we say that the philosophers were blind in their fine observation and artful description of nature? Shall we say that those men were devoid of understanding who conceived the art of disputation and taught us to speak reasonably? Shall we say that they are insane who developed medicine, devoting their labor to our benefit? What shall we say of all the mathematical sciences? Shall we consider them the ravings of madmen? No, we cannot read the writings of the ancients on these subjects without great admiration.[52]

> Whenever we come upon these matters in secular writers, let that admirable light of truth shining in them teach us that the mind of man, though fallen and perverted from its wholeness, is nevertheless clothed and ornamented with God's excellent gifts.[53]

Calvin further argued that "all of us have a certain aptitude" in the liberal and manual arts, and that "this evidence clearly testifies to a universal apprehension of reason and understanding by nature implanted in men" which "is bestowed indiscriminately upon pious and impious."[54] Indeed, Calvin maintained that the great abilities of the human mind are indicators that humanity was created in the image of God.[55] Calvin was exuberant over the accomplishments of human reason, even fallen human reason as found among unbelievers, but his enthusiasm extended only to the application of such reason to "earthly" subjects which did not yield "spiritual" wisdom.

For what is more noble than the reason of man, by which he stands out far above all other animals? How greatly deserving of honor are the liberal sciences, which refine man in such a way as to make him truly human! Besides, what a great number of rare products they yield! Who would not use the highest praise to extol statesmanship, by which states, empires and kingdoms are maintained?—to say nothing of other things! I maintain that the answer to this question is obvious from the fact that Paul does not utterly condemn, either the natural insight of men, or wisdom gained by practice and experience, or education of the mind through learning; but what he affirms is that all those things are useless for obtaining spiritual wisdom.[56]

In fact, Calvin asserted that "knowledge of all the sciences is so much smoke apart from the heavenly science of Christ,"[57] and he asked rhetorically, "For though we have all the sciences in the world stuffed inside our heads, what help will that be when life fails us?"[58] Calvin's point was that "although we are naturally endued with the greatest acuteness, which is also his [God's] gift, yet we may call it a limited endowment, as it does not reach to the heavens."[59] According to Calvin, true wisdom is absent where true knowledge of God in Christ is absent, whatever other knowledge may be present.[60] In Calvin's view, fallen humans often exhibit marvelous comprehension in understanding "earthly things." The problem is that understanding earthly things is of very limited value in fulfilling the eternal purposes of human existence.[61] Calvin was convinced that the fallen human mind is less careful and less skillful in investigating matters "above the level of the present life" than "things below."[62] When it comes to "the kingdom of God and all that relates to the spiritual life," Calvin believed that, "the light of human reason differs little from darkness."[63]

We must now analyze what human reason can discern with regard to God's kingdom and to spiritual insight. This spiritual insight consists chiefly in three things: (1) knowing God; (2) knowing his fatherly favor in our behalf, in which our salvation consists; (3) knowing how to frame our life according to the rule of his law. In the first two points—and especially in the second—the greatest geniuses are blinder than moles.[64]

Calvin understood Paul "to teach that human intelligence is useless for assessing the teachings of religion,"[65] such that Paul "brings down all the natural ability of men, so that it counts for nothing in the kingdom of God."[66] Beyond the apostle Paul, Calvin also found support for his position in Augustine, who "recognizes this inability of the reason to understand the things of God."[67] Within the overall category of "the things of God" or "things above" or "heavenly things," Calvin made some distinctions.[68] Nonetheless, in the end he concluded that sin distorts humanity's understanding of all "heavenly matters." Calvin wrote:

And if we want to measure our reason by God's law, the pattern of perfect righteousness, we shall find in how many respects it is blind! Surely it does not at all comply with the principal points of the First Table such as putting our

faith in God, giving due praise for his excellence and righteousness, calling
upon his name, and truly keeping the Sabbath. What soul, relying upon natural
perception, ever had an inkling that the lawful worship of God consists in these
and like matters…. Men have somewhat more understanding of the precepts of
the Second Table because these are more clearly concerned with the
preservation of civil society among them. Yet even here one sometimes detects
a failure to endure.[69]

Calvin observed that such a "failure to endure" was often evident when it
came to humans applying God's law to themselves. Calvin noted that "men
seldom err in general principles, and therefore, with one mouth, confess that
every man ought to receive what is his due; but as soon as they descend to their
own affairs, perverse self-love blinds them, or at least envelops them in such
clouds that they are carried in an opposite course."[70] Centuries before the
popularization of "hermeneutics of suspicion" and critical insights from the
sociology of knowledge, Calvin recognized the blinding effect of self-interest.

In reply to the general question, every man will affirm that murder is evil. But
he who is plotting the death of an enemy contemplates murder as something
good. The adulterer will condemn adultery in general, but will privately flatter
himself in his own adultery. Herein lies man's ignorance: when he comes to a
particular case, he forgets the general principle that he has just laid down.[71]

In the end Calvin's position was that the gospel "is at once too profound,
and too lofty to be grasped by the human mind,"[72] that "all the mysteries of God
far exceed the comprehension of our natural capacity,"[73] and that "the riches of
the wisdom of God are too deep for our reason to be able to penetrate them."[74]
Calvin concluded that "human reason, therefore, neither approaches, nor strives
toward, nor even takes a straight aim at, this truth: to understand who the true
God is or what sort of God he wishes to be toward us."[75] Because Calvin
believed that heavenly things were beyond the reach of fallen human reason, he
insisted that it was foolish for fallen humans to attempt to understand heavenly
things via this impaired faculty.

And it is certainly madness for any one to presume to ascend to heaven, relying
on his own acumen, or the help of learning; in other words, to investigate the
secret mysteries of the kingdom of God, or force his way through to a
knowledge of them, for they are hidden from human perception.[76]

In Calvin's view, because fallen human reason could not attain true
knowledge of heavenly things, another way to this knowledge must be found. Or
perhaps because this other way is only possible by God's grace, for Calvin it
may be more proper to say that the knowledge of heavenly things must be *given*
to us. Calvin was quite clear "that only those to whom it is given can
comprehend the mysteries of God."[77] As the next sub-section will show, Calvin
believed that fallen humans could attain true and saving knowledge of God only

through the Word of God and the regenerating work of the Spirit which renews our reason and "lifts us up to heaven with the wings of faith."[78]

C. Redeemed Human Reason

Calvin was convinced that fallen humans must renounce their "natural" fallen reason before they could rightly understand God's works or acquire true spiritual wisdom. Calvin claimed that it was "in vain for any to reason as philosophers on the workmanship of the world, except those who, having been first humbled by the preaching of the gospel, have learned to submit the whole of their intellectual wisdom (as Paul expresses it) to the foolishness of the cross, (I Cor. i. 21)."[79] In Calvin's view, "to be adequate disciples of him [Christ], we must put away all confidence in our own intellect and seek light from heaven."[80] Calvin maintained that "we must give up our understanding and renounce the wisdom of the flesh and offer to Christ empty minds that he may fill them."[81]

This filling, according to Calvin, was to be a filling with the Word of God. Calvin warned that "the church should not be wise of itself, should not devise anything of itself but should set the limits of its own wisdom where Christ has made an end of speaking. In this way the church will distrust all the devisings of its own reason."[82] Calvin maintained that "men can do nothing but err when they are guided by their own opinion without the Word or command of God," so that "all who forsake the Word fall into idolatry."[83] Hence, Calvin urged his readers "to reject all inventions of the human mind (from whatever brain they have issued) in order that God's pure Word may be taught and learned in the believers' church."[84]

According to Calvin, fallen humans were hopelessly lost in their search for God, if they undertook this search apart from the guidance of Scripture. Employing a famous metaphor, Calvin said that, "just as eyes when dimmed with age or weakness or by some other defect, unless aided by spectacles, discern nothing distinctly; so such is our feebleness, unless Scripture guides us in seeking God, we are immediately confused."[85] In short, Calvin believed that "the human mind because of its feebleness can in no way attain to God unless it be aided and assisted by his sacred Word."[86]

Calvin further argued, in parallel fashion, that just as the Word was necessary for fallen humans to attain true and saving knowledge of God, so also was the Spirit. He asserted that "flesh is not capable of such lofty wisdom as to conceive God and what is God's, unless it be illumined by the Spirit of God."[87] Calvin's belief in the absolute necessity of the Spirit's illumination is reflected in his pronouncement that, "all who have not been born anew of the Spirit of Christ" may be condemned for vanity of mind.[88] In fact, Calvin went so far as to say that apart from the Holy Spirit, humanity's "gifts are darkness of mind and perversity of heart."[89]

Calvin believed that "the way to the kingdom of God is open only to him whose mind has been made new by the illumination of the Holy Spirit."[90] In Calvin's view, the Spirit "may rightly be called the key that unlocks for us the treasures of the kingdom of heaven (cf. Rev. 3:7); and his illumination, the keenness of our insight."[91] Calvin spoke of the "heavenly Spirit, who begets in us another and a new mind."[92] In fact, Calvin argued that in the matter of persuading people of the truthfulness of Scripture, "the testimony of the Spirit is more excellent than all reason."[93]

This last statement highlights a vitally important part of Calvin's teaching: that the Word of God is ineffective revelation apart from the Spirit of God regenerating the fallen human mind. According to Calvin, "the gospel cannot be properly known except by the illumination of the Spirit,"[94] and the whole teaching of salvation "would have been set before us in the Scriptures uselessly, if God does not lift up our minds to him by his Spirit."[95] Calvin held that God "shines forth upon us in the person of his Son by his gospel, but that would be in vain, since we are blind, unless he were also to illuminate our minds by his Spirit."[96] In short, Calvin believed that the testimony of the Word of God and the testimony of the Spirit of God were completely harmonious,[97] and both were necessary for attaining the right knowledge of God, which comes by faith.[98]

So, in Calvin's view, the Word of God and the Spirit of God were indispensable to faith in God, and faith was crucial because "it belongs to faith to penetrate into heaven, in order to find the Father there."[99] However, Calvin emphasized not some sort of generalized faith in God and knowledge of God, but rather specific faith in Christ and knowledge of Christ.[100] This point was especially important for Calvin since he believed that "a supposed knowledge of God outside Christ will be a deadly abyss,"[101] and "apart from Christ the saving knowledge of God does not stand."[102] In brief, for Calvin, "all the reason or understanding that we have is mere darkness, till we have been enlightened by Christ."[103]

One of the ways Calvin believed people are enlightened by Christ is through sound doctrinal instruction.[104] Though it is frequently overlooked, Calvin taught that another way in which God enlightens people's minds is through the church's sacraments.[105] According to Calvin, "the function of the sacrament is to help the otherwise weak mind of man so that it may rise up to look upon the height of spiritual mysteries."[106] Our faith in Christ, produced by the united work of the Word and the Spirit, can be sustained, confirmed, nourished, and even increased through participating in the sacraments of baptism and the Lord's Supper.[107]

It is evident from the preceding analysis that Calvin believed that right knowledge of God was a special kind of knowledge marked by particular characteristics. Calvin was convinced that "all right knowledge of God is born of obedience."[108] Calvin declared that "we must join practice to our doctrine in order to know what we have been shown and taught."[109] This belief in the inseparability of creed and deed helps to explain Calvin's insistence that "in order to be good theologians, it is necessary for us to lead a holy life."[110] For Calvin, humans could know God rightly and personally only by God's gift of faith,[111] and this special epistemological avenue for knowing God rightly was required for two reasons. First, Calvin claimed that humans needed faith because, due to the noetic effects of sin, their impaired faculty of reason cannot know God rightly.[112]

> But our mind has such an inclination to vanity that it can never cleave fast to the truth of God; and it has such a dullness that it is always blind to the light of God's truth. Accordingly, without the illumination of the Holy Spirit, the Word can do nothing. From this, also, it is clear that faith is much higher than human understanding. . . . [F]aith is a singular gift of God, both in that the mind of man is purged so as to be able to taste the truth of God and in that his heart is established therein.[113]

Second, Calvin claimed that humans needed faith because God was a unique object of knowledge.[114] Calvin believed that "the divine nature is infinitely exalted above the comprehension of our understanding,"[115] but faith is especially well suited to knowing God because "it does not stop short at the immediate sight but penetrates even to heaven, so as to believe what is hidden from the human senses."[116] Calvin was convinced that "it is the true nature of faith" that "faith sees things in God higher and more hidden than our senses can perceive."[117] In brief, our dullness (due to the noetic effects of sin) and God's greatness make faith a necessity for humans to know God rightly.[118]

It might be expected that Calvin would develop an additional reason that faith is necessary to know God rightly; namely, that even if humanity's capacity to reason were restored to its original rectitude, the creation is now cursed or fallen so that it is no longer such a "magnificent theater" in which humans may behold God's glory, nor such a spotless "mirror" through which humans may come to know God aright. It is noteworthy that despite his strong emphasis on the ways in which the fall problematizes our knowledge of God, Calvin did not argue for the fallenness of creation as a significant barrier to true knowledge of God.[119]

Through faith and the renewal of our reason, then, Calvin believed that the noetic effects of sin may be gradually reversed. Calvin taught that in the redeemed person, "the mind, illumined by the knowledge of God, is at first wrapped up in much ignorance, which is gradually dispelled."[120] Indeed, Calvin held that "the purpose of the gospel is the restoration in us of the image of God which had been canceled by sin and that this restoration is progressive and goes on during our whole life, because God makes his glory to shine in us little by little."[121]

Yet, Calvin insisted also that regenerate humans who possessed faith and a redeemed capacity to reason were still limited in their understanding of God. Hence, Calvin urged "in all religious doctrine, that we ought to hold to one rule of modesty and sobriety: not to speak, or guess, or even to seek to know, concerning obscure matters anything except what has been imparted to us by God's Word."[122] Calvin exhorted his readers with this remark: "Let us then learn not to make inquiries concerning the Lord, except so far as he has revealed them by Scripture. Otherwise we enter a labyrinth from which retreat will not be easy."[123]

Four particularly treacherous labyrinths against which Calvin warned were God's providence, God's predestination, God's essence, and God's hidden counsel/secret will.[124] Concerning God's providence, Calvin maintained that "the sluggishness of our mind lies far beneath the height of God's providence,"[125] from which we ought to learn "how reverently and modestly we must reflect upon the providence of God, viz., that no one may dare, in view of the pride of human nature, to demand from God a reason for his actions."[126] On the subject of predestination, Calvin remarked "that all human beings are wholly prevented by their blindness from examining the predestination of God by their own judgment."[127] Calvin exhorts us to "keep our minds within this limit, lest in investigating predestination, we go beyond the oracles of God, while we learn that in this matter men can discern no more than a blind man in darkness."[128] As to God's essence, Calvin argued that "we cannot fully comprehend God in his greatness, but that there are certain limits within which men ought to confine themselves. . . . Only fools, therefore, seek to know the essence of God."[129] Lastly, in regard to God's hidden counsel or secret will, Calvin was convinced that God "does indeed have his own hidden counsel, by which he orders all things as he pleases; but because it is incomprehensible to us, we should know that we are debarred from a too curious investigation into it."[130]

Calvin was concerned that believers recognize the limits of the knowledge which they could obtain by their faith and redeemed faculty of reason. Calvin insisted that "we should willingly remain ignorant of the matters which he [God] keeps from us"[131] and should "seek to know nothing but what the Lord has been willing to reveal to his Church. Let that be the limit of our knowledge."[132] When God grants the gift of faith to a sinner and redeems a sinner's reason, that person is given true and saving knowledge of God, but Calvin insisted that this knowledge of God must remain within the proper bounds of God's self-revelation in God's Word as illumined by God's Spirit.

D. Summary of Calvin's Teaching

To recap briefly, Calvin taught that at creation God gave the faculty of reason to humanity alone, with the intention that humanity use this gift to know God (especially God's paternal benevolence), through contemplating God's magnificent works. At the fall, humanity failed to believe God, was drawn away from God, and experienced extensive depravity, which included the impairment of its reason. This impairment of humanity's reason was brought about by the harmonious "workings" of humanity, Satan, and God. After the fall, human reason was so impaired as to become ineffective in the practical matter of attaining saving knowledge of God, but fallen humanity is without excuse because it is responsible for its original sin and its actual sins and their effects, one of which is the noetic effect of being unable to perceive rightly God's clear self-revelation.

Calvin's disparaging comments about fallen human reason must be understood in light of the distinction which he drew between fallen reason's capacities in "earthly matters" and fallen reason's capacities in "heavenly matters." In the former, matters pertaining to the present life such as the mechanical and liberal arts, Calvin was optimistic about the abilities of fallen human reason. Here the Holy Spirit has granted wonderful insights to believers and unbelievers alike. However, in the latter, matters pertaining to the future life such as the mysteries of the heavenly kingdom, Calvin was pessimistic about the abilities of fallen human reason. Here the unregenerate human mind is stupid, like a labyrinth, unable to penetrate to heaven, and often opposed to God's wisdom. Calvin taught that humanity's sin has variable noetic effects, impairing the knowledge of heavenly things more than the knowledge of earthly things.

In Calvin's view, unregenerate humans cannot, by themselves, know God aright. However, through salvation, which includes the redemption of human reason, God has provided a way for humans to attain right knowledge of God. This unique way of knowing is through faith in Christ, which depends on God's self-revelation in God's Word, illumined by God's Spirit, and strengthened by the Church's sacraments. When God grants the gift of faith to a sinner and redeems a sinner's reason, that person is given assurance of God's fatherly favor and is given knowledge of God's will as it is revealed in Scripture, while still being barred from knowledge of God's essence or of God's secret and hidden purposes. Calvin was convinced that, with redemption, the noetic effects of sin are progressively reversed by the Holy Spirit, so that believers may know God rightly and savingly, but Calvin insisted that this knowledge of God ought to remain within the proper bounds of God's self-revelation in God's Word.

In sum, Calvin maintained a basic division between knowledge of earthly things and knowledge of heavenly things. In the former, fallen human reason is ingenious and is to be lauded. In the latter, fallen human reason is more faulty, though here an additional division must be made between the precepts of the second table of the law (those concerned with the preservation of civil society—in which fallen human reason possesses some ability) and the principal points of the first table of the law (e.g., putting our faith in God, giving due praise for God's excellence and righteousness, calling upon God's name, and truly keeping the Sabbath—in which fallen human reason is severely impaired). Calvin's central ideas on the noetic effects of sin may be schematized as follows. Movement from left to right in the diagram indicates an increase in the noetic effects of sin.

Lesser ← Noetic Effects Of Sin → Greater

Earthly Things/Things Below	Heavenly Things/Things Above
(matters relating to this life)	(matters relating to the future life)
	/ \
	2nd table of the law 1st table of the law

2nd table of the law   1st table of the law
(knowing how to frame   (knowing God and
our lives according to   God's fatherly favor)
God's law)

III. Critical Evaluation

Thus far this chapter has set forth Calvin's view of human reason, giving special attention to his view of how reason is affected by sin (in hopes of filling an important gap in present Calvin scholarship). However, Calvin's view is not merely a matter of historical interest. His teachings on the noetic effects of sin, while open to criticism on several fronts and in need of some updating, provide a perspective which needs to be heard in the contemporary academic scene. The final section of this chapter undertakes a brief critical evaluation of Calvin's teachings on the subject.

In regard to his broad teachings on human reason, Calvin has been criticized on several points. For instance, he has been criticized for inconsistency in formally rejecting reason as an authority but nonetheless employing it authoritatively in practice.[133] Calvin also has been criticized for being a rationalist and thereby contributing to the rise of rationalism in the eighteenth century.[134] Because the main interest of this chapter is in Calvin's narrower teachings on how human reason is affected by sin, the task of assessing other aspects of Calvin's thought will be left to others, and the assessment here will be limited to evaluating Calvin's central ideas on the noetic effects of sin.

Calvin was essentially correct that reason is a good gift of God but it has been corrupted by sin. I agree with Calvin that the human fall into sin (original sin) introduced distortion into our thinking, and this distortion is further compounded by our own actual sins. I also concur with him that the noetic effects of sin are variable, and that sin distorts our knowledge of God more seriously than it distorts our knowledge of other matters. Calvin was also right that God's gracious redemption gradually restores our capacity to know God rightly, though this knowledge has its limits. In these observations Calvin offers a helpful framework for understanding how sin affects our thinking. Other elements of Calvin's understanding, however, are problematic.

First, Calvin's most basic division between the knowledge of earthly things and the knowledge of heavenly things is insufficiently precise. For instance, Calvin describes "earthly things" as "those which do not pertain to God or his kingdom," and Calvin includes in this category "government, household management, all mechanical skills, and the liberal arts." In my view, these areas of human endeavor *do* pertain to God's kingdom, and should not be categorized as "merely earthly matters." These areas of knowledge, skill, and stewardship are not just "secular" or "earthly" affairs. Rather, they are intimately connected to our service in God's kingdom and have important implications for our lives as faithful followers of Christ (I Corinthians 10:31; Colossians 3:17-25).

In addition to questioning whether Calvin's distinction between earthly and heavenly knowledge was adequate in his day, it must be asked whether this dichotomous model is workable in our day. This question may be highlighted by asking whether current disciplines such as philosophy, history, anthropology, and psychology deal with earthly knowledge, and hence are *not* distorted by sin, or deal with heavenly knowledge (whether precepts of the first table or the second table of the law) and hence *are* distorted by sin. The difficulty of fitting such disciplines, or even branches within these disciplines, into Calvin's categories illustrates the ways in which Calvin's earthly/heavenly distinction is too simplistic to account adequately for the many varieties of human knowledge and whether or not they are affected by sin.

Second, Calvin's view of sin is not comprehensive enough. He appears to have worked nearly exclusively with an individualistic concept of sin which ignored the corporate aspects of sin. While Calvin did offer a corporate treatment of human reason and the fall of human reason in original sin (via his connection between Adam and Eve and the rest of the human race), he did not extend this analysis to an investigation of the corporate nature of many actual sins (economic oppression, racism, sexism, etc.). Nor did Calvin examine the ways in which reason is dependent on human traditions (as recognized by contemporary philosophers and sociologists of knowledge), and the ways in which these traditions can be corporately sinful and/or corporately redeemed. In this respect, Calvin's concept of sin neglects the corporate manifestations of sin and redemption.

The third and final problem is that, as Dewey Hoitenga has observed, "Calvin fails to explain exactly what he thinks grace implies for the renewal of human reason."[135] For Calvin, the loss of faith (that is, faithlessness or unbelief) is the root cause of sin, which in turn has distorting noetic effects. So it would be expected that the gift of faith, by which salvation is received, would have redemptive noetic effects, reversing the distortions of sin and permitting again right knowledge of God. Though Calvin hints at this, he does not develop this theme with great clarity (see note 112). As Hoitenga puts it, "Calvin fails to work out the noetic consequences of redemption as clearly as he does the noetic consequences of the fall. . . . For all the attention Calvin gives to the noetic effects of the fall, he gives surprisingly little to the noetic effects of grace and redemption."[136]

Of course, it must be acknowledged, as Stuermann says, that "it is altogether too easy for a man removed by four centuries from another adversely to criticize the latter's ideas, assumptions, or arguments."[137] So it should be understood that in my criticisms I am not asserting that Calvin should have anticipated modern developments and concerns, but I am asserting that if we are to appropriate Calvin's useful insights for our current situation, we must do so by way of critical appropriation and modification. This opening chapter sets forth Calvin's central teachings on the subject as a helpful starting point for establishing a contemporary model of the noetic effects of sin. The next chapter examines the ideas of two more recent Reformed theologians as a prelude to proposing a new model of how sin affects our thinking.

Notes

1. In my review of the secondary literature on this topic, I searched several pertinent computer databases and consulted the following Calvin and Reformation bibliographies: *Archiv für Reformationsgeschichte, Beiheft, Literaturbericht*, Jahrgang 1 (1972), and successive years through 1998; R. Bainton and E. W. Gritsch, *Bibliography of the Continental Reformation*, second edition (Hamden, CT: Archon Books, 1972), 161-181; Commission internationale d'histoire ecclésiastique comparée, *Bibliographie de la Réforme, 1450-1648, Ouvrages parus de 1940 à 1955*, premier fascicule (Leiden: E. J. Brill, 1958), also deuxième fascicule—1960, quatrième fascicule—1963, sixième fascicule—1967; P. DeKlerk, "Calvin Bibliography 1972," *Calvin Theological Journal* 8 (1973): 221-250, and successive years through 1998; E. A. Dowey Jr., "Survey—Continental Reformation: Works of General Interest. Studies in Calvin since 1948," *Church History* 24 (1955): 360-367; E. A. Dowey Jr., "Survey—Continental Reformation: Works of General Interest. Studies in Calvin since 1955," *Church History* 29 (1960): 187-204; A. Dufour, "Bibliographie calvinienne en 1959," *Bibliothèque d'humanisme et renaissance* 21 (1959): 619-642; A. Erichson, *Bibliographia Calviniana* (Nieuwkoop: B. De Graaf, 1955), originally published in Berlin in 1900; P. Fraenkel, "Petit Supplément aux bibliographies calviniennes, 1901-1963," *Bibliothèque d'humanisme et renaissance* 33 (1971): 385-413; D. Kempff, *A Bibliography of Calviniana, 1959-1974* (Leiden: E. J. Brill, 1975); A. Lang, "Recent German Books on Calvin," *Evangelical Quarterly* 6 (1934): 64-81; J. T. McNeill, "Thirty Years of Calvin Study," *Church History* 17 (1948): 207-240, and "Addendum," *Church History* 18 (1949): 241; W. Niesel, *Calvin—Bibliographie, 1901-1959* (München: Kaiser, 1961); T. H. L. Parker, "A Bibliography and Survey of the British Study of Calvin, 1900-1940," *Evangelical Quarterly* 18 (1946): 123-131; K. E. Rowe, *Calvin Bibliography* (Madison, NJ: Drew University, 1967); H. Rueckert, "Calvin-Literatur seit 1945," *Archiv für Reformationsgeschichte* 50 (1959): 64-74; D. C. Steinmetz, "The Theology of Calvin and Calvinism," in S. Ozment (ed.), *Reformation Europe: A Guide to Research* (St. Louis: Center for Reformation Research, 1982), 211-232; J. N. Tylenda, "Calvin Bibliography, 1960-1970," *Calvin Theological Journal* 6 (1971): 156-193; P. Vogelsanger, "Neuere Calvin-Literatur," *Reformatio* 8 (1959): 362-366; J. N. Walty, "Calvin et le calvinisme," *Revue des sciences philosophiques et théologiques* 49 (1965): 245-287; and R. White, "Fifteen Years of Calvin Studies in French (1965-1980)," *Journal of Religious History* 12 (1982): 140-161.

Note that despite the absence of any published monographs on the subject other than Nixon's book, there are four masters theses which address Calvin's view of sin and/or reason: A. L. Anderson, "Calvin's Conception of Sin and Guilt" (Master of theology thesis, Union Theological Seminary, 1947); H. M. Conn, "The Concept of the Reason in the Theology of John Calvin" (Master of theology thesis, Westminster Theological Seminary, 1958); C. H. Stinson, "Reason and Sin According to Calvin and Aquinas" (Master of arts thesis, The Catholic University of America, 1966); and Y. I. Kim, "Luther and Calvin on Human Reason" (S.T.M. thesis, Concordia Seminary, St. Louis, 1971).

Another work which is frequently indexed in Calvin bibliographies under the subject heading of reason is J. M. Jones, "The Problem of Faith and Reason in the Thought of John Calvin" (Ph.D. diss., Duke University, 1942). However, its title notwithstanding, this dissertation devotes only one chapter out of five explicitly to

Calvin's view of reason, and within this chapter there are only a few scattered references to Calvin's teachings on the noetic effects of sin.

    Two studies published this decade also touch on Calvin's teachings on reason and the noetic effects of sin. Dewey Hoitenga Jr. uses a creation-fall-redemption schema to interpret Calvin, though Hoitenga's work is centered primarily on the themes of the immediacy and vitality of human knowledge of God (D. J. Hoitenga Jr., *Faith and Reason from Plato to Plantinga* [Albany: State University of New York Press, 1991], 143-174). Paul Helm also makes use of the creation and fall categories, though Helm's emphasis is on Calvin's view of the *sensus divinitatis* (P. Helm, "John Calvin, the *Sensus Divinitatis*, and the Noetic Effects of Sin," *International Journal for Philosophy of Religion* 43 [1998]: 87-107).

    2. L. Nixon, "John Calvin's Teachings on Human Reason and Their Implications for Theory of Reformed Protestant Christian Education: A Problem in Philosophy of Religion Studied for Its Possible Implications for Theory of Religious Education" (Ph.D. diss., School of Education of New York University, 1960), and three years later, L. Nixon, *John Calvin's Teachings on Human Reason* (New York: Exposition Press, 1963). My citations of Nixon refer to the latter work.

    3. For a complete listing of the sources which Nixon uses in constructing his categories, see Nixon, 272-275.

    4. Nixon, 130.

    5. An explicit differentiation between reason at creation, after the fall, and after redemption is found in Calvin's eucharistic polemics with Heshusius, in which Calvin stated: "Three kinds of reason (*tres rationis gradus*) are to be considered, but he [Heshusius] at one bound overleaps them all. There is a reason naturally implanted which cannot be condemned without insult to God, but it has limits which it cannot overstep without being immediately lost. Of this we have a sad proof in the fall of Adam. There is another kind of reason which is vicious, especially in a corrupt nature, and is manifested when mortal man, instead of receiving divine things with reverence, would subject them to his own judgment. This reason is mental intoxication, or pleasing insanity, and is at eternal variance with the obedience of faith, since we must become fools in ourselves before we can begin to be wise unto God. In regard to heavenly mysteries, therefore, we must abjure this reason, which is nothing better than mere fatuity, and if accompanied with arrogance, grows to the height of madness. But there is a third kind of reason, which both the Spirit of God and Scripture sanction. Heshusius, however, disregarding all distinction, confidently condemns, under the name of human reason, everything which is opposed to the frenzied dream of his own mind" ("The True Partaking of the Flesh and Blood of Christ in the Holy Supper," in *Calvin's Tracts and Treatises*, trans. H. Beveridge [Grand Rapids: Eerdmans, 1958], vol. 2, 512; *CO* IX: 474). See also Calvin's *Commentary on Genesis*, Argument; *CO* XXIII: 11-12.

    6. *Institutes*, I. xv. 4; *CO* II: 139.

    7. This gap in present Calvin scholarship, substantiated by the research alluded to in the first endnote, is further highlighted by the publication this decade of R. C. Gamble (ed.), *Articles on Calvin and Calvinism* (New York: Garland Publishing, 1992). In this fourteen volume anthology, which contains approximately two hundred articles on Calvin's theology produced by scholars over the past thirty years, there is not a single publication on Calvin's view of sin or its noetic effects.

    8. In this expositional portion of the chapter, my aims are remarkably similar to those described by T. F. Torrance in his study of *Calvin's Doctrine of Man* (Westport,

CT: Greenwood Press, 1977), originally published by Eerdmans in 1957: "It has been my attempt to lay bare Calvin's own thought and to present it as far as possible in his own way and in his own words. . . . I am conscious that in the very arrangement of this material, as also in the exposition, interpretation has been unavoidable, but it is, I believe, in the direction which Calvin's own thought moves as it is drawn out, particularly in its relevance to the modern theological debate" (7).

9. *Institutes*, II. ii. 12; *OS* III: 255.

10. *A Harmony of the Gospels*, Matthew 6:22; *CO* XLV: 207.

11. *Institutes*, I. xv. 8; *OS* III: 185.

12. *Commentary on Genesis*, 11:1; *CO* XXIII: 164. The exceptional case of the cognitively impaired is acknowledged, somewhat insensitively, in *Institutes*, II. ii. 14; *OS* III: 257-258.

13. *Institutes*, II. ii. 12; *OS* III: 255. See also *Institutes*, II. ii. 17; *OS* III: 259 and *Commentary on John*, 1:4; *CO* XLVII: 5.

14. *Commentary on Acts*, 17:28; *CO* XLVIII: 417.

15. *Institutes*, II. i. 1; *OS* III: 228-229. According to Calvin, if Adam had obeyed God, "he would have passed into heaven without death, and without injury" (*Commentary on Genesis*, 2:16; *CO* XXIII: 45).

16. *Commentary on Isaiah*, 29:9; *CO* XXXVI: 490. See also Calvin's *Commentary on Hebrews*, 11:3; *CO* LV: 144, where he asked rhetorically, "Why are men endowed with reason and intellect except for the purpose of recognizing their creator?"

17. *Commentary on I Corinthians*, 1:21; *CO* XLIX: 326 ("*salvificam Dei notitiam*").

18. *Institutes*, II. iii. 13; *OS* III: 289-290.

19. *Institutes*, I. ii. 1; *OS* III: 34. Talbot characterizes Calvin's view thus: "Undamaged by sin, each of us would really believe *in* God; we would know the God who actually exists and trust Him as our Father" (M. Talbot, "Is it Natural to Believe in God?" *Faith and Philosophy* 6 [1989]: 157).

20. Calvin was appreciative of Augustine's suggestion "that pride was the beginning of all evils, and that by pride the human race was ruined" (*Commentary on Genesis*, 3:6; *CO* XXIII: 60). However Calvin refined this hypothesis in suggesting, as Luther had, that "unbelief was the root of defection" (*Commentary on Genesis*, 3:6; *CO* XXIII: 60). Calvin argues that, "Adam would never have dared oppose God's authority unless he had disbelieved God's Word" (*Institutes*, II. i. 4; *OS* III: 232). This, of course, begs the question of how Adam, with an upright mind, will, and body, and with every reason to trust in God and obey God, might disbelieve God's Word. Apropos here is the comment of J. M. Jones that "Calvin does not offer a complete explanation of man's first sin. He merely accepts it as a fact and asserts that responsibility for it can be attributed neither to God nor nature" (110). See also the remark of Charles Partee that "Calvin asserts (epistemologically) but does not explain (ontologically) how sin is able to enter the world which God created" ("Calvin, Calvinism, and Rationality," in H. Hart [ed.], *Rationality in the Calvinian Tradition* [Lanham, MD: University Press of America, 1983]: 8).

21. *Commentary on Genesis*, 3:6; *CO* XXIII: 59.

22. *Institutes*, II. ii. 4; *OS* III: 245. See also *Institutes*, II. i. 9; *OS* III: 238.

23. *Commentary on Genesis*, 1:26; *CO* XXIII: 27. See also Calvin's *Commentary on Romans*, 7:14; *CO* XLIX: 128, where he declared that "we are so

completely driven by the power of sin, that our whole mind, our whole heart, and all our actions are inclined to sin."

24. *Commentary on Genesis*, 6:3; *CO* XXIII: 114.

25. T. F. Torrance asserts that for Calvin, "knowledge of God is reached primarily by hearing rather than by seeing" ("Knowledge of God and Speech about Him, According to John Calvin," *Revue d'histoire et de philosophie religieuses* 44 [1964]: 412). W. J. Bouwsma also claims that Calvin frequently expressed "a preference for the ear over the eye as the primary human instrument for knowing, a major departure from the traditional position" ("Calvin and the Renaissance Crisis of Knowing," *Calvin Theological Journal* 17 [1982]: 204). Certainly passages supportive of this view, even beyond those cited by Torrance and Bouwsma, might be gathered from Calvin's writings (for instance, *Institutes*, III. xiii. 4; *OS* IV: 219 and *A Harmony of the Last Four Books of Moses*, Exodus 33:19; *CO* XXV: 109).

Such evidence notwithstanding, M. P. Engel denies Bouwsma's claim that Calvin "relied more on audial than visual metaphors" (*John Calvin's Perspectival Anthropology* [Atlanta: Scholars Press, 1985], 18). My study of this matter lends support to Engel's position, as is evident in the exposition, which reflects a proportionately higher frequency of language concerning blindness and restored sight, as over against deafness and restored hearing.

26. *Commentary on Ezekiel*, 18:20; *CO* XL: 441. See also Calvin's earlier statement in his *Commentary on Ezekiel*, 11:19-20; *CO* XL: 245.

27. *Commentary on Ephesians*, 4:18; *CO* LI: 206. In his comment on the following verse, Calvin implies that "the second blindness" which mars the minds of fallen humans is the punishment for our actual sins (*Commentary on Ephesians*, 4:19; *CO* LI: 206).

28. *A Harmony of the Gospels*, Matthew 6:22; *CO* XLV: 206.

29. *Institutes*, II. ix. 1; *OS* III: 399.

30. *The Mystery of Godliness and Other Selected Sermons*, 78; *CO* LIV: 493. See also *Commentary on Genesis*, 6:22; *CO* XXIII: 126.

31. *Commentary on II Thessalonians*, 2:11; *CO* LII: 204. See also *A Harmony of the Gospels*, Matthew 13:11; *CO* XLV: 358.

32. *Commentary on Romans*, 11:8; *CO* XLIX: 217.

33. *Commentary on I Corinthians*, 1:19; *CO* XLIX: 323. See also *Commentary on Isaiah*, 19:14; *CO* XXXVI: 338.

34. *Institutes*, I. xvii. 2; *OS* III: 205. See also *Commentary on Romans*, 1:28; *CO*: XLIX: 28 and *Commentary on Isaiah*, 19:14; *CO* XXXVI: 338.

35. In *Institutes*, II. iv. 2; *OS* III: 292, Calvin comments, on the plundering of Job's goods, that "we see no inconsistency in assigning the same deed to God, Satan, and man; but the distinction in purpose and manner causes God's righteousness to shine forth blameless there, while the wickedness of Satan and of man betrays itself by its own disgrace." For other passages in which Calvin addresses in a single paragraph the respective roles of humanity, Satan, and God, see *Commentary on Romans*, 1:24; *CO* XLIX: 27 and *Commentary on II Corinthians*, 4:4; *CO* L: 51. Curiously, although this notion of "triple agency" is a serious and sustained concern of Calvin, it is a facet of his thought which is rarely, if ever, noted in the secondary literature on Calvin.

36. *Commentary on Romans*, 1:24; *CO* XLIX: 27. See also *Commentary on II Corinthians*, 4:4; *CO* L: 51.

37. *Institutes* I. v. 15; *OS* III: 59.

38. *Commentary on Romans*, 1:28; *CO* XLIX: 29.
39. *A Harmony of the Last Four Books of Moses*, Deuteronomy 29:4; *CO* XXIV: 243.
40. *Commentary on Ezekiel*, 12:1-2; *CO* XL: 254.
41. *Commentary on John*, 1:5; *CO* XLVII: 6.
42. *Institutes*, I. v. 14; *OS* III: 58-59. See also *Institutes*, II. v. 19; *OS* III: 319.
43. *Commentary on Ephesians*, 4:17; *CO* LI: 205. See also *Commentary on Ezekiel*, 11:19-20; *CO* XL: 245-246.
44. *Institutes*, II. ii. 25; *OS* III: 267. See also *Institutes*, II. v. 19; *OS* III: 319.
45. *Commentary on John*, 1:5; *CO* XLVII: 6.
46. For an example of this distinction between the "earthly" and the "heavenly" in Luther, see *Luther's Works* 33: 98; *Martin Luthers Werke* 18: 659.
47. The "earthly/heavenly" distinction occupies only one sentence in the fifteen pages of Partee's "Calvin, Calvinism, and Rationality." It receives only passing allusions (138, 149) in E. A. Dowey, *The Knowledge of God in Calvin's Theology* (New York: Columbia University Press, 1952), and it is entirely ignored in William Bouwsma's "Calvin and the Renaissance Crisis of Knowing." Ignoring this distinction leads Bouwsma (202-203) to claim mistakenly that "Calvin's doubts about the possibility of knowing anything notably extended to physical nature. . . . The discernment of uniformities in nature, from this [Calvin's] standpoint, would have involved an impossible claim to penetrate the mind of Creator; scientific knowledge was thus out of the question, and to seek it, like grappling with the mysteries of theology, could only involve the mind in a *labyrinth*, one of Calvin's favorite words for expressing the disorientation he seems often to have felt in a world that surpassed all human understanding."
    I believe that the subsection (I.B) on the variable abilities of fallen human reason demonstrates that Calvin did *not* doubt the "possibility of knowing anything notably" about physical nature, and that, for Calvin, attempting to discern uniformities in nature would not necessarily involve one in the same sort of labyrinth that attends grappling with the unrevealed mysteries of theology.
48. *Concerning Scandals*, trans. J. W. Fraser (Grand Rapids, MI: Eerdmans, 1978), 23; *CO* VIII: 19.
49. *Institutes*, II. ii. 13; *OS* III: 256. See also the *Sermon on Job*, 27:19-28:9; *CO* 34:503 where Calvin states that "l'esprit humain de nature est capable de cognoistre les choses d'ici bas, et qui concernent la vie presente."
50. *Commentary on Titus*, 1:12; *CO* LII: 414-415. See also *Institutes*, II. ii. 16; *OS* III: 259.
51. *Commentary on Genesis*, 4:20; *CO* XXIII: 100. See also *Commentary on I Corinthians*, 1:17; *CO* XLIX: 321.
52. *Institutes*, II. ii. 15; *OS* III: 258. See also *Commentary on Isaiah*, 28:29; *CO* XXXVI: 483-484.
53. *Institutes*, II. ii. 15; *OS* III: 258. See also *Institutes*, II. ii. 16; *OS* III: 259.
54. *Institutes*, II. ii. 14; *OS* III: 257-258. See also the related proofs for the universality of human rationality found in *Institutes*, II. ii. 13; *OS* III: 256-257 and *Commentary on Acts*, 17:28; *CO* XLVIII: 417.
55. *Institutes*, I. v. 5; *OS* III: 49. Calvin's laudatory comments about the capacities of fallen human reason prompt Dewey Hoitenga to criticize Calvin for failing

to develop a parallel account of the capacities of fallen human will (*John Calvin and the Will: A Critique and Corrective* [Grand Rapids, MI: Baker, 1997], especially 119-121).

56. *Commentary on I Corinthians*, 1:20; *CO* XLIX: 325. Calvin argued similarly in his *Commentary on Isaiah*, 19:11; *CO* XXXVI: 334, that "their wisdom is nothing but empty smoke. There is no wisdom but that which is founded on the fear of God, which Solomon declares to be the chief part of wisdom."

57. *Commentary on I Corinthians*, 1:20; *CO* XLIX: 325 (*coelestis Christi scientia*).

58. *Sermon on Luke*, 2:1-14, *CO* XLVI: 958. See also *Commentary on Hosea*, 14:9; *CO* XLII: 511-512.

59. *Commentary on Daniel*, 2:30; *CO* XL: 588.

60. See Calvin's *Commentary on Isaiah*, 33:6; *CO* XXXVI: 563, where he declared that "where Christ is not known, men are destitute of true wisdom, even though they have received the highest education in every branch of learning; for all their knowledge is useless till they truly 'know God.'"

61. As Trinkaus puts it, Calvin "simultaneously appreciates the objective results of human activity and discounts its ultimate meaning" by teaching "that man by his own efforts in science and material activities had some possibility of realizing limited worldly goals, but none at all of achieving moral and spiritual ends" (C. E. Trinkaus, "Renaissance Problems in Calvin's Theology," *Studies in the Renaissance* 1 [1954]: 78).

62. *Institutes*, II. ii. 13; *OS* III: 256-257.

63. *Commentary on Ephesians*, 4:17; *CO* LI: 204. See also *Institutes*, I. v. 12; *OS* III: 56.

64. *Institutes*, II. ii. 18; *OS* III: 260. See the similar animal analogy in the *Commentary on I Corinthians*, 1:20; *CO* XLIX: 325, where Calvin stated "that man with all his shrewdness is as stupid about understanding by himself the mysteries of God as an ass is incapable of understanding musical harmony."

65. *Commentary on I Corinthians*, 2:15; *CO* XLIX: 345 (*nihil valere carnis prudentiam iniudicanda pietatis doctrina*).

66. *Commentary on I Corinthians*, 1:20; *CO* XLIX: 324.

67. *Institutes*, II. ii. 25; *OS* III: 268. See also *Institutes*, II. ii. 18; *OS* III: 261.

68. *Institutes* II. ii. 22; *OS* III: 264-265 and *Institutes* II. ii. 24; *OS* II: 266-267.

69. *Institutes*, II. ii. 24; *OS* III: 266-267. See also *Commentary on I Corinthians*, 1:21; *CO* XLIX: 326 and *Commentary on John*, 18:38; *CO* XLVII: 405-406.

70. *Commentary on Genesis*, 29:14; *CO* XXIII: 401-402.

71. *Institutes* II. ii. 23; *OS* III: 265.

72. *Commentary on I Corinthians*, 2:14; *CO* XLIX: 344.

73. *Commentary on Romans*, 11:34; *CO* XLIX: 231. See also *Institutes*, I. viii. 11; *OS* III: 79, where Calvin spoke of "heavenly mysteries above human capacity."

74. *Commentary on Romans*, 11:33; *CO* XLIX: 230.

75. *Institutes*, II. ii. 18; *OS* III: 261. See also Calvin's *Commentary on John*, 1:5; *CO* XLVII: 6 and *A Harmony of the Gospels*, Matthew 13:12; *CO* XLV: 359.

76. *Commentary on I Corinthians*, 1:20; *CO* XLIX: 325. See also *Commentary on I Corinthians* 2:7; *CO* LXIX: 337.

77. *Institutes*, I. vii. 5; *OS* III: 71. See also *Commentary on John*, 8:12; *CO* XLVII: 191 and *Institutes*, IV. i. 6; *OS* V: 11-12.

78. *Commentary on Acts*, 17:24; *CO* XLVIII: 411. See also *Institutes*, III. ii. 34; *OS* IV: 45.

79. *Commentary on Genesis*, Argument; *CO* XXIII: 9-10.

80. *A Harmony of the Gospels*, Luke 24:45; *CO* XLV: 816.

81. *Commentary on II Corinthians*, 10:5; *CO* L: 116. Calvin believed that such a renunciation of our own fallen human wisdom was particularly difficult for those in the early church at Corinth (*Commentary on I Corinthians*, 3:1; *CO* XLIX: 346).

82. *Institutes*, IV. viii. 13; *OS* V: 147. See also *Commentary on Romans*, 1:22; *CO* XLIX: 25.

83. *Commentary on John*, 4:22; *CO* XLVII: 87.

84. *Institutes*, IV. viii. 9; *OS* V: 140.

85. *Institutes*, I. xiv. 1; *OS* III: 153. See also *Institutes*, I. vi. 1; *OS* III: 60.

86. *Institutes*, I. vi. 4; *OS* III: 64. See also *Institutes*, I. xiv. 1; *OS* III: 153.

87. *Institutes*, II. ii. 19; *OS* III: 261.

88. *Commentary on Ephesians*, 4:17; *CO* LI: 204.

89. *Institutes*, III. i. 3; *OS* IV: 4-5.

90. *Institutes*, II. ii. 20; *OS* III: 263.

91. *Institutes*, III. i. 4; *OS* IV: 6.

92. *Commentary on Ephesians*, 4:23; *CO* LI: 208 (*qui aliam in nobis ac novam mentem genrat*). This language raises questions which are addressed in note 112.

93. *Institutes*, I. vii. 4; *OS* III: 70. See also *Institutes*, I. vii. 5; *OS* III: 70 and *Institutes*, I. viii. 13; *OS* III: 81.

94. *Commentary on Hebrews*, 6:4; *CO* LV: 71.

95. *Commentary on I Corinthians*, 2:10; *CO* XLIX: 341.

96. *Commentary on II Corinthians*, 4:6; *CO* L: 53. See also *A Harmony of the Gospels*, Luke 24:45; *CO* XLV: 816.

97. *Institutes*, I. ix. 1; *OS* III: 82-83. See also *Treatises against the Anabaptists and against the Libertines*, 224; *CO* VII: 175.

98. For Calvin's insistence on the close connection between the Word of God and faith, see *Institutes*, III. ii. 6; *OS* IV: 14. On the intimate link between the Spirit of God and faith, see *Institutes*, III. i. 4; *OS* IV: 5.

99. *Commentary on I Peter*, 1:20-21; *CO* LV: 227.

100. *Institutes*, II. vi. 2-4; *OS* III: 321-326 and *Institutes*, III. ii. 1; *OS* IV: 6-9.

101. *Commentary on John*, 6:46; *CO* XLVII: 150-151, where Calvin inveighed against *Dei cognitio extra Christum*. See also *Commentary on I Peter*, 1:20-21; *CO* LV: 226.

102. *Institutes*, II. vi. 4; *OS* III: 325.

103. *Commentary on Isaiah*, 40:14; *CO* XXXVII: 17.

104. *Commentary on II Thessalonians*, 2:9; *CO* LII: 202.

105. It is striking that most modern studies on Calvin's view of the knowledge of God neglect any serious analysis of the role of the sacraments. See, as one example, the conspicuous absence of the sacraments in the statement of Parker that "by continual study of the Scriptures, by lifelong repentance, by discipline, by prayer, by all those practices of the Christian life which he [Calvin] enumerates in the third book of the *Institutio*, our knowledge of God becomes stronger in proportion as our ignorance is dispelled and our pride of mind is humbled" (T. H. L. Parker, *Calvin's Doctrine of the Knowledge of God*, second edition [Edinburgh: Oliver and Boyd, 1969], 144, originally published by Oliver and Boyd in 1952). Indeed, when I perused Parker's copious footnotes I did not find a single reference to book four of the *Institutes* (*OS* V). Much the same may be said of the work of Dowey and Torrance. The one exception which I found

to the general neglect of this subject is the brief chapter on the sacraments and faith in V. A. Shepherd, *The Nature and Function of Faith in the Theology of John Calvin* (Macon, GA: Mercer University Press, 1983).

106. *Institutes*, IV. xvii. 36; *OS* V: 398. See also *Institutes*, IV. xv. 2; *OS* V: 286.

107. See *Institutes*, IV. xiv. 7; *OS* V: 264, *Institutes*, IV. xiv. 9; *OS* V: 266, and *Commentary on Genesis*, 9:11-13; *CO* XXIII: 149.

108. *Institutes*, I. vi. 2; *OS* III: 63.

109. *Sermon LVIII, Sur Le Deuteronome, CO* XXVI: 584-585: "Il faut donc que la prattique soit coniointe à la doctrine: car autrement nous ne pourrons pas cognoistre ce qui nous aura esté monstré et enseigné."

110. *Sermon XXIV, Sur La Seconde A Timothée, CO* LIV: 292 ("pour estre bons theologiens, il nous faut mener une saincte vie"). Lobstein remarks aptly that, for Calvin, "nous ne pouvons saisir la vérité divine que dans la mesure où nous vivons de la vie divine" (P. Lobstein, "La connaissance religieuse d'après Calvin." *Revue de Théologie et de Philosophie* 42 [1909]: 64).

111. Calvin was insistent that "faith is a unique and precious gift of God" (*Instruction in Faith*, 39; *CO* V: 334). See also Calvin's *Commentary on Acts*, 16:14 (*CO* XLVIII: 377), where he stated that "not only faith, but also all understanding of spiritual things, is a special gift of God (*peculiare donum Dei*)."

112. To my knowledge, Calvin nowhere offered an explicit discussion of the relation of redeemed reason to faith, though the two both appear to function as means to the right knowledge of God. Calvin's failure to clarify his position in this matter explains why a substantial portion of my exposition of "redeemed reason" is devoted to the subject of faith, and it also explains the variety of scholarly opinion concerning how Calvin envisioned the relationship between redeemed reason and faith.

Muller argues that, for Calvin, *faith enlightens reason*; faith functions as "a gift that awakens all the powers of the soul, intellect and will, so that both are enlightened and moved, each in its own way, to grasp the gift of God in Christ" ("*Fides* and *Cognitio* in Relation to the Problem of Intellect and Will in Calvin," *Calvin Theological Journal* 25 [1990]: 224). In contrast, Hoitenga argues that, for Calvin, *faith complements reason*, such that "the proper knowledge of God is *beyond* even any restored capacities of reason; reason even when restored to its original 'nobility' requires the assistance of faith" ("Faith and Reason in Calvin's Doctrine of the Knowledge of God," in H. Hart [ed.], *Rationality in the Calvinian Tradition* [Lanham, MD: University Press of America, 1983]: 36). Jones argues, in a slightly different manner, that for Calvin *reason complements faith* in such a way that "faith should be brought by reason to *full* understanding" (217) because through redeemed reason humans "may gain such a religious knowledge as fills full and confirms the knowledge apprehended by faith from the Scripture" (207).

Hoitenga highlights the interpretive problem in his finding that Calvin "*locates* the 'proper knowledge of God' in the redemption made possible by faith, without, however, connecting that faith to the functions of reason" so that "the new relationship in the redeemed man between such faith and restoration of the natural gifts [e.g., reason] he leaves obscure" ("Faith and Reason in Calvin's Doctrine of the Knowledge of God," 35, 32).

In my view, Gerrish's assessment of Luther in this matter applies equally to Calvin: "Sometimes Luther oscillates between two kinds of statement: (1) that the old light (reason) is *extinguished*, and a new light (faith) is kindled; and (2) that the old light is *transformed* into the new light. Partly, the ambiguity is in the concept of regeneration, which may be thought of either as a new birth or as renewal. . . . Clearly, what has happened [in Luther's writings] is that the notion of 'regenerate reason' tends to coalesce with the notion of 'faith' itself. This, doubtless, hardly makes for lucidity" (B. Gerrish, *Grace and Reason* [New York: Oxford University Press, 1962], 23-24). One example of this is found in Calvin's statement in *Institutes*, II. i. 9; *OS* III: 239 that the mind both "needs to be healed and also to put on a new nature." In short, Calvin oscillated between speaking of redeemed reason and speaking of faith as means to the right knowledge of God, without specifying the relation between the two.

113. *Institutes*, III. ii. 33; *OS* IV: 44. Note that here faith purges the human mind, thus permitting right knowledge of God (cf. the extended discussion in the previous note). See also *Commentary on I Corinthians*, 2:10; *CO* XLIX: 341, where the certainty of faith is said to be negatively correlated with the mind's certainty and sharpness.

114. In his *Commentary on I Peter*, 1:20-21; *CO* LV: 226, Calvin asserted that "there are two reasons why faith cannot be in God, unless Christ intervenes as a mediator. First, the greatness of the divine glory must be taken into account, and at the same time the littleness of our capacity."

115. *Commentary on Psalms*, 86:8; *CO* XXXI: 794.

116. *Commentary on John*, 20:29; *CO* XLVII: 445.

117. *Commentary on Hebrews*, 11:27; *CO* LV: 163.

118. See *Institutes*, III. ii. 33; *OS* IV: 44 and *Commentary on I Peter*, 1:20-21; *CO* LV: 226.

119. In his *Commentary on Romans*, 8:21; *CO* XLIX: 153, Calvin did offer the following acknowledgment: "[A]ll innocent creatures from earth to heaven are punished for our sins. It is our fault that they struggle in corruption. The condemnation of the human race is thus imprinted on the heavens, the earth, and all creatures." But in his comments on the "fallenness of creation" Calvin did not develop the idea that this fallenness of God's magnificent theater is a serious hindrance to humanity's right knowledge of God.

The idea seems to comport so well with Calvin's overall thinking that it is tempting to read it into his thought, as does Demarest when he claims that, according to Calvin, "nature in its cursed condition occasionally miscommunicates information. The propositional revelation of Scripture provides the necessary clarification of nature's testimony, which is garbled at its source" (B. A. Demarest, *General Revelation* [Grand Rapids: Zondervan, 1982], 56). Torrance does the same when he infers from Calvin's statements about the "inversion" of the created order that "therefore any attempt to know God out of the perverted order of nature can only partake of its perversity. It can only succeed in inverting the truth of God" (*Calvin's Doctrine of Man*, 164). Thus Torrance (169) concludes that, according to Calvin, "there can be no knowledge of God apart from atonement, for through the death of Christ the perverted order of the world is restored to its original rectitude, and true knowledge of God becomes possible."

Neither Demarest nor Torrance supplies any references to Calvin which support this inference, because this inference, however logical it may seem to interpreters of Calvin, is one which was not developed by Calvin himself, at least not in the places where one would expect to find it (Calvin's *Institutes*; *Commentary on Genesis*, 1-11; or *Commentary on Romans*, 8). As D. C. Steinmetz puts it, "in spite of the human fall into sin, the created order continues to function as a theater of God's glory" ("Calvin and the Natural Knowledge of God" in H. A. Oberman and F. A. James III [eds.], *Via Augustini* [Leiden: E. J. Brill, 1991]: 156). S. Schreiner observes correctly that Calvin "never directly addresses how nature remains a mirror of God's glory when it has been disordered by sin" ("The Theater of His Glory: Nature and the Natural Order in the Thought of John Calvin," Ph.D. diss., Duke University, 1983, 186-187).

The closest that Calvin came to arguing for the cursedness of creation as a hindrance to right knowledge of God was in a passage (cited by neither Demarest nor Torrance) in his *Commentary on Genesis*, 3:17; *CO* XXIII: 73: "Before the fall, the state of the world was a most fair and delightful mirror of the divine favor and paternal indulgence towards man. Now, in all the elements we perceive that we are cursed. . . . the blessing of God is never seen pure and transparent as it appeared to man in innocence."

120. *Institutes*, III. ii. 19; *OS* IV: 29. In *Institutes*, III. xvi. 1; *OS* IV: 249, Calvin taught that "Christ justifies no one whom he does not at the same time sanctify."

121. *Commentary on II Corinthians*, 3:18; *CO* L: 47. Schreiner (173-174) observes that, for Calvin, "the noetic effects of sin are gradually corrected in that reordering of the soul into the image of God." Shepherd notes similarly that, in Calvin's view, although "true faith continues to be error—and ignorance—beclouded" it is nevertheless the case that "true faith continues to advance so as to shrink, proportionately, the element of error and ignorance" (2).

122. *Institutes*, I. xiv. 4; *OS* III: 156.

123. *Commentary on Romans*, 11:33; *CO* XLIX: 230. A nearly identical exhortation is found in *Institutes*, I. xiii. 21; *OS* III: 137: "Let it be remembered that men's minds, when they indulge their curiosity, enter into a labyrinth. And so let them yield themselves to be ruled by the heavenly oracles, even though they may fail to capture the height of the mystery."

124. While these four related areas were of special concern to Calvin, he also issued warnings concerning audacious inquiries into God's foreknowledge and into God's reasons for creating when God did. On the former, see Calvin's *Commentary on Ephesians*, 3:9; *CO* LI: 181-182. On the latter, see *Institutes*, I. xiv. 1; *OS* III: 152-153.

125. *Institutes*, I. xvi. 9; *OS* III: 200.

126. *Commentary on Acts*, 17:30; *CO* XLVIII: 420. See also *Institutes*, I. xvii. 2; *OS* III: 203-204.

127. *Commentary on Romans*, 11:34; *CO* XLIX: 230-231. See also *Institutes*, III. xxi. 2; *OS* IV: 371.

128. *Commentary on Romans*, 11:34; *CO* XLIX: 231. When he spoke of predestination in *Institutes*, III. xxiii. 8; *OS* IV: 403, Calvin declared that "of those things which it is neither given nor lawful to know, ignorance is learned; the craving to know, a kind of madness."

129. *Commentary on Romans*, 1:19; *CO* XLIX: 23. See also *Institutes*, I. xi. 3; *OS* III: 90.

130. *Commentary on Romans*, 8:7; *CO* XLIX: 143. See also *Commentary on Romans*, 11:34; *CO* XLIX: 231.

131. *Commentary on Acts*, 1:7; *CO* XLVIII: 9.

132. *Commentary on II Corinthians*, 12:4; *CO* L: 138.

133. See J. M. Jones, 248-249; J. H. Leith, "Calvin's Theological Method and the Ambiguity in his Theology," in F. H. Littell (ed.), *Reformation Studies: Essays in Honor of Roland H. Bainton* (Richmond: John Knox Press, 1962), 112; and R. H. Ayers,

"Language, Logic and Reason in Calvin's *Institutes*," *Religious Studies* 16 (1980): 283-298.

134. See H. J. Weber, "The Formal Dialectical Rationalism of Calvin," *Papers of the American Society of Church History* (n.p.: 1928): 26; S. Fowler, "Martin Luther: Faith Beyond Reason," in T. Van der Walt (ed.), *Our Reformational Tradition: A Rich Heritage and Lasting Vocation* (Potchefstroom: Institute for Reformational Studies, 1984), 107-108; L. A. Belford, "Foreword," in Nixon, vi; and Q. Breen, *John Calvin: A Study in French Humanism*, 2nd edition (Hamden, CT: Archon Books, 1968), 153.

135. Hoitenga, *Faith and Reason From Plato to Plantinga*, 147.

136. Hoitenga, *Faith and Reason From Plato to Plantinga*, 168, 170.

137. W. E. Stuermann, *A Critical Study of John Calvin's Concept of Faith* (Tulsa, OK: University of Tulsa Press, 1952), 367. See also Torrance's observation that "it is easy to criticize after centuries of discussion of problems which were not acute and demanded no immediate solution in the sixteenth century" (*Calvin's Doctrine of Man*, 8).

Chapter 2

Kuyper, Brunner, and a New Model of How Sin Affects Our Thinking

I. Introduction

In the past, Christian scholars considered sin to be a topic of utmost importance, and they examined the ways in which sin affects human thinking. Recently, however, the subject of sin and its attendant noetic effects has received relatively little attention.[1] Because the Christian Scriptures and church tradition acknowledge the fact that sin distorts our thinking, the topic of the noetic effects of sin is first and foremost a *Christian* topic (see appendix two). It seems, however, that the most detailed reflection on how sin affects our thinking is found within the *Reformed* (or Calvinistic) tradition of Christianity.

Chapter one of this book examined the teachings of John Calvin, the founding figure for Reformed theology. This chapter will continue to probe the Reformed tradition by assessing the teachings of Abraham Kuyper (section II) and Emil Brunner (section III) on the noetic effects of sin. Although many thinkers have commented on the topic, there are two reasons for focusing on Kuyper and Brunner in the present chapter. First, they have formulated the most detailed models of exactly how sin affects thinking about different fields of study. Second, they represent two models of the noetic effects of sin which have strongly influenced the thinking of late twentieth-century Christian scholars. In each case, an exposition is followed by a critical evaluation to discern what these thinkers contribute to current inquiry into the noetic effects of sin.

Section IV of this chapter proposes a new model of how sin affects our thinking. The new model attempts to ameliorate the problems identified in previous treatments of the subject, while preserving and extending the useful insights others have to offer. The proposed model relates the noetic effects of sin to the complex interaction between the object of knowledge and the knowing subject. The new view is further distinguished from preceding models by attending carefully to the noetic effects of corporate (not just individual) sin.

II. Kuyper on the Noetic Effects of Sin

A. Description

Abraham Kuyper (1837-1920) is widely recognized as the leading figure of the nineteenth-century revival of neo-Calvinism in Holland. Kuyper was trained as a theologian, and served as a pastor in the national Dutch Reformed Church, founder and editor of a daily newspaper (*De Standaard*) and a weekly magazine (*De Heraut*), founder and professor at the Free University of Amsterdam, prime minister of the Netherlands, and a delegate in the Dutch Parliament. In several of his writings Kuyper reflected on the noetic effects of sin.[2] His thinking on the subject may be schematized as follows.

Kuyper's Model

Matters of observation and logic (mathematics and natural/physical sciences)	Agree by common grace	Regenerate Christians (abnormalists) ← and → unregenerate non-Christians (normalists)	Disagree due to the noetic effects of sin	Matters of principle (theology, philosophy, history, or humanities)

At the very center of Kuyper's thought, and at the center of the diagram, is the conviction that before there is any human thinking, there are human thinkers whose subjectivity influences their thinking.[3] According to Kuyper, these thinkers may be divided into two groups: regenerate Christians and unregenerate non-Christians. Kuyper was forthright in his assertion that "'regeneration' breaks humanity into two, and repeals the unity of the human consciousness."[4] In Kuyper's view, Christian thinkers may be characterized as abnormalists in the sense that they believe the world in its present state is abnormal, that is, fallen and in need of renewal. Conversely, non-Christian thinkers may be characterized as normalists in the sense that they believe the world in its present state is normal, that is, not in need of radical renewal.[5]

Kuyper believed that regenerate and unregenerate thinkers were fundamentally different in their outlooks, and therefore in almost all cases, these two groups would disagree with one another. Because there are two kinds of humans (regenerate and unregenerate), Kuyper concluded that there must be two kinds of thinking. He declared that "the fact that there are two kinds of *people* occasions of necessity the fact of two kinds of human *life* and *consciousness* of life, and of two kinds of *science*."[6] Wolterstorff aptly characterizes this outlook in his statement that, "there is Christian learning and there is non-Christian learning; only religious conversion will change that."[7] As indicated on the right side of the diagram, Kuyper maintained that Christians and non-Christians differ not only in their views of theology, but also of history, philosophy, and all of the humanities.[8] Herein, there are two kinds of scholarship (*tweeërlei wetenshap*): one arising from a regenerate heart and standing under the authority of Scripture and the other arising from an unregenerate heart and rejecting the authority of Scripture.[9] This was Kuyper's famous principle of antithesis between Christian and non-Christian thought, and it was his prime motivation for establishing the Free University of Amsterdam as a center for distinctively Christian thought.[10]

As indicated on the left side of the diagram, however, Kuyper believed that there were two exceptions to this principle of antithesis. In matters of pure sensory observation and in matters of pure logical reasoning (as opposed to higher matters of principle), Kuyper believed that the noetic effects of sin were restrained by God's common grace.[11] In these matters (e.g., mathematics and the natural or physical sciences), agreement was possible between regenerate and unregenerate thinkers.[12]

B. Critical Evaluation

Kuyper was correct in noting that ultimately there are two kingdoms or dominions at war with one another in the cosmos. This idea is taught in the Christian Scriptures and developed in Christian theology.[13] Kuyper also was correct in drawing attention to the important subjective influences on people's thinking. As Klapwijk observes, "Kuyper single-handedly battled the entire educated world of his time, an age which swore by the supposed objectivity and impartiality of all science."[14] Similarly, Ratzsch remarks that "fifty years before many Western philosophers, Kuyper had already seen that 'values' and even metaphysical principles play a proper, ineradicable role in science, that there are legitimate subjective factors in science."[15] The purpose of this chapter, however, is not to determine whether Kuyper was epistemically praiseworthy or blameworthy within his historical setting, but rather to critically appropriate his useful insights for application today. A necessary first step in such critical appropriation is to highlight several problematic aspects of Kuyper's model.

First, although Kuyper did recognize a corporate element in the sanctification of believers' thinking (note 9), he, like Calvin before him, worked with an individualistic concept of sin, which tended to overlook corporate or communal sin. Kuyper's incomprehensive view of sin neglected the corporate manifestations of sin and the noetic effects of corporate sin. (The concept of corporate sin and its noetic effects is developed at more length in section IV below, especially on pages 38-39.)

Second, there are two ways in which Kuyper's view of human thinking is suspect. On the one hand, Kuyper held to a romantic, expressivist view of thinking, according to which the contents of one's consciousness determine the outcome of one's thinking.[16] This view overemphasizes the subjective nature of human thinking and underemphasizes the objective aspects of human thinking— how the object of study influences the outcome of one's thinking. Put theologically, human thinking is grounded in our common creation and not solely in the presence or absence of people's redemption.[17]

On the other hand, Kuyper exempted the processes of observation and formal thought ('logic') from the noetic effects of sin. This exemption mistakenly denies the extensiveness of human depravity. There is now abundant evidence that observation is not a purely passive, objective process. Rather, it is an active process that includes subjective elements, in which we very often see only what we are looking for or want to see.[18] Kuyper was incorrect in his assertion that "the formal process of thought has *not* been attacked by sin."[19] Rather, as Wolters explains, "fallacies and error (understood as incorrect inferences from the available evidence or from justified premises) manifest the fallenness of human rationality."[20] So, Kuyper was mistaken to assert that the human activities of observation and formal thought are completely immune to the noetic effects of sin.

Third, and most importantly, although Kuyper eschewed Calvin's bifurcation between earthly and heavenly knowledge, he replaced it with a sharp division between the thinking of regenerate Christians and unregenerate non-Christians. Kuyper moved too quickly and without qualification from the fact that there are ultimately two kingdoms or dominions at war with one another in the cosmos, to his claim that there are two types of thinking at war with one another which can be found in Christians on one side and non-Christians on the other.[21] Put simply, Kuyper exaggerated the antithesis between the thinking of Christians and non-Christians. As Wolterstorff explains, Kuyper's principle of antithesis surely "is flagrantly false to the experience of all of us. All of us who are Christian scholars find ourselves agreeing with our non-Christian colleagues on vastly more than the deliverances of the senses and 'reason.'"[22]

Kuyper also overestimated the uniformity within "Christian thinking" and within "non-Christian thinking." It is true that Kuyper acknowledged a degree of diversity of thought within the Christian camp (note 10), but his principle of antithesis implies that the basic division in all thinking is between Christian thinking and non-Christian thinking. As Wolters observes, Kuyper failed to account adequately for the fact that "Christians and non-Christians also differ among *themselves*."[23] Wolterstorff is right that "even if we set aside the deliverances of the senses and 'reason' [Kuyper's two exceptions] consensus and dissension in the sciences are not to be found neatly along the fault lines of the break between Christian and non-Christian."[24] Differences of thought are many and varied, and are not always sufficiently explained by the labels "Christian" and "non-Christian." This was recognized early on by Kuyper's colleague Herman Bavinck, who took exception to Kuyper's teaching that there were two kinds of people and therefore two kinds of thinking. [25]

Kuyper's model fails to account adequately for the many types of thinking which exist in the world and the tremendous complexity of agreements and disagreements within and between different groups. The cosmic struggle between the kingdom of God and the kingdom of Satan simply does not filter down neatly into the struggle of two kinds of people who express themselves in two kinds of thinking. These inadequacies in Kuyper's model lead us to examine an alternative model of the noetic effects of sin proposed by Emil Brunner.

III. Brunner on the Noetic Effects of Sin

A. Description

Heinrich Emil Brunner (1889-1966) is perhaps the best known twentieth-century theologian to give extended consideration to the noetic effects of sin. After earning his Th.D. from the University of Berlin, Brunner taught in England, participated in the Swiss militia, served as a pastor in Switzerland, worked as a professor of systematic and practical theology at the University of Zurich, and taught as a visiting professor in Tokyo. In several of his writings Brunner devoted attention to the noetic effects of sin. [26]

Like Kuyper before him, Brunner maintained that "reason is never neutral," but rather "in all that reason does it is making a response—whether in sin or in faith." [27] Like Calvin, Brunner recognized that "our reason, apart from its restoration through the Word of grace, is always sinfully self-sufficient, a reason infected with rationalism and unbelief." [28] Also like his predecessors Calvin and Kuyper, Brunner argued that sin has noetic effects which are not constant, but variable. Brunner envisioned the variability of sin's noetic effects in a way that can be illustrated by a series of concentric circles, as in the diagram on the following page.

In the outermost circle are mathematics and the natural sciences. Brunner believed that "the disturbance of rational knowledge by sin" reaches "its minimum in the exact sciences, and zero in the sphere of the formal [logic]. Hence, it is meaningless to speak of 'Christian mathematics.'" [29] In this statement it is possible to read Brunner as arguing that the exact or natural sciences (*die exacte Wissenschaft*) are minimally disturbed by sin but that mathematics (included *im Bereich des Formalen*) is completely untouched by sin, such that mathematics should be placed in a circle of its own further removed from the center of the noetic effects of sin than the natural sciences. [30] This possible interpretation notwithstanding, the grouping of mathematics with

Brunner's Model

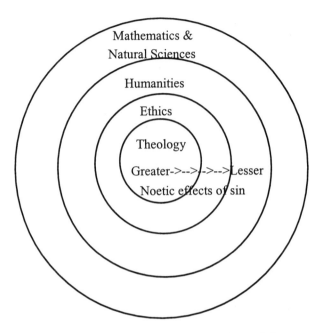

the natural sciences is warranted by Brunner's coupling of these two areas of knowledge in many statements elsewhere. Note, for instance, the grouping of mathematics with physics, chemistry, and anatomy in quotations below.

Brunner maintained that "through Christ we do not receive a different mathematics, physics, or chemistry,"[31] so that "if a person studies anatomy or physics it will be impossible to tell from his scientific work, pure and simple, whether he is a Christian or unbeliever."[32] To Brunner, it was "self-evident that there is practically no conflict between mathematics and theology, between physics, chemistry and theology, because here the autonomy of the sciences, even from the point of view of the Christian faith, is almost complete."[33] According to Brunner, in these areas there was a scientific neutrality (*wissenschaftliche Neutralität*)[34] in accordance with his principle that "the more that knowledge has to do with the world as world, the further it is removed from the sphere of sin, and therefore the more 'neutral' it becomes."[35] Brunner believed that "the more impersonal the sphere [of knowledge], the less disturbance there is [due to sin]; the more personal, the greater is the disturbance,"[36] so that "sin does not hinder men from knowing the things of the world, the laws of nature, the facts of nature, and man in his natural, historical and cultural manifestations."[37] Brunner argued vigorously that "whether men know God or not, they can in any case know the things of this world; and that means, to know them aright."[38] Briefly, Brunner held that sin scarcely influences human thinking in the outermost circle of mathematics and science.

In the next circle, nearer to the center, are the humanities. Brunner was convinced that the humanities were more affected by sinful blindness than mathematics and the natural sciences.[39] "In the sphere of natural science," Brunner asserted, "it makes practically no difference whether a scholar is a Christian or not; but this difference emerges the moment that we are dealing with problems of sociology, or law, which affect man's personal and social life."[40] In Brunner's schema, the study of law, the state, history and other such disciplines lies midway between reason's knowledge of the world and faith's knowledge of God.[41] Hence, Brunner believed there must be an accounting for the noetic effects of sin in these subjects.[42]

In the next circle, almost at the center, is ethics. Here Brunner argued that the noetic effects of sin were even greater than in the humanities.[43] Brunner believed that through Christ "we do find a different kind of marriage, family life, a different relation to our fellow men, and hence, influenced by that, a different kind of public justice."[44] So, according to Brunner, "it is significant and necessary to distinguish the Christian conceptions of freedom, the good, community, and still more the Christian idea of God from all other conceptions."[45]

Finally, in the innermost circle is theology. Brunner argued that "the more we are dealing with the inner nature of man, with his attitude to God, and the way in which he is determined by God, it is evident that this sinful illusion becomes increasingly dominant."[46] Brunner believed that "the nearer we come to the sphere of that which is connected with the personal being of God and man, which can no longer be perceived by reason but only by faith, the more we shall see that the self-sufficient reason is a source of error."[47] Hence, in Brunner's view "the disturbance of rational knowledge by sin" attained "its maximum in theology."[48]

Brunner referred to his model of the noetic effects of sin as "the law of the closeness of relation" («*Gesetz der Beziehungsnähe*»), which served as his "guiding principle for all problems that concern the relation between the Christian and the world."[49] It is summed up succinctly in the following statement.

> The more closely a subject is related to man's inward life, the more natural human knowledge is 'infected' by sin while the further away it is, the less will be its effect. Hence we find the maximum of sinful blindness in the knowledge of God itself. Hence mathematics and the natural sciences are much less affected by this negative element than the humanities, and the latter less than ethics and theology. In the sphere of natural science, for instance—as opposed to natural philosophy—it makes practically no difference whether a scholar is a Christian or not; but this difference emerges the moment that we are dealing with problems of sociology, or law, which affect man's personal and social life.

In the doctrine of God, however, this difference becomes a sharp contradiction.[50]

B. Critical Evaluation

Of the three models examined thus far, Brunner's schema best explains the variability of the noetic effects of sin on different areas of human knowledge. Brunner's model is more useful than Calvin's in explaining how sin affects human thinking within current disciplines of knowledge. Brunner's schema is also superior to Kuyper's, in that it avoids the exaggerated principle of antithesis and the excessively expressivist view of human thinking.

However, as with Calvin and Kuyper, Brunner's study of this subject is inadequately attentive to the noetic effects of corporate sin. In addition, Brunner fails to offer an extended treatment of the noetic consequences of regeneration and sanctification. He focuses so much on the object of study as to virtually ignore the knowing subject, outside of the one question of whether the knower is a Christian.

Beyond this oversight, the main problem with Brunner is that he too easily oscillates between discussing whether sin distorts human thinking in a particular discipline and whether a particular discipline is marked by disagreement between Christians and non-Christians. The following quotations exemplify the way in which Brunner moves, without qualification, from the question of sin's noetic effects to the question of the distinctiveness of Christian thought in various spheres of knowledge.

> The nearer anything lies to that center of existence where we are concerned with the whole, that is, with man's relation to God and the being of the person, the greater is the disturbance of rational knowledge by sin; the farther away anything lies from this center, the less is the disturbance felt, and the less difference is there between knowing as a believer or as an unbeliever.[51]

> If a person studies anatomy or physics it will be impossible to tell from his scientific work, pure and simple, whether he is a Christian or unbeliever. But his faith or unbelief will come out very clearly in his way of thought and life as a man. The more that knowledge has to do with the world as world, the further it is removed from the sphere of sin, and therefore the more 'neutral' it becomes.[52]

> Hence mathematics and the natural sciences are much less affected by this negative element [sinful blindness] than the humanities, and the latter less than ethics and theology. In the sphere of natural science, for instance—as opposed to natural philosophy—it makes practically no difference whether a scholar is a Christian or not.[53]

Brunner's idea is that if a particular area of thought is *not* affected by sin (for instance, mathematics), then we should expect no systematic differences between Christian and non-Christian thought. Conversely, if a particular area of thought *is* affected by sin (for instance, ethics), then we should expect noticeable differences between the thinking of Christians and non-Christians. The hidden premise, of course, is that the thinking of Christians is less affected by sin than is the thinking of non-Christians. While this assumption certainly contains an element of truth, it can also be dangerous in what it overlooks.

The element of truth is that in one sense Christians have died to sin and have been freed from sin so that it is no longer necessary for them to be slaves to sin, with sin as their master.[54] Whereas the unbeliever is under the dominion of sin, the believer has been set free from bondage to sin.[55] Indeed, it may even be said that believers may be distinguished from unbelievers because believers do not keep on sinning.[56] Moreover, as John Frame has noted, the Bible teaches that "the 'mind of Christ,' His wisdom, is communicated to believers (Matt. 11:25ff.; Luke 24:45; I Cor. 1:24, 30; 2:16; Phil. 2:5; Col. 2:3)."[57] So, with Brunner, we might expect that if a discipline of knowledge is susceptible to the noetic effects of sin, the thinking of Christians will be less affected by sin and, therefore, different than the thinking of non-Christians.

In another sense, however, Christians are not immune to sin and its effects. Indeed, those who claim to be without sin may be described as self-deceived.[58] The Christian Scriptures teach that believers may be immature and slow to learn,[59] as well as mistaken in many matters (demonstrated by the high proportion of Paul's correspondence aimed at correcting the mistaken beliefs of Christians). In short, believers' minds are still in need of renewal.[60] The fact that believers' thinking continues to be distorted by sin is precisely the crucial point that is overlooked in Brunner's analysis. Nowhere does he speak of the noetic effects of sin in believers' thinking. Brunner's argument is always from the noetic effects of sin to the distinctiveness of Christian thinking. The great danger for Christians here is that of a Pharisaic finger-pointing at the way sin may distort unbelievers' thought without attending to how sin distorts their own thought. (Precisely this tendency has been manifested in the writings of Kuyper, Van Til, and others in the neo-Calvinist tradition.[61]) Brunner may unwittingly exacerbate this problem by his own failure to address the noetic effects of sin in the thinking of Christians. Such shortcomings in Brunner's model, as well Kuyper's earlier model, highlight the need for a new model of the ways in which sin affects our thinking.

IV. A Constructive Model of the Noetic Effects of Sin

In my view, sin is a multifaceted concept that cannot be easily explained. Because the Bible describes sin in several ways (breaking a covenant, transgressing a law, hardening a heart, missing a target, etc.), I do not believe that sin can be defined comprehensively in a single sentence. Nevertheless, as

Ted Peters notes, "despite the inherently mysterious or impenetrable character of sin, we can still say something about it."[62] When I speak of sin in this constructive section of the chapter, my usage will be akin to that of Cornelius Plantinga Jr.: "Let us say that *a* sin is any thought, desire, emotion, word, or deed—or its particular absence—that displeases God and deserves blame. Let us add that *sin* is the disposition to commit sins. And let us use the word *sin* for instances of either."[63]

I do not believe that it is possible to predict, with a high degree of accuracy, how the noetic effects of sin will be manifested in any particular situation, though I do believe that some broad generalizations are possible. Beyond such generalizations (to be noted below), I believe that the noetic effects of sin vary according to the complex interplay of many factors, as will be explained by the proposed model. I recognize that by its very nature a simple, static, two-dimensional diagram runs the risk of misrepresenting the complex, active, dynamic, interactive model which I wish to describe. Nonetheless the following diagram may be of heuristic value, as the skeletal picture is fleshed out by a verbal description of the model.

The Proposed Model

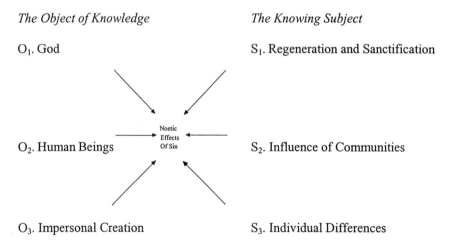

The Object of Knowledge	*The Knowing Subject*
O_1. God	S_1. Regeneration and Sanctification
O_2. Human Beings	S_2. Influence of Communities
O_3. Impersonal Creation	S_3. Individual Differences

A. The Object of Knowledge

Calvin, Kuyper, and Brunner were all correct in observing that sin disturbs human thinking in some areas more than others. This insight is reflected on the left side of the proposed model, with its tripartite division of various "objects" of human knowledge. Of course, the "object" of knowledge is very often a "subject" in its own right, as with humans or God. In the absence of a better alternative, I simply employ the phrase "object of knowledge" to designate the entity which is known, whether this entity be impersonal or personal. According to the proposed model, the noetic effects of sin generally are expected to be most evident in the knowledge of God (O_1), less evident in the knowledge of human beings (O_2), and least evident in the knowledge of impersonal aspects of creation (O_3).

In the critical evaluation of Calvin's model, I argued that his earthly/heavenly distinction was too simplistic to adequately account for the many varieties of human knowledge and whether or not they were affected by sin. The proposed model instead suggests a tripartite division to better account for the ways in which sin affects modern disciplines of study (anthropology, psychology, etc.) which cannot be easily fitted into Calvin's two categories. The proposed model also does not exempt any area of study completely from the potential distorting effects of sin, as does Kuyper's bifurcation of knowledge into matters of observation and logic in contrast to matters of principle. The proposed schema further diverges from Brunner's tendency to generalize about broad fields of study (e.g., sociology) because subdisciplines within these fields may differ significantly in their foci. What the proposed model suggests may be illustrated with examples from three subdisciplines within the field of psychology.

Working from the bottom up, the proposed model suggests, in general, that when examining impersonal creation (O_3), scholars are minimally affected by the distorting effects of sin.[64] For example, sin is expected to have little impact on psychologists' investigation into the communicative action of neurons or the learning patterns of pigeons. However, when scholars examine human beings (O_2), as a general rule, more distorting effects of sin are anticipated. That is, sin likely interferes to a greater degree in psychologists' investigation of the nature of human motivation or the definition of optimal mental health for humans. Finally, when scholars examine matters related to God (O_1), the greatest distorting effect of sin is generally anticipated. Thus, sin is expected to interfere the most in psychologists' investigation of the function of worshipping God or the significance of believing in God.

As the diagram indicates, however, the proposed model suggests that the object of knowledge is not the only factor related to the noetic effects of sin. This is the reason that the expectations in the preceding paragraph are couched as generalizations. The expectations generated by factors related to the object of knowledge (the left side of the model) interact in complex ways with the expectations generated by factors related to the knowing subject (the right side of the model).[65]

B. The Knowing Subject

The first subjective factor (S_1) concerns a person's regeneration and sanctification. Humans' capacity to reason is not an isolated faculty. As John Cooper notes, human thinking "functions correlatively with other capacities of human nature—psychological, social, cultural, and crucially, religious."[66] A person's thinking cannot be completely dissociated from the rest of his or her life, including the "spiritual" aspects of his or her life. Hoffecker was correct when he said that "the intellect cannot be surgically separated from the will. Since we know that human beings have willfully turned from God, their rebellion has not only moral and spiritual but epistemological consequences."[67]

Apart from the freedom available in Jesus Christ, humans are in bondage to sin and all of its effects, including the noetic effects of sin. Human self-centeredness distorts human thinking.[68] Moreover, our sinful decisions and behaviors may also have distorting noetic effects. As Talbot argues, "If I were to decide to cheat often enough, I would probably leave myself ill-disposed to believe that cheating is wrong."[69] Talbot's argument finds support in the biblical notion that people who sin and do not repent can develop consciences that are corrupted (Titus 1:15) or seared (1 Timothy 4:2).

All of this simply acknowledges that there is a moral dimension to human knowledge, especially knowledge of certain objects. Our moral and spiritual state affects what we think. As John Frame puts it, "morality influences intellectual judgments."[70] It follows then that people's thinking is influenced by their relationship with God, specifically (1) whether or not they have been regenerated by the work of the Holy Spirit, and (2) to what degree they are sanctified. As I use the terms here, regeneration denotes the work of the Holy Spirit in bringing about a new birth in which a person's basic direction in life is changed from the pursuit of sin to the pursuit of righteousness, and sanctification denotes one's subsequent progressive growth in holiness. [71]

Kuyper stressed the importance of regeneration and Brunner acknowledged it, but neither developed the significance of ongoing sanctification to reverse the noetic effects of sin on Christians' thinking. According to the proposed model, a person who is unregenerate and living in persistent rebellion against God (evidenced by the acts of the sinful nature in Galatians 5:19-21) is likely to have a more distorted knowledge of God than someone who is regenerated but immature in the faith (I Corinthians 14:20, Hebrews 5:11-14), who in turn is more likely to misconstrue God's nature than a person who is further along in the process of sanctification (evidenced by the fruit of the Spirit in Galatians 5:22-23).

Second, there is the related matter of how people are influenced by the communities in which they participate (S_2). In the critical evaluations of Calvin, Kuyper, and Brunner, I argued that all three thinkers paid insufficient attention to the communal aspects of sin, including its concomitant noetic effects. The new model attempts to ameliorate this pretermission by incorporating insights from recent scholarship on the communal aspects of human knowing. Alasdaire MacIntyre, among others, has demonstrated that human thinking is always embedded in historical traditions such that human standards of rationality are always dependent on some tradition or another.[72] What needs to be added to

MacIntyre's analysis is the observation that sinful elements in human traditions have distorting noetic effects on the thinking of people within those traditions.

Thus, according to the proposed model, sin and sanctification are not merely individual matters, but also are corporate issues. As Plantinga Jr. observes, "moral evil is social and structural as well as personal; it comprises a vast historical and cultural matrix that includes traditions, old patterns of relationship and behavior, atmospheres of expectation, social habits."[73] Jürgen Habermas is right that "from everyday experience we know that ideas serve often enough to furnish our actions with justifying motives in place of the real ones. What is called rationalization at this level is called ideology at the level of collective action."[74] A major function of the Old Testament prophets was a denunciation of the Israelites' corporate sin.[75]

Within Christian theology, a doctrine of extensive human depravity demands serious analysis of corporate and systemic sin.[76] Montgomery is right that, "on the basis of their own doctrine of sin, church people should be in the forefront of those who are self-critical in raising questions about their biases."[77] As Stephen Mott says, "we should become more self-probing and self-critical of our class, racial, sexual, and national biases."[78] Recent analyses of corporate sin have helped uncover the workings of corporate and systemic sins such as racism, sexism, and economic exploitation.[79]

These insights are incorporated into the new model in the recognition that the knowing subject is influenced by the communities in which he or she participates. Clark and Gaede (following Gregory Baum) are correct that "error and cultural blindness are profoundly rooted in our social histories as nations and churches."[80] Within the proposed model, there is a general expectation that communal sins distort the thinking of the members of the community, as within Nazi Germany or the Ku Klux Klan.[81]

It should be added, however, that our communities do not always exercise a negative influence on our thinking or lead us astray. As Clark and Gaede point out, "our social location, the interests, values, opportunities, and incentives of our social context may be the social basis for obtaining truth as well as error."[82] While our corporate sin has adverse noetic effects, our corporate redemption has positive noetic effects. Indeed, John Baillie has argued that "only when I am in *fellowship* with my fellow men does the knowledge of God come to me individually," and this "means the necessity of the Church and the rejection of religious individualism."[83] Hence, a person may enjoy redemptive noetic effects through participation in communities of those who have been redeemed from their sins and are in the process of being sanctified. In short, the model proposed here accounts for both the sinful and the redemptive ways our communities shape our thinking.

Third, the proposed model acknowledges individual differences in the outworkings of the noetic effects of sin (S_3). As mentioned earlier, it is not always possible to predict, with a high degree of accuracy, how the noetic effects of sin will be manifested in any particular situation. Although human beings are characterized by many commonalities, they also are characterized by marked individual differences. Individuals entangled in a similar sin may not experience similar noetic effects of the sin. For instance, several biblical scholars may all be involved in extramarital affairs. One may distort the biblical teaching in such a way that it does not condemn his adulterous behavior. Another may admit that the Bible condemns adultery, but may simply dismiss the Bible as an authoritative guide for her life. Still another may simply avoid any serious study or reflection on what the Bible teaches about adultery. Sin has volitional as well as noetic effects, and it is no easy matter to predict how people's wills and minds may influence one another.[84]

It is certainly the case that our personal interests—as well as cultural, religious, social, psychological, political, and economic influences—affect our understanding of Scripture.[85] When these influences are sinful (whether personal or corporate sin), either our understanding of Scripture is distorted (the noetic effects of sin) and/or our obedience to Scripture is undermined (the volitional effects of sin). As sinners we are ingenious in inventing many ways of dealing with our sin, such that there is not a uniform manifestation of the noetic effects of sin among us. The model proposed here recognizes that there will be idiosyncratic individual differences in the manifestations of the noetic effects of sin.

Acknowledgment of individual differences is related closely to the final point of the proposed model, namely, that the noetic effects of sin vary according to the complex interplay of multiple factors. This final point is illustrated pictorially by the six arrows pointing toward the center of the proposed model, indicating that people's thinking may be influenced by the complicated and unpredictable interaction of several factors related to the object of knowledge and the knowing subject. One scholar who is studying human motivation (an aspect of O_2) may be regenerate but immature in the faith (S_1), a longtime member of the American Psychological Association, a recent member of a Southern Baptist Church, and a Skinnerian by graduate training (S_2), who is a natural extrovert, still drawn to some materialistic career goals (S_3). Another scholar who is studying God's immutability (O_1) may be a mature believer noted for her genuine holiness of life (S_1), recently making strides in overcoming a painfully shy disposition (S_3), and staunch Calvinist with a Wesleyan childhood, conducting her sabbatical investigation as part of an interdenominational seminar at Fuller Theological Seminary (S_2). According to the proposed model, it is not possible to forecast exactly how sin may distort the thinking of these scholars in these particular situations.

Despite such predictive uncertainty, some broad generalizations can be made with respect to the noetic effects of sin. According to the proposed model it is generally true that sin distorts human knowledge of God more than human knowledge of the material world. The model further indicates that, in general, a person who is redeemed and is growing in sanctification through participation in a holy community will have his or her thinking less distorted by sin than a person who lives in persistent rebellion against God and participates in an evil community. Due to the complex interplay of many factors, including "individual differences," however, particular cases may defy these general rules. Hence, the model proposed here concurs with John Frame's reflections on the relationship between holiness and reasoning.

> Are the most sanctified people always the best reasoners? No. (a) For sanctification is not the only factor bearing on reason. A person's intelligence, his access to data, his education and training, his experience in reasoning, all these play a role as well. (b) For sanctification bears on all areas of human life, not only reasoning. And it affects these areas of life sometimes unevenly: a person may show his holiness by helping the poor, while not being as faithful in other areas of life. Yet sanctification *can* be an epistemological advantage, for it opens our eyes to relate our experiences to God.[86]

C. Addendum: Sin, Finitude, and Error

This book argues that sin is an important and often ignored cause of erroneous thinking. Because the book focuses solely on the noetic effects of sin, it may convey the impression that all of the mistakes and limitations of human thinking may be ascribed specifically to sin. In this brief addendum I wish to acknowledge that sin is only one factor that contributes to erroneous thinking.

Another key source of error in human thinking is human finitude. As Arthur Holmes observes, sometimes an intellectual "difficulty has more to do with limited access to evidence and arguments than with moral turpitude or willful rebellion against God."[87] Holmes is right that "error is not all due to sin and unbelief or to the misuse of human free will. Some error is due, like natural evil, to human finiteness, to the highly complicated nature of things, and to the impracticability of always suspending judgment."[88] This line of reasoning supports Holmes' conclusion that "human finiteness is not a moral failing, however, and no guilt attaches itself to errors we could not avoid."[89] Holmes' perspective on human finitude and error is echoed by John Frame.

> [Among other sources,] errors in our knowledge arise from immaturity and weakness. Even if Adam had not fallen, the acquisition of knowledge would not have taken place all at once. It would have been a historical process, part of the "subduing of the earth" (Gen. 1:28; cf. 2:19f.). Even Jesus "grew" in wisdom and stature (Luke 2:52) and "learned" obedience (Heb. 5:8) in His life as a perfect man. Certainly, then, even apart from sin, human knowledge may be incomplete; we may be ignorant in comparison to what we may know later. Thus I see no reason why even an unfallen race may not have proceeded by the method of trial and error in the continuing quest for knowledge. Error as such need not cause pain or wrongdoing; to make an honest mistake is not in itself sinful.[90]

Hence, the position taken in this book is that, as Robert Adams puts it, "not all cognitive failures are moral faults."[91] More specifically, the proposed model does not claim that all cognitive failures are *caused* by moral faults or sins. Not all intellectual mistakes should be attributed to sin. Mental errors are the products of human finitude as well as human fallenness.

Notes

1. K. Menninger, *Whatever Became of Sin?* (New York: Hawthorne Books, 1973). Though they do not address themselves directly to sin's noetic effects, the studies this decade by Peters and Plantinga may at least signal a renewed theological interest in the subject of sin (T. Peters, *Sin: Radical Evil in Soul and Society* [Grand Rapids: Eerdmans, 1994]; C. Plantinga Jr., *Not the Way It's Supposed to Be: A Breviary of Sin* [Grand Rapids: Eerdmans, 1995]).

2. This study of Kuyper focuses primarily on his extensive treatment of the noetic effects of sin in his *Principles of Sacred Theology*, trans. J. H. De Vries (Grand Rapids: Eerdmans, 1954), originally published in Dutch in 1894. As it applies to the subject at hand, I also draw occasionally from Kuyper's *Lectures on Calvinism* (Grand Rapids: Eerdmans, 1931), originally delivered as the Stone Lectures at Princeton University in 1898.

3. Kuyper, *Principles of Sacred Theology*, 178.

4. Kuyper, *Principles of Sacred Theology*, 152.

5. Kuyper, *Principles of Sacred Theology*, 118, 219-220; and *Lectures on Calvinism*, 131-141.

6. Kuyper, *Principles of Sacred Theology*, 154; see also 168, 226, 679.

7. N. Wolterstorff, "On Christian Learning," in P. A. Marshall, S. Griffioen, and R. J. Mouw (eds.), *Stained Glass: Worldviews and Social Sciences* (Lanham, MD: University Press of America, 1989), 58.

8. Kuyper, *Principles of Sacred Theology*, 103, 602, 613.

9. A. Wolters, "Dutch Neo-Calvinism: Worldview, Philosophy and Rationality," in H. Hart (ed.), *Rationality in the Calvinian Tradition* (Lanham, MD: University Press of America, 1983), 123. In regard to the first group, Kuyper believed that there was a corporate element in the sanctification of believers' thinking, stating that "in the circle of the 'enlightened' the Holy Spirit operates not merely in individuals, but also in groups and in the whole circle" (*Principles of Sacred Theology*, 290; see also 289).

10. On the principle of antithesis, see *Principles of Sacred Theology*, 168, 176 and *Lectures on Calvinism*, 130-141. Kuyper recognized the fact that the "two kinds of thinking" remained interlaced, but he attributed this to regeneration working as a continual process rather than as a complete instantaneous change (*Principles of Sacred Theology*, 162-163, 179).

It should further be acknowledged that Kuyper denied the existence of completely uniform thinking among the regenerate because he believed that regeneration "does *not* alter the differences of temperament, of personal disposition, of position in life, nor of concomitant circumstances which dominate the investigation," such that "subjective divergence continues to exist in every way" and "different schools have formed themselves" (*Principles of Sacred Theology*, 170; see also 169, 171, 177, 178).

11. As to the first exception, Kuyper asserted that "in the present dispensation palingenesis [regeneration] works no change in the senses" such that "the entire empiric investigation of the things that are perceptible to our senses (simple or reinforced) has nothing to do with the radical difference which separates the two groups" (*Principles of Sacred Theology*, 157).

In regard to the second exception, Kuyper denied that "we have lost the capacity of thinking logically," and argued contrariwise that "the logica has *not* been impaired by sin" (*Principles of Sacred Theology*, 110). Because he maintained that "the formal process of thought has *not* been attacked by sin," Kuyper held that "palingenesis [regeneration] works no change in this mental task" (*Principles of Sacred Theology*, 159).

12. Kuyper, *Principles of Sacred Theology*, 104, 157, 600.

13. On this, see Colossians 1:13, Luke 11:14-23, and Acts 26:18, as well as Augustine's characterization of the history of the world as a conflict between the *civitas dei* and the *civitas mundi*.

14. J. Klapwijk, "Rationality in the Dutch Neo-Calvinist Tradition," in H. Hart (ed.), *Rationality in the Calvinian Tradition* (Lanham, MD: University Press of America, 1983), 98.

15. D. Ratzsch, "Abraham Kuyper's Philosophy of Science," *Calvin Theological Journal* 27 (1992): 301.

16. On this, see Kuyper's *Lectures on Calvinism*, 136-137.

17. As Marsden argues, "our common humanity guarantees us considerable commonality of thought" (G. Marsden, "The Collapse of American Evangelical Academia," in A. Plantinga and N. Wolterstorff [eds.], *Faith and Rationality* [Notre Dame: University of Notre Dame Press, 1983], 256).

18. The notion that there are no neutral, uninterpreted facts observed by a neutral eye, but that observation itself is a theory-laden activity was perhaps most widely popularized by Thomas Kuhn, *The Structure of Scientific Revolutions* (Chicago: University of Chicago Press, 1962), especially chapters VI and X. On perception as an active and selective process, see Bert Hodges, "Perception, Relativity, and Knowing and Doing the Truth," in S. L. Jones (ed.), *Psychology and the Christian Faith* (Grand Rapids: Baker, 1986), 51-77.

19. Kuyper, *Principles of Sacred Theology*, 159.

20. Wolters, "Dutch Neo-Calvinism," 129.

21. Kuyper, *Lectures on Calvinism*, 132. This same extreme bifurcation is found in Cornelius Van Til, "Antitheses in Education," in L. Berkhof and C. Van Til, *Foundations of Christian Education* (Phillipsburg, NJ: Presbyterian and Reformed, 1990), 3-24. In fact Van Til even goes beyond Kuyper in arguing for an antithesis even in mathematics, for instance that "the fact that two times two are four does not mean the same thing to you as a believer and to someone else as an unbeliever" (7).

22. Wolterstorff, "On Christian Learning," 69.

23. Wolters, "Dutch Neo-Calvinism," 129.

24. Wolterstorff, "On Christian Learning," 69.

25. E. P. Heideman, *The Relation of Revelation and Reason in E. Brunner and H. Bavinck* (Assen, Netherlands: Van Gorcum, 1959), 209, note 6. Wolters (103) explains that "for Bavinck, the kingdom of truth can no more be equated with those who have

been born again than can the kingdom of Satan with those who have not been born again; among the former there is in fact much error present, among the latter much truth."

26. This study of Brunner focuses primarily on his treatment of the noetic effects of sin in three of his major works: *Der Mensch im Widerspruch* (Berlin: Furche-Verlag, 1937); *Offenbarung und Vernunft* (Zürich: Zwingli-Verlag, 1941); and *Die christliche Lehre von Schöpfung und Erlösung*, Dogmatik Band II (Zürich: Zwingli-Verlag, 1950). The respective English translations, all completed by Olive Wyon, are *Man in Revolt* (Philadelphia: Westminster, 1939); *Revelation and Reason* (Philadelphia: Westminster, 1946); and *The Christian Doctrine of Creation and Redemption*, Dogmatics: Volume II (Philadelphia: Westminster, 1952).

27. Brunner, *Revelation and Reason*, 55, note 11; *Offenbarung und Vernunft*, 56, note 11. See also Brunner's related claim that "in the New Testament there is an 'instrumental' conception of reason: it is good when it is rightly used; it is bad when it is controlled by the sinful heart in a sinful way" (*Revelation and Reason*, 310, continuation of note 1 from 309; *Offenbarung und Vernunft*, 306, continuation of note 1 from 305).

28. Brunner, *Man in Revolt*, 254; *Der Mensch im Widerspruch*, 257. In Brunner's view such "*eine rationalistisch verseuchte, eine ungläubige Vernunft*" found its antidote in faith. Brunner believed that faith rids reason of its sinful misuses and illusions, purifying it in such a way that "reason is not annihilated by faith, but it is set free" (*Revelation and Reason*, 429; *Offenbarung und Vernunft*, 424).

29. Brunner, *Revelation and Reason*, 383; *Offenbarung und Vernunft*, 378.

30. On this, see also *Revelation and Reason*, 386, note 23; *Offenbarung und Vernunft*, 381, note 23.

31. Brunner, *Revelation and Reason*, 429; *Offenbarung und Vernunft*, 425.

32. Brunner, *Man in Revolt*, 255; *Der Mensch im Widerspruch*, 257.

33. Brunner, *Man in Revolt*, 62; *Der Mensch im Widerspruch*, 50.

34. Brunner, *Man in Revolt*, 247-248; *Der Mensch im Widerspruch*, 249.

35. Brunner, *Man in Revolt*, 255; *Der Mensch im Widerspruch*, 257. Almost identical language is found in *Revelation and Reason*, 384; *Offenbarung und Vernunft*, 379.

36. Brunner, *Revelation and Reason*, 429; *Offenbarung und Vernunft*, 425.

37. Brunner, *The Christian Doctrine of Creation and Redemption*, 27; *Die christliche Lehre von Schöpfung und Erlösung*, 34.

38. Brunner, *The Christian Doctrine of Creation and Redemption*, 26; *Die christliche Lehre von Schöpfung und Erlösung*, 33.

39. Brunner, *The Christian Doctrine of Creation and Redemption*, 27; *Die christliche Lehre von Schöpfung und Erlösung*, 34.

40. Brunner, *The Christian Doctrine of Creation and Redemption*, 27; *Die christliche Lehre von Schöpfung und Erlösung*, 34.

41. Brunner, *Revelation and Reason*, 383-384; *Offenbarung und Vernunft*, 379. Within these disciplines Brunner further distinguished between (1) neutral subjects (e.g., in linguistics, the "empirical description of the actual situation of language study or the growth of language" or, in law, matters of "juridical technique"), where there were no Christian distinctives, and (2) more central or fundamental questions (e.g., in linguistics, "the real kernel of the phenomenon of language" or, in law, "the nature and obligations of law and of the State") where "the difference between a Christian and a non-Christian

understanding of man comes out plainly" (*Revelation and Reason*, 385-386; *Offenbarung und Vernunft*, 380-381).

42. For example, in philosophy, Brunner argued that "even the *formal* concepts of every philosophical ontology are positions of *sinful* reason, from which, it is true, not *reason* but *sin* must be eliminated" (*Man in Revolt*, 546; *Der Mensch im Widerspruch*, 557).

43. Brunner, *The Christian Doctrine of Creation and Redemption*, 27; *Die christliche Lehre von Schöpfung und Erlösung*, 34.

44. Brunner, *Revelation and Reason*, 429; *Offenbarung und Vernunft*, 425.

45. Brunner, *Revelation and Reason*, 383; *Offenbarung und Vernunft*, 378. Statements such as this one, in which Brunner clearly differentiated theology proper from related ethical matters, led me to distinguish the two areas in my schematization, despite his occasional grouping of the two together. On this point, see also the quotations in the following paragraph of the text.

46. Brunner, *The Christian Doctrine of Creation and Redemption*, 27; *Die christliche Lehre von Schöpfung und Erlösung*, 34.

47. Brunner, *Man in Revolt*, 248; *Der Mensch im Widerspruch*, 250.

48. Brunner, *Revelation and Reason*, 383; *Offenbarung und Vernunft*, 378.

49. Brunner, *Revelation and Reason*, 383, note 20; *Offenbarung und Vernunft*, 379, note 20.

50. Brunner, *The Christian Doctrine of Creation and Redemption*, 27; *Die christliche Lehre von Schöpfung und Erlösung*, 34. For earlier statements of this "law of the closeness of relation," which are less elaborate but essentially the same, see *Man in Revolt*, 248, 255 (*Der Mensch im Widerspruch*, 249-250, 257); and *Revelation and Reason*, 429 (*Offenbarung und Vernunft*, 425).

51. Brunner, *Revelation and Reason*, 383; *Offenbarung und Vernunft*, 378.

52. Brunner, *Man in Revolt*, 255; *Der Mensch im Widerspruch*, 257.

53. Brunner, *The Christian Doctrine of Creation and Redemption*, 27; *Die christliche Lehre von Schöpfung und Erlösung*, 34.

54. Romans 6:1-14.

55. Romans 6:15-23.

56. 1 John 3:4-10.

57. J. Frame, *The Doctrine of the Knowledge of God* (Phillipsburg, NJ: Presbyterian and Reformed, 1987): 153.

58. 1 John 1:8-10.

59. 1 Corinthians 14:20; Hebrews 5:11-14.

60. Romans 12:2, Ephesians 4:23. As Frame acknowledges, there is a need not only for noetic regeneration but also for noetic sanctification (*The Doctrine of the Knowledge of God*, 154).

61. See, for example, the Kuyperian comment of Ratzsch (301) that "as we go up the scale of disciplines and out into the further, more global theoretical reaches of each of the individual disciplines, our Christian antennae must be increasingly sensitive (just as those most keenly aware of the antithesis claim), for it is in those areas that unbelieving subjectivity can (and perhaps eventually must) make its appearance." Here the "Christian antennae" tune in to the effects of "unbelieving subjectivity" in "the science of unbelievers" (301), but not the effects of sin on the work of Christian scientists.

62. Peters, *Sin*, 10.

63. Cornelius Plantinga Jr., "Not the Way It's S'pposed to Be: A Breviary of Sin," *Theology Today* 50 (July 1993): 184.

64. As Buber argues, our knowledge of the impersonal world (I-It) is qualitatively different than our knowledge of other human beings and God (I-Thou) (M. Buber, *I and Thou* [New York: Scribner, 1937]).

65. On the subjective or personal factors in human knowledge, see M. Polanyi, *Personal Knowledge* (Chicago: University of Chicago Press, 1958).

66. J. Cooper, "Agreeing to Disagree," *The Reformed Journal* 31 (1981): 12-13.

67. W. A. Hoffecker, "Augustine, Aquinas, and the Reformers," in W. A. Hoffecker (ed.), *Building a Christian World View*, vol. 1 (Phillipsburg, NJ: Presbyterian and Reformed, 1986), 257. See also related observations in A. Holmes, *Contours of a World View* (Grand Rapids: Eerdmans, 1983), 131; R. Pazmiño, *Principles and Practices of Christian Education* (Grand Rapids, MI: Baker, 1992), 30; and R. Pazmiño, *By What Authority Do We Teach?* (Grand Rapids, MI: Baker, 1994), 108, 130.

68. N. F. S. Ferré, *Faith and Reason* (New York: Harper and Brothers, 1946): 234.

69. Talbot, M. "Is It Natural to Believe in God," *Faith and Philosophy* 6 (1989): 163-164.

70. J. Frame, "Van Til and the Ligonier Apologetic," *Westminster Theological Journal* 47 (1985): 291.

71. Zemek's study supports the proposed model in his conclusion that regeneration establishes an initial reorientation of people's mental capacities, but continued sanctification is required for further growth in godliness (G. J. Zemek, "Aiming the Mind: A Key to Godly Living," *Grace Theological Journal* 5 [1984]: 205).

72. A. MacIntyre, *Whose Justice? Which Rationality?* (Notre Dame: University of Notre Dame Press, 1988).

73. Plantinga Jr., *Theology Today*, 191.

74. J. Habermas, *Knowledge and Human Interests* (Boston: Beacon Press, 1971), 311.

75. On the correspondence between Israel's corporate sin and Yahweh's judgment, see Patrick D. Miller Jr., *Sin and Judgment in the Prophets* (Chico, CA: Scholars Press, 1982). In regard to terminology, I take it that my preferred phrase "corporate sin" is synonymous with "communal sin," "collective sin," "social sin," and "communitarian sin." I take it that phrases such as "systemic sin" or "structural sin" designate the institutionalized manifestations of (mainly corporate) sin. On the history and interrelationship of these terms, see Marciano Vidal, "Structural Sin: A New Category in Moral Theology?" in R. Gallagher and B. McConvery (eds.), *History and Conscience* (Dublin, Ireland: Gill and MacMillan, 1989), 181-198.

76. S. C. Mott, "Biblical Faith and the Reality of Social Evil," *Christian Scholar's Review* 9 (1980): 235.

77. R. L. Montgomery, "Bias in Interpreting Social Facts: Is it a Sin?" *Journal for the Scientific Study of Religion* 23 (1984): 290.

78. Mott, "Biblical Faith," 237. See also Merold Westphal's related argument that Marx, Nietzsche, and Freud may aid Christians in detecting corrupt uses of religion

(M. Westphal, *Suspicion and Faith: The Religious Uses of Modern Atheism* [Grand Rapids: Eerdmans, 1993]).

79. For example, on racism, see C. V. Willie, "Getting a Handle on Institutional Sin," *The Witness* 64 (March 1981): 17-18. On sexism, see B. Greene, "Women, Men and Corporate Sin," *Daughters of Sarah* 4 (May 1978): 5-6, and 4 (July 1978): 5-7. On economic exploitation, see J. Sobrino, "500 Years: Structural Sin and Structural Grace," *SEDOS Bulletin* 24 (May 15, 1992): 151-156. Related observations may be found in J. N. Poling, *Deliver Us from Evil* (Minneapolis: Augsburg Fortress, 1996), especially part one.

80. R. Clark and S. Gaede, "Knowing Together: Reflections on a Holistic Sociology of Knowledge," in H. Heie and D. Wolfe (eds.), *The Reality of Christian Learning* (Grand Rapids: Eerdmans, 1987), 69.

81. For a dramatic recognition of corporate sin, see the Confessing Church's "Intercession Liturgy" of September 1938 in P. Matheson (ed.), *The Third Reich and the Christian Churches* (Grand Rapids: Eerdmans, 1981), 77-78.

82. Clark and Gaede, "Knowing Together," 68.

83. J. Baillie, *Our Knowledge of God* (New York: Charles Scribner's Sons, 1959), 179.

84. Daniel Fuller makes the provocative argument that unbelievers who reject the authority of the Bible and regard it as foolishness have no need to distort the Bible's teachings and may exegete it accurately (presence of volitional effects of sin render noetic effects of sin less likely). Conversely, believers who accept the authority of the Bible and realize that they ought to submit to its teachings are at special risk for distorting the Bible's teachings whenever it clashes with their sinful egos (absence of volitional effects of sin render noetic effects of sin more likely). On this, see D. P. Fuller, "The Holy Spirit's Role in Biblical Interpretation," in W. W. Gasque and W. S. LaSor (eds.), *Scripture, Tradition, and Interpretation* (Grand Rapids: Eerdmans, 1978), 189-198, especially 197-198. Another intriguing analysis of the bidirectional interplay between reason and will may be found in T. D. Cuneo, "Combating the Noetic Effects of Sin: Pascal's Strategy for Natural Theology," *Faith and Philosophy* 11 (1994): 645-662.

85. W. M. Swartley, *Slavery, Sabbath, War, and Women* (Scottdale, PA: Herald Press, 1983), especially 22, 62, 185, 208, 227, and 230-231.

86. J. Frame, "Rationality and Scripture," in H. Hart (ed.) *Rationality in the Calvinian Tradition* (Lanham, MD: University Press of America, 1983), 309. The position taken in the present study is much the same in regard to the "epistemological privilege of the poor," as it is discussed, for instance, by Hugo Assman. The model proposed here agrees that "the value-laden viewpoint of the oppressed is less distorted than that of the oppressors whose vision propagates the interests of the powerful at the expense of the weak" (E. Schmidt, "In Candid Conversation: Theology and Sociology of Knowledge," in B. Hargrove [ed.], *Religion and the Sociology of Knowledge* [New York: The Edwin Mellen Press, 1984], 22-23). Because "prosperity and power can distort our thinking" (Clark and Gaede, 81), there is a sense in which being oppressed provides one with an advantageous viewpoint from which to apprehend God, although those who are oppressed will not *always* be the best theologians, due to the complex interplay of the multiple factors discussed in the proposed model.

87. A. Holmes, *All Truth Is God's Truth* (Grand Rapids: Eerdmans, 1977), 52.

88. Holmes, *All Truth Is God's Truth*, 66.

89. Holmes, *Contours of a World View*, 134.
90. Frame, *The Doctrine of the Knowledge of God*, 20.
91. R. M. Adams, "The Virtue of Faith," *Faith and Philosophy* 1 (1984): 4.

Chapter 3

Pannenberg's Rationalist Theology

The first two chapters of this book provide an exposition and critical evaluation of the teachings of Calvin, Kuyper, and Brunner on how our thinking is affected by sin. The second chapter also proposes a new contemporary model of the noetic effects of sin. The next three chapters use the new model as a basis for critical reflection on prominent current ideas in theology, philosophy, and psychology respectively. In each case, it is argued that the noetic effects of sin have been overlooked or minimized. This chapter focuses on the rationalist theology of Wolfhart Pannenberg.

I. Description

A. Background

Pannenberg was born in 1928 in Stettin, Germany. After studying philosophy and theology under (among others) Karl Jaspers, Karl Barth, Gerhard von Rad, and Edmund Schlink, Pannenberg has served as professor of systematic theology at Wuppertal, Mainz, and Munich.[1] Pannenberg is a significant figure in the contemporary theological scene. As Stanley Grenz notes: "Wolfhart Pannenberg has distinguished himself as one of the most creative theologians of the post-Barthian era, and his program offers promise of exerting lasting influence on the theological world."[2]

It is recognized that Pannenberg "defies categorization into the traditional schools of theological thought."[3] The difficulty of classifying Pannenberg's thought was evident very early in his career, as is manifest in Carl Braaten's assessment in 1965.

The neo-fundamentalists would enjoy his position on the historical verifiability of the resurrection as a datable event of past history. The orthodox would like the sound of *notitia, assensus,* and *fiducia* but wouldn't know what to do about his antisupernaturalism. *Heilsgeschichte* theologians would endorse his stress on history but generally not approve of eliminating the prophetic word from the definition of revelation. Historians would applaud his devotion to the facts, but few would succeed in reading revelation right off the facts of history. Those who see Pannenberg's theology as a revival of conservatism need only to meet his doctrine of scripture and of the confessions to be disabused of any illusions. Pannenberg's theology obviously escapes ready-made labels.[4]

Over twenty years later, in 1986, William Placher's observations reflected the continuing difficulty in classifying Pannenberg's theological orientation.

Pannenberg has often been misunderstood in this country [the United States]. First he was classified with the theology of hope, and then some conservatives found comfort in his historical arguments for Jesus' resurrection. But theologians of hope like Moltmann and Metz have more in common with the theology of liberation, while Pannenberg's politics are rather conservative. And the important feature of his discussion of Jesus' resurrection was his emphasis on argument and historical evidence. More than anything else he is an Hegelian.[5]

Yet, even Placher's characterization of Pannenberg as an Hegelian is disputed. Merold Westphal has described Pannenberg as "the most articulate anti-Hegelian since Kierkegaard."[6]

The perspective taken in this chapter is that, whatever else he is, Pannenberg is an apologist and a rationalist. Grenz is right that as an apologist Pannenberg's "central purpose is to demonstrate the intellectual respectability of Christian faith in a secular society, both within the walls of the church and in the marketplace of ideas."[7] Pannenberg is pessimistic in his assessment of how the "general public today" views theology, arguing that "in the public mind statements about God are mere assertions which are ascribed to the subjectivity of the speaker" such that "the truth claims of statements about God are not even worth discussing publicly."[8] In response to this bleak situation, Pannenberg operates as an apologist for Christianity, both to the academy and to the general public. According to Pannenberg, the task of theology today is to "make the primacy of God and his revelation in Jesus Christ intelligible, and validate its truth claim, in an age when all talk about God is reduced to subjectivity."[9] Pannenberg believes that theology in which "the result is a foregone conclusion, independent of the cogency of the arguments," tragically "has helped to discredit theology in the public mind."[10] Pannenberg opposes the privatization of religion, and insists that theology be a public discipline, and "as a public theology Pannenberg's dogmatics focuses on reason."[11] As Placher puts it, Pannenberg may be classified "as a theologian of reason."[12]

In this chapter, Pannenberg's ideas will be analyzed through an examination of (1) his methodological statements about the role of reason in theology, (2) his doctrinal assertions concerning sin, and (3) his substantive claims for revelation as history.[13] The subsections describing Pannenberg's viewpoint will be followed by corresponding subsections criticizing his outlook. The main argument of the critical sections is that in a variety of ways Pannenberg has not accounted adequately for the noetic effects of sin, and that his theology could be further strengthened by incorporating insights from the proposed model of the noetic effects of sin.

B. Methodological Statements about the Role of Reason in Theology[14]

Pannenberg acknowledges that he very much "wishes to escape from the religious subjectivism which lies at the root of modern Protestant dogmatics."[15] He characterizes religious subjectivism as "irrational fanaticism" which "hands the Christian faith over to an atheistic psychology of religion which traces the irrational need to believe back to secular roots."[16] Along with Loescher, Schäder, and Barth before him, Pannenberg is critical of "the Pietist linking of the possibility of theology to the believing subject" because this "involves a false anthropocentrism which contradicts the implications of serious discourse about God."[17] In Pannenberg's view, "the subjectivization and individualization of piety," which argues that "the content of faith is present only for the pious subjectivity, so that its truth cannot be presented in a way that can claim universal binding force" has threatened the very life of the Christian church.[18]

As an antidote to the evils of religious subjectivism, Pannenberg argues that "to the presentation of church doctrine, then, there must be added a critical element. It must be tested against scripture in accordance with the claim of the confessional writings themselves. Its inner coherence and its relation to the truths of reason (*Vernunftwahrheiten*) must also be investigated."[19] Pannenberg is convinced that in order for the church to avoid being criticized for "mere assertion" which is indistinguishable from fanaticism (a criticism to which Barth is vulnerable, according to Pannenberg), what is needed is the mediation of reasoning.[20]

Pannenberg argues that human reason possesses a demand for "a final explanation of the world's existence,"[21] and he spares no effort in the attempt to demonstrate that Christian doctrine agrees with "the principles of reason."[22] Hence, Pannenberg is attracted to the demand "that in the field of rational argumentation theology should examine what it believes subjectively by reason alone (*sola ratione*). It may not, then, make the subjective presupposition of faith the starting point of the argument. The force of the argument alone is what counts."[23] Given that in the modern consciousness God is no longer a self-evident presupposition, Pannenberg believes that "every theological statement must prove itself on the field of reason, and can no longer be argued on the basis of unquestioned presuppositions of faith."[24]

Pannenberg also recognizes, however, that "reason alone" has its limits. He finds that "the rational theology of the Enlightenment" was not cogent because it was unable to "prove the existence of God by strict reason."[25] Pannenberg additionally acknowledges the possible existence of a mistaken universal human consensus grounded in an invincible human prejudice,[26] the relativity of hermeneutical perspectives,[27] and the subjective conditioning of human judgments about what is true or false.[28] For these reasons, Pannenberg concedes "the impossibility of a theology that is based on pure reason,"[29] and he grants that it is proper for Christians to exhibit "intellectual humility which does not directly equate personal teaching with divine truth."[30]

Pannenberg's recognition of the limits of human reason is rooted primarily in his recognition of the limits that characterize human finitude. According to Pannenberg, "the finitude of theological knowledge" is grounded in "the limitation of information" about God, and even more importantly, in "the time-bound nature of the knowledge."[31] For Pannenberg, "the historicity of human experience and reflection forms the most important limit of our human knowledge of God. Solely on account of its historicity all human talk about God unavoidably falls short of full and final knowledge of the truth of God."[32] Pannenberg argues that "recognizing the finitude and inappropriateness of all human talk about God is an essential part of theological sobriety."[33]

In accordance with such sobriety, Pannenberg contends that all Christian dogma (human knowledge of God in the present) is preliminary and provisional,[34] so that "epistemologically the statements of dogmatics and the theses of the Christian doctrine which it presents are given the status of hypotheses."[35] In Pannenberg's schema, human finitude, which is grounded in human historicity, dictates that all human knowledge of God "will always be preliminary so long as time and history endure."[36] Pannenberg finds that when it is compared to the definitive revelation of God at the eschaton, "the knowledge of Christian theology is always partial."[37]

Briefly, in his methodological statements about the role of reason in theology, Pannenberg does lean in a "rationalist" direction in making "reason alone" the final court of appeal for theological argumentation, and he leans in this direction in self-conscious reaction to what he perceives as the excesses of religious subjectivism. However, Pannenberg also recognizes that human reason is limited because of human finitude, which he understands primarily in terms of human historicity.

C. Doctrinal Assertions Concerning Sin[38]

In Pannenberg's view, human sin is one of the two basic anthropological topics in Christian theology (the creation of humans in the image of God being the other).[39] Pannenberg further observes that human sin is a topic which has been obscured,[40] and that in the modern world it is exceedingly difficult "to win new credibility for the core content of traditional Christian terms in this field."[41] According to Pannenberg, one major factor which has obscured this topic and reduced its credibility is the traditional teaching of an original state of human perfection followed by a fall and the subsequent transmission of sin which results in the depravity of the entire human race.[42] Pannenberg himself rejects this traditional teaching.[43] Pannenberg denies Jürgen Moltmann's view "that human personality, other than in the case of the incarnation, is necessarily characterized by the sin of egocentricity," in favor or the view that "we are sinners only as in our defectiveness we strive after autonomy and make ourselves absolute."[44] Despite his rejection of the doctrine of original sin, Pannenberg does maintain the universality of human sin.[45] In Pannenberg's view, sin is "the universal human failure to achieve our human destiny" which is often manifest in "a life in anxiety, unbridled desire, and aggressiveness" and is only rarely manifest in "the naked hubris of our human wanting to be as God."[46]

Pannenberg is convinced not only that sin is a universal phenomenon, but also that sin has a pervasive influence on human existence. In this regard, Pannenberg believes that there is a corporate or social dimension to sin.[47] He argues that "as there can be no separating individual and social life, the former being always co-constituted by social relations, so sin also works itself out in the social forms of life."[48]

Pannenberg doubts whether "Kant really grasped the radicalness of evil and its root in human life" and criticizes Kant for not perceiving "in its comprehensive significance for all aspects of human life the contradiction present in the self-realization of the ego."[49] Pannenberg finds Augustine's "explanation of the moral perversity of the ego" much more satisfactory than Kant's.[50] Pannenberg also criticizes Hobbes for viewing reason "as an agency that is free of the biases of the passions," arguing that "there is a contradiction on this point between Hobbes's anthropology and that of Christian theology."[51]

Pannenberg contends that "sin is located in the will" because it is in our wills that we fail to "correspond to our destiny."[52] Pannenberg speaks of "the enslavement of the will" and "the will's bondage, which leaves intact the power to choose, that is, the formal act of self-transcendence, but reduces its range."[53] In Pannenberg's schema, it follows that "the bondage of the will calls, therefore, for a liberation and, in the radical case, for a redemption that will establish the will's identity anew."[54]

D. Substantive Claims for Revelation As History[55]

According to Pannenberg, revelation is a necessary prerequisite for human knowledge of God. As Pannenberg puts it, "God can be known only if he gives himself to be known. The loftiness of the divine reality makes it inaccessible to us unless it makes itself known. . . . Hence the knowledge of God is possible only by revelation."[56] The question then arises as to exactly how God is revealed to humans. Pannenberg's response may be summarized in four main ideas.

First, Pannenberg argues that Yahweh is revealed as God by Yahweh's historical deeds, especially those historical deeds which were foretold by the prophets. Pannenberg states frankly that Yahweh "showed himself to be God by the historical deeds he performed. In what way? By the fact that the events announced in his name in fact took place."[57] Hence, Pannenberg understands revelation to be "the self-demonstration of God by his historical action, the results of which are disclosed in advance to the prophet or apocalyptic seer."[58]

Second, Pannenberg denies that God's various historical actions are all of equal value in revealing God to us. For Pannenberg, Jesus' resurrection is the decisive act in which God's power and love are revealed to us, and in comparison to Jesus' resurrection, all of God's earlier actions of self-revelation are purely provisional (*vorläufig*).[59] Pannenberg contends that unlike previous self-disclosures of God, "what happened in and through Jesus cannot, however, be superseded by any future events because in him precisely the end of all things has occurred. Consequently Jesus' resurrection, and in its light the rest of his history and actions, is the one unique revelation of the deity of the one God."[60]

Third, Pannenberg argues that God's revelation is indirect, such that "his deeds indirectly throw light back on him."[61] Pannenberg believes that "the indirectness of God's self-revelation" is supported by "the biblical texts themselves" in which the direct content of revelation "is not God himself but ourselves and our world."[62]

Fourth, Pannenberg argues that only at the end of history, when God's self-revealing acts are finished, will people have a full knowledge of God. He states that "it is only when the revealing events are completed that they can produce knowledge of the deity of Yahweh as, so to speak, their last act."[63] Pannenberg defends the thesis that "revelation is not comprehended completely in the beginning, but at the end of the revealing history."[64] In a sentence, Pannenberg maintains that God is revealed through God's historical actions, the most important action being Jesus' resurrection, though God's revelation must be understood as indirect and incomplete prior to the end of history.

In regard to the human reception of God's self-revelation, Pannenberg insists that the facts of history themselves demonstrate God's deity. Pannenberg makes a sustained argument that "no special 'supernatural' presuppositions are necessary in order to recognize the deity of Yahweh in the events announced, only the language of the facts themselves which will take place before the eyes of all," that "the facts themselves preach the message announced by Paul," and that "Christians ought surely to be the last faint-heartedly to minimize the universal truth of the revelation of God in the Christ-event, as though the facts themselves did not demonstrate God's deity, as though a pious interpretation was needed for that."[65]

In Pannenberg's view, humans have no need of supernatural, pious interpretation to properly understand God's self-revelation.

The events in which God demonstrated his deity are self-evident as they stand within the framework of their own history. It does not require any kind of inspired interpretation to make these events recognizable as revelation. R. Rothe's assertion of the need for an inspiration that would supplement the outer proclamation of the manifestation and make it into a recognizable manifestation of God is an assertion that misses the point.[66]

According to Pannenberg, Israel had no need for a prophetic word to properly interpret historical events.[67] Likewise, Christians had no need to "wait for an experience of the Spirit in order to come to know God in Jesus."[68] Indeed, Pannenberg believes that "it is precisely the other way round; the Spirit is present when anyone recognizes Jesus' life-history as a revelation of God. Only through the Gospel of Jesus Christ and faith in it, is the Spirit bestowed (Ga. 3.2, 14)."[69]

Pannenberg asserts that unprejudiced historical research is sufficient to see God at work in God's historical acts. Pannenberg is emphatic that "the rational (*vernünftige*), unprejudiced (*vorurteilslose*) consideration of what happened [in the events of Jesus' history], must recognize in them the demonstration of the deity of the God of Israel."[70] Pannenberg contends that "as long as historiography does not begin dogmatically with a narrow concept of reality according to which 'dead men do not rise,'" it will conclude that, in light of the appearance tradition and the empty tomb tradition (which are independent and mutually complementary), the reality of Jesus' resurrection is "historically very probable, and that always means in historical inquiry that it is to be presupposed until contrary evidence appears."[71]

Pannenberg goes so far as to say that it is historical research alone, unsupplemented by faith, which can rightly determine the proper meaning of historical events. He insists that nothing should be given priority over "the instruments of historical criticism" in determining the certainty of a past event:

Whether or not a particular event happened two thousand years ago is not made certain by faith but only by historical research, to the extent that certainty can be attained at all about questions of this kind. . . . The only method of achieving at least approximate certainty with regard to the events of a past time is historical research.[72]

If, however, historical study declares itself unable to establish what "really" happened on Easter, then all the more, faith is not able to do so; for faith cannot ascertain anything certain about events of the past that would perhaps be inaccessible to the historian.[73]

Pannenberg believes that for Jesus' Jewish contemporaries, and also for unprejudiced historians today, Jesus' resurrection is a self-interpreting event which is unambiguous in its meaning.[74] Pannenberg boldly asserts that "in the context of Jewish experience the meaning of the event [Jesus' resurrection] was so clear that no one to whom the Lord appeared could acknowledge the event and remain an unbeliever."[75] According to Pannenberg, "in distinction from special manifestations of the deity, the historical revelation is open to anyone who has eyes to see. It has a universal character."[76] In this way, God's historical self-revelation is accessible to all people.

II. Criticisms

A. Initial Remarks

Pannenberg is without a doubt a profound and creative thinker. His knowledge of exegesis, historical theology, and contemporary theology, coupled with his ability to interact skillfully with "non-theological" disciplines, is perhaps unparalleled in the late twentieth century. As Placher puts it, Pannenberg "seems almost casually the master of biblical research, patristic and medieval texts, Protestant scholasticism, the 19th century. It's hard to think of anything he doesn't know. Pannenberg may well be the most erudite living Christian theologian."[77]

Pannenberg has unquestionably done much in accomplishing his goal to "make the primacy of God and his revelation in Jesus Christ intelligible, and validate its truth claim, in an age when all talk about God is reduced to subjectivity."[78] David Holwerda puts it this way:

> Pannenberg is to be commended for grasping the theological pendulum and pushing it in the opposite direction. In a world which has come to doubt that the Gospel makes any claims concerning truth, in which certain theologians even have thought it necessary to surrender virtually all claims to the historical truth of the Gospel in order to preserve the authority of the kerygma, a theology trying to demonstrate the contrary is absolutely essential.[79]

Pannenberg has been (and continues to be) a significant apologist, primarily to academicians and secondarily to the educated public. There is much in Pannenberg's outlook to be appreciated. Hence, the remarks that follow should be understood as constructive criticisms, which are intended to further strengthen his viewpoint.

B. Methodological Statements about the Role of Reason in Theology

My main criticism of Pannenberg's methodological statements is that in his zeal to avoid the "ruinous consequence" of an extreme subjectivism,[80] he neglects the subjective and personal components in human thinking, including, notably, the noetic effects of sin. I argue that (1) human finitude is significant in limiting our knowledge of God, and (2) sin is significant in distorting our thinking about God. Pannenberg argues only for the former.[81]

Pannenberg's imbalance in this regard is evident in his treatment of Romans 1:18ff. When Pannenberg addresses this important Pauline passage, his sole concern is to establish the existence of universal knowledge of God received by the light of human reason from the works of creation.[82] To my knowledge, Pannenberg never addresses himself in any sustained way to the sinful repression and distortion of the "natural knowledge of God," despite the fact that this is such a prominent feature of Paul's argument in these verses. Paul's statements that people "suppressed the truth by their wickedness" (v. 18), that people's "thinking became futile" (v. 21), that people "became fools" (v. 22), and that people "exchanged the truth of God for a lie" (v. 25) receive practically no comment from Pannenberg.[83] According to the proposed model of the noetic effects of sin (specifically, the component concerning regeneration and sanctification of the knowing subject, as diagrammed on page 36), Pannenberg needs to attend more carefully to the subjective and personal aspects of human thinking. He needs to recognize not only that human finitude (or human historicity) limits our knowledge of God, but also that human sin distorts our thinking about God.

A second criticism of Pannenberg concerns the way in which he frequently hypostatizes "reason." As was evident in the descriptive section (I.B), Pannenberg speaks freely of "the principles of reason (*Prinzipien der Vernunft*),"[84] "the truths of reason (*Vernunftwahrheiten*),"[85] and "the need for meaning of human reason (*das Sinnbedürfnis der menschlichen Vernunft*)."[86] Indeed, such a hypostatization of "reason" is necessary if Pannenberg is to meet the demand "that in the field of rational argumentation theology should examine what it believes subjectively by reason alone (*sola ratione*)."[87] To paraphrase MacIntyre, the question which Pannenberg must answer here is "Whose reason?"[88]

At times Pannenberg appears to recognize the impropriety of speaking simply of "reason."[89] For instance, he criticizes Kant's position as erroneous in claiming "that the reason is the same in all men because its basic structures are supposed to be established *a priori* and to precede all experience."[90] Pannenberg asserts that, "Kant remained in the grip of the Enlightenment at this point in that he had not yet recognized the real root of the spontaneity of reason, which is its historicness."[91] Similarly Pannenberg questions Hume for positing a monolithic entity known as "*the* modern reason" which foredooms the Christian faith as nothing more than "a subjectivity which lacks any intersubjective binding force."[92] Pannenberg contends that "upon closer inspection, 'reason' is by no means a uniformly determined entity," but, ironically, on the same page, he also states that "every theological statement must prove itself on the field of reason."[93] So, he equivocates between acknowledging variety in human standards of rationality (which he attributes principally to human historicity) and speaking of human reason in universal terms (his more normal usage of the term).[94]

The model proposed in the preceding chapter (especially the three components concerning the knowing subject) indicates that human thinking is a dynamic, complex process influenced by multiple factors, including sin. Hence, it is preferable to speak of human thinking (or perhaps "reasoning" as a verb) instead of speaking of "reason" (as a noun, connoting a hypostatized entity). In short, Pannenberg needs to speak less of the abstract item "reason" and more of the concrete process of "reasoning." He also needs to recognize that not just human historicity, but also human sin, contributes to differences in people's thinking, especially their thinking about God.

A third criticism of Pannenberg's methodological statements concerns his failure to account for the ways in which regeneration and sanctification influence human thinking, especially human thinking about God. Through his study of Luther's view of reason,[95] Pannenberg is aware of some of the issues at stake here, but he steadfastly refuses to make humans' fallenness, regeneration, and sanctification significant categories in his analysis of reason. For instance, Pannenberg acknowledges that Luther and Melanchthon distrusted reason because it "was enslaved and blinded after the fall," and was therefore "unreliable in matters of the knowledge of God."[96] Yet Pannenberg himself is not so distrustful of the thinking of sinful humans. Pannenberg also acknowledges that Luther "spoke of a renewal of reason by faith."[97] Yet Pannenberg himself rarely speaks of the need for reason to be renewed by faith. Pannenberg realizes that Luther and early Lutheran dogmatics emphasized "the concrete rooting of the actual use of reason in the prevailing total orientation of people as sinners or believers."[98] However, it is precisely such an analysis of how people's spiritual state influences their thinking that is so conspicuously absent in Pannenberg's writings.[99] Pannenberg recognizes that Luther "praise[d] reason illuminated by faith as much as he disparaged natural reason."[100] Nevertheless, Pannenberg eschews categories such as natural (or fallen) reason and illuminated (or regenerated) reason in favor of speaking of reason in universal terms, and this with very little disparagement. So, a third implication of the model proposed in this study (in particular, the assertions regarding the object of knowledge and the assertions regarding the spiritual state of the knowing subject) is that Pannenberg needs not only to acknowledge but also to adopt some of Luther's insights and to attend more carefully to the ways in which sin, regeneration, and sanctification influence human thinking, especially human thinking about God.

C. Doctrinal Assertions Concerning Sin

From my perspective, Pannenberg is to be applauded for realizing that human sin is a topic which is central to Christian anthropology, and for emphasizing the pervasive way in which sin influences human existence. The problem is that Pannenberg has neglected one of the important ways in which sin influences human existence, namely, the way in which sin influences human thinking. As was noted in the descriptive section (I.C), Pannenberg speaks freely of the bondage of the will which calls for a liberation or for "a redemption that will establish the will's identity anew,"[101] but he does not speak of the need for a liberation or redemption of human thinking to reorient it or establish its identity anew. Pannenberg is right that the will's bondage leaves the power to choose intact, but reduces its range.[102] He simply needs to extend his analysis to include the parallel reality that when people's minds are in bondage to sin, their power to think is left intact, but the range of their thought is reduced. Pannenberg fails to acknowledge that godly thinking is not possible apart from the regenerating and sanctifying work of the Spirit.

Pannenberg hits the mark in arguing that new birth is necessary to liberate human eros from sin and its egoism.[103] Again, what is needed is to extend these claims to the realm of human thinking. In short, though Pannenberg asserts the pervasiveness of sin, he fails to apply this doctrine sufficiently when it comes to the area of human thought.

I believe Pannenberg also is quite right to criticize Kant for not accounting adequately for sin's "comprehensive significance for all aspects of human life."[104] However, Pannenberg himself does not account adequately for the significance of sin for human thinking. Similarly, Pannenberg is correct to observe that Christian theology contradicts Hobbes' anthropology (in which reason is viewed as an agency which is "free of the biases of the passions").[105] The problem is that Pannenberg himself does not fully incorporate this insight of Christian theology (that human thinking is biased by passions) into his own system. In the hundreds of pages of his anthropological writings, the only clear reference to this phenomenon which I have been able to locate is Pannenberg's teaching, following Paul, that our reason "is hopelessly subject to the blind drive for self-fulfillment."[106]

Pannenberg properly objects to the Enlightenment view of humanity because "it found no more than a minor place for the brokenness of human reality. It did not let this affect its trust in reason."[107] Nevertheless, Pannenberg also neglects the effects of sin on human thinking and does not allow the reality of human sin to substantially affect his own trust in "reason." In the concluding paragraph to the chapter on anthropology in his *Systematic Theology*, Pannenberg remarks that reason (and law) can restrain the destructive effects of sin,[108] but he fails to acknowledge that human thinking ("reason") itself is affected by the distorting power of sin. In brief, Pannenberg himself is subject to several criticisms which he levels at others for their deficiencies in developing comprehensive accounts of sin and "reason."

D. Substantive Claims for Revelation As History

One criticism of Pannenberg's view of revelation as history is that it simply does not square with the experience of many Christian believers. Pannenberg implies that the way that people ought to come to faith in Christ (confessing Christ's deity) is by calmly weighing arguments on the historicity of the resurrection of Jesus of Nazareth.[109] Pannenberg insinuates that the only legitimate way that people can know that Jesus is alive today as the risen and exalted Lord is by careful historical investigation and close scholarly reasoning.[110] The problem for Pannenberg here is that in reality most Christians do not come to faith in Christ solely or even primarily as the result of deliberate historical research. Avery Dulles is properly critical of "Pannenberg's contention that critical historical research is the only reliable avenue of access to the past."[111]

> With this assertion he apparently rejects the trustworthiness of other channels, such as the apostolic witness, the Christian tradition, and the creeds. Yet it is on these other sources that most Christians rely for their convictions about the saving events that sustain their faith. Very few have the skills or leisure to conduct personal research evaluating the authenticity of the Gospel accounts. . . . Rare indeed is the individual who comes to Christian faith from a detached historical analysis of Christian origins such as one finds in the work of E. P. Sanders. The ordinary catalyst of faith is the religious testimony of convinced believers.[112]

Pannenberg has attempted to respond to this criticism by distinguishing between what he calls "the psychology of faith" and "the logic of faith." According to this distinction, the logic of faith dictates that trust (*fiducia*) must be grounded on some previous knowledge (*notitia*).[113] Otherwise, a ruinous subjectivism results.[114] However, in the psychology of faith, Pannenberg indicates that an "ordinary Christian believer" might come to trust in Christ initially without extensive historical investigation into Jesus of Nazareth and his resurrection, in the expectation that when he or she undertook such an investigation he or she would find strong evidence in support of his or her beliefs. According to Pannenberg, here "one conjecturingly anticipates the result, but must then confirm this conjecture, find verification of it."[115]

Alternatively, an "ordinary Christian believer" might come to trust in Christ without extensive historical investigation into Jesus of Nazareth and his resurrection on the assumption that his or her source of information (Bible, friend, clergy, etc.) is reliable. Pannenberg acknowledges that "believing trust can also arise in such a way that the believer does not always have to prove on his own the trustworthiness of the knowledge presupposed therein. It is the special task of theology to do this. Not every individual Christian needs to undertake this task."[116] According to Pannenberg, knowledge (obtained by historical research) logically must precede faith (believing trust), but faith psychologically may precede knowledge.[117] In Pannenberg's view, this explains both the necessity for careful historical inquiry, as well as the experience of many Christian believers.

A second, and closely related criticism brought against Pannenberg's view of revelation as history is that it does not square with the experience of many non-Christian historians. In some of his writings Pannenberg gives the impression that one should be able to demonstrate the divinity of Jesus to any rational inquirer.[118] The problem, of course, is that many people, including well-trained, competent historians, who examine the evidence for Jesus' resurrection remain unconvinced by it. Hence, Ernst Fuchs asks, "if the resurrection of Jesus is an event that can be historically verified, why is it that those who are the best trained in historical science are the blindest?"[119] Likewise, Frederick Herzog asserts that, "the meaning of the resurrection is not something that everyone can read off the bare events of history, if only he uses the right method."[120]

Pannenberg has attempted to respond to this criticism by distinguishing between what he calls *"mere* historical faith" and "saving faith," and by discussing the psychological (but not logical) necessity of illumination by the Holy Spirit.[121] As Pannenberg describes it, an unbelieving historian might possess *mere* historical faith "which is satisfied with the establishment that the event happened and does not allow itself to be grasped by this event," but "the real defect of *mere* historical faith is that it stops at the level of historical knowledge, and does not let itself be drawn into the event but instead gapes at it as if it were only a theatrical production, so to speak."[122] In saving faith, by contrast, one "trustingly takes this event [of God's revelation] as the ground on which he stands," such that "salvation is received only in the act of trust, which is essentially self-surrender."[123] What the unbelieving historian lacks, presumably, is the illumination which is psychologically necessary "in order for that which is true in itself to appear as evident in this character to a man."[124]

Pannenberg comes very close to a recognition of the noetic effects of sin in his acknowledgment that "not infrequently the way to insight into a truth that is in itself most evident is barred by pre-judgments. And the more vital the interest accompanying a specific question, the more do the pre-judgments have a habit of being stiff-necked."[125] In regard to Jesus' resurrection, Pannenberg contends that "anyone who will not trust himself to the God revealed in Jesus' resurrection will also obscure for himself any recognition of the history which reveals God, even if he once possessed it."[126] Pannenberg even gives a material example of this in his claim that Jews who were afraid of the consequences of the resurrection of Jesus tried to deny the facts of the resurrection.[127] However, Pannenberg never identifies human pre-judgments, or failures to trust in God, or fears which lead to an obscuring or a denial of facts as being sinful or as being due to the noetic effects of sin.

Closely related to these two criticisms (made by others) is the main concern raised by this present study, namely, that Pannenberg fails to recognize how the noetic effects of sin can help to account for the variety of human perceptions of

God's revelation. As was noted in the descriptive section (I.D), Pannenberg defends the thesis that "in distinction from special manifestations of the deity, the historical revelation is open to anyone who has eyes to see. It has a universal character."[128] Pannenberg asserts that the "truth of God's revelation in the fate of Jesus" is "open to general reasonableness (*allgemeinen vernünftigen*)."[129]

> There is no need for any additional perfection of man as though he could not focus on the 'supernatural' truth with his normal equipment for knowing. The event, which Paul witnessed, took place totally within the realm of that which is humanly visible. In particular, the Holy Spirit is not an additional condition without which the event of Christ could not be known as revelation.[130]

Against this outlook, a clear implication of the model of the noetic effects of sin proposed in this study (including claims made both for the object of knowledge and the knowing subject) is that in order for fallen sinners to rightly know God, the regenerating and sanctifying work of the Holy Spirit is very much required to repair or restore people's "normal equipment for knowing" because fallen sinners' noetic faculties are seriously impaired.

Pannenberg does acknowledge (following Paul's reflections in 2 Corinthians 4:4) that God's revelatory events are "veiled" from many people, and Pannenberg explains how the veil is to be "lifted."

> That these and other [revelatory] events are veiled from many men, indeed, from most men, does not mean that this truth is too high for them, so that their reason must be supplemented by other means of knowing. Rather it means that they must use their reason in order to see correctly. If the problem is not thought of in this way, then the Christian truth is made into a truth for the in group, and the church becomes a gnostic community.[131]

In short, Pannenberg's remedy for the veiling of God's revelatory events is that people "use their reason." According to the model proposed in the present study, however, it may very well be the case that it is precisely people's fallen sinful thinking (reason, for Pannenberg) which is causing them to see incorrectly. As Ross puts it, "from the biblical point of view man refuses to believe not because of a lack of historical evidence but because he is morally and spiritually corrupt."[132]

Pannenberg does affirm "the dependence of reason on the working of the Spirit as the basis of our subjective freedom."[133] However, Pannenberg here envisions the Spirit functioning as a sort of prime mover which quickens human reason just as it quickens "every other vital function."[134] The Spirit's work of regeneration and sanctification per se is not in view. According to the model proposed in this book, the remedy is not merely a matter of people "using their reason," but of having their thinking set straight through the Spirit's work of regeneration and sanctification.

Pannenberg seems to be aware that his subject matter here calls for a discussion of something like the noetic effects of sin. However, he states that "the relationship of the event of revelation to the sin of man cannot be developed here in the particulars."[135] To my knowledge Pannenberg never analyzes the relationship between God's revelation and humanity's sin, and it is the suggestion of this chapter that just such an analysis would further strengthen his theology.

Lastly, while I share Pannenberg's concern that the Christian Church not degenerate into a gnostic community, I do not believe it gnostic to assert that a change in the knowing subject is requisite to a proper reception of a generally available revelation.[136] My model of the noetic effects of sin implies that the failure of people to rightly understand God's revelation is not due so much to the fact that people are not "using their reason" as it is due to the fact that people's sin distorts (in multifarious ways) their reception of God's revelation. In short, Pannenberg's rational theology would be further strengthened by including an account of the noetic effects of sin, which provides a key explanatory concept for the variety of biases and distortions in humans' thinking. For instance, in reference to Pannenberg's appeals to "the facts themselves" concerning Jesus' resurrection and the "datum itself" concerning human spirituality (note 65), an account of the noetic effects of sin helps to explain why many historians remain unconvinced that Jesus is the resurrected Lord and why many social scientists do not arrive at a theistic interpretation of human behavior. The next chapter argues similarly that Reformed epistemology could also be strengthened by incorporating into its perspective a more developed account of the noetic effects of sin.

Notes

1. More details on Pannenberg's life can be found in his autobiographical remarks in "God's Presence in History," *The Christian Century* 98 (March 11, 1981): 260-263, as well as the more recent "An Autobiographical Sketch," in C. E. Braaten and P. Clayton (eds.), *The Theology of Wolfhart Pannenberg* (Minneapolis: Augsburg Publishing House, 1988), 11-18.

2. S. J. Grenz, *Reason for Hope* (New York: Oxford University Press, 1990), 212.

3. S. J. Grenz, "The Appraisal of Pannenberg: A Survey of the Literature," in C. E. Braaten and P. Clayton (eds.), *The Theology of Wolfhart Pannenberg* (Minneapolis: Augsburg Publishing House, 1988), 28.

4. C. Braaten, "The Current Controversy in Revelation: Pannenberg and His Critics," *Journal of Religion* 45 (1965): 233-234.

5. W. C. Placher, "Review of *Anthropology in Theological Perspective*, by Wolfhart Pannenberg," *Encounter* 47 (1986): 173.

6. M. Westphal, "Hegel, Pannenberg, and Hermeneutics," *Man and World* 4 (1971): 276. Pannenberg himself states, "I never became a Hegelian," though he understands how "the tenacious prejudice of my alleged Hegelianism developed" ("An Autobiographical Sketch," 16).

7. Grenz, *Reason for Hope*, 218.

8. W. Pannenberg, *Systematic Theology*, vol. 1, trans. G. W. Bromiley (Grand Rapids: Eerdmans, 1991), 64/*Systematische Theologie*, Band 1 (Göttingen: Vandenhoeck & Ruprecht, 1988), 74.

9. *Systematic Theology*, vol. 1, 128/*Systematische Theologie*, Band 1, 143.

10. *Systematic Theology*, vol. 1, 51/*Systematische Theologie*, Band 1, 61.

11. Grenz, *Reason for Hope*, 9.

12. W. C. Placher, "Revealed to Reason: Theology as 'Normal Science,'" *The Christian Century* 109 (February 19, 1992): 192. While I think that it is fair to characterize Pannenberg as "a theologian of reason," I am less sure of Placher's labeling of Pannenberg as "a theologian of the Enlightenment" (192).

13. I believe that this approach to analyzing Pannenberg's thought is in keeping with his own statement that his "[methodological] reflections need to be based on interaction with the subject matter and presentation" (*Systematic Theology*, vol. 1, xii/*Systematische Theologie*, Band 1, 9).

14. For Pannenberg's methodological statements about the role of reason in theology I will focus on three sources: (1) the essay "Insight and Faith" in *Basic Questions in Theology*, vol. II, trans. G. H. Kehm (Philadelphia: Fortress Press, 1971), 28-45/ "Einsicht und Glaube," in *Grundfragen systematischer Theologie* (Göttingen: Vandenhoeck & Ruprecht, 1967/1979), 223-236; (2) the essay "Faith and Reason" in *Basic Questions in Theology*, vol. II, trans. G. H. Kehm (Philadelphia: Fortress Press, 1971), 46-64/ "Glaube und Vernunft," in *Grundfragen systematischer Theologie* (Göttingen: Vandenhoeck & Ruprecht, 1967/1979), 237-251; and (3) the first two chapters of *Systematic Theology*, vol. 1, 1-118/*Systematische Theologie*, Band 1, 11-132.

15. *Systematic Theology*, vol. 1, 45/*Systematische Theologie*, Band 1, 55.

16. *Systematic Theology*, vol. 1, 47-48/*Systematische Theologie*, Band 1, 57. On the atheistic critiques of religion by Feuerbach, Marx, Nietzsche, and Freud, see *Systematic Theology*, vol. 1, 152ff./*Systematische Theologie*, Band 1, 167ff.

17. *Systematic Theology*, vol. 1, 45/*Systematische Theologie*, Band 1, 55.

18. "Insight and Faith," 43/"Einsicht und Glaube," 235.

19. *Systematic Theology*, vol. 1, 40/*Systematische Theologie*, Band 1, 50.

20. *Systematic Theology*, vol. 1, 48, 127/*Systematische Theologie*, Band 1, 57,
142
21. *Systematic Theology*, vol. 1, 94/*Systematische Theologie*, Band 1, 106.

22. Pannenberg contends that "the underlying interest in the systematic unity of Christian doctrine and its agreement with the principles of reason (*Prinzipien der Vernunft*) remains permanently valid" (*Systematic Theology*, vol. 1, 20/*Systematische Theologie*, Band 1, 30).

23. *Systematic Theology*, vol. 1, 51/*Systematische Theologie*, Band 1, 61. That he is in agreement with the demand is confirmed by Pannenberg's later statement in his section on Christological method that "only arguments count in theology" (*Systematic Theology*, vol. 2, trans. G. W. Bromiley [Grand Rapids: Eerdmans, 1994], 287/*Systematische Theologie*, Band 2 [Göttingen: Vandenhoeck & Ruprecht, 1991], 326).

24. "Faith and Reason," note 15, 53-54/"Glaube und Vernunft," note 10, 243.

25. *Systematic Theology*, vol. 1, 106/*Systematische Theologie*, Band 1, 119. However, this critical assessment must be read in light of Pannenberg's appreciative assessment that "in its day this natural theology did at least support the claim of Christian talk about God to universality. Barth has little to offer in this regard but rhetoric" (*Systematic Theology*, vol. 1, 106/*Systematische Theologie*, Band 1, 119).

26. *Systematic Theology*, vol. 1, 12-13/*Systematische Theologie*, Band 1, 22-23. See also "Insight and Faith," 40-41/"Einsicht und Glaube," 232-233.

27. *Systematic Theology*, vol. 1, 15/*Systematische Theologie*, Band 1, 24.

28. *Systematic Theology*, vol. 1, 52/*Systematische Theologie*, Band 1, 62.

29. *Systematic Theology*, vol. 1, 107/*Systematische Theologie*, Band 1, 120.

30. *Systematic Theology*, vol. 1, 10/*Systematische Theologie*, Band 1, 20.

31. *Systematic Theology*, vol. 1, 54/*Systematische Theologie*, Band 1, 64. Related to this, see the way in which Pannenberg adduces evidence for "the historicity of reason itself" in Schleiermacher's "historical relativizing of philosophical theology (in terms of the history of religion)" (*Systematic Theology*, vol. 1, 98/*Systematische Theologie*, Band 1, 111).

32. *Systematic Theology*, vol. 1, 55/*Systematische Theologie*, Band 1, 65. Pannenberg makes the same point in "Response to the Discussion," in J. M. Robinson and J. B. Cobb, Jr. (eds.), *Theology as History* (New York: Harper & Row, 1967), 242.

33. *Systematic Theology*, vol. 1, 55/*Systematische Theologie*, Band 1, 65.

34. *Systematic Theology*, vol. 1, 16/*Systematische Theologie*, Band 1, 26.

35. *Systematic Theology*, vol. 1, 56/*Systematische Theologie*, Band 1, 66.

36. *Systematic Theology*, vol. 1, 16/*Systematische Theologie*, Band 1, 26.

37. *Systematic Theology*, vol. 1, 55/*Systematische Theologie*, Band 1, 65. It is perhaps noteworthy that Pannenberg provides "consolation for theologians" in his observation that while theologians' perceptions are limited, so are the perceptions of theologians' critics (*Systematic Theology*, vol. 1, 60/*Systematische Theologie*, Band 1, 71).

38. For Pannenberg's doctrinal assertions concerning sin I will focus on two sources: (1) the monograph *Anthropology in Theological Perspective*, trans. M. J. O'Connell (Philadelphia: Westminster, 1985)/*Anthropologie in theologischer Perspektive* (Göttingen: Vandenhoeck & Ruprecht, 1983); and (2) the eighth chapter of *Systematic Theology*, vol. 2, 175-275/*Systematische Theologie*, Band 2, 203-314. A third source which might have been employed here is Pannenberg's earlier and briefer anthropological study *What is Man?*, trans. D. A. Priebe (Philadelphia: Fortress Press, 1970)/*Was ist der Mensch?* (Gottingen: Vandenhoeck & Ruprecht, 1962). However, I have omitted explicit reference to this work because I concur with Walsh's assessment that "all of the major themes introduced in *What is Man?* are taken up, expanded, developed, and deepened in *Anthropology in Theological Perspective*. I can detect no significant deviation from his earlier position" (B. J. Walsh, "A Critical Review of *Anthropology in Theological Perspective*," in *Christian Scholar's Review* 15 [1986]: 248). Pannenberg himself acknowledges a strong continuity between the two works in the concluding note to his introduction of *Anthropology in Theological Perspective*, 23, note 9/*Anthropologie in theologischer Perspektive*, 23, note 9).

39. *Systematic Theology*, vol. 2, 180/*Systematische Theologie*, Band 2, 208. See also *Anthropology in Theological Perspective*, 20/*Anthropologie in theologischer Perspektive*, 20.

40. *Systematic Theology*, vol. 2, 231/*Systematische Theologie*, Band 2, 266.

41. *Systematic Theology*, vol. 2, 236/*Systematische Theologie*, Band 2, 271.

42. *Systematic Theology*, vol. 2, 231-232/*Systematische Theologie*, Band 2, 266-267.

43. *Systematic Theology*, vol. 2, 212ff./*Systematische Theologie*, Band 2, 243ff. In Pannenberg's view, "Adam was simply the first sinner. In him began the temptation by the power of sin that still seduces us all today. All of us sin because we think we can attain a full and true life thereby. In this sense the story of Adam is the story of the whole race. It is repeated in each individual. The point is not Adam's first state of innocence in contrast to that of all his descendants" (*Systematic Theology*, vol. 2, 263/*Systematische Theologie*, Band 2, 301).

44. *Systematic Theology*, vol. 2, 294, note 64/*Systematische Theologie*, Band 2, 332-333, note 64. While Pannenberg denies that "the self-centeredness of life is itself sinful" he admits that insofar as this dimension of human life is the occasion of sinful self-willing which degenerates into unrestricted self-affirmation, "sin is bound up with the natural conditions of human existence" (*Systematic Theology*, vol. 2, 260-261/*Systematische Theologie*, Band 2, 298-299). On the latter point, see also *Anthropology in Theological Perspective*, 108/*Anthropologie in theologischer Perspektive*, 105-106.

45. *Systematic Theology*, vol. 2, 238/*Systematische Theologie*, Band 2, 273.

46. *Systematic Theology*, vol. 2, 252/*Systematische Theologie*, Band 2, 289. See also Pannenberg's discussion of sin as the distortion in which "human beings wrench their life away from its source in the divine spirit and try to ground it in itself" (*Anthropology in Theological Perspective*, 529/*Anthropologie in theologischer Perspektive*, 514).

47. *Anthropology in Theological Perspective*, 120/*Anthropologie in theologischer Perspektive*, 117.

48. *Systematic Theology*, vol. 2, 255/*Systematische Theologie*, Band 2, 293.

49. *Anthropology in Theological Perspective*, 86/*Anthropologie in theologischer Perspektive*, 83.

50. *Anthropology in Theological Perspective*, 86/*Anthropologie in theologischer Perspektive*, 83.

51. *Anthropology in Theological Perspective*, 171, note 33/*Anthropologie in theologischer Perspektive*, 165, note 32.

52. *Anthropology in Theological Perspective*, 108/*Anthropologie in theologischer Perspektive*, 105-106.

53. *Anthropology in Theological Perspective*, 119/*Anthropologie in theologischer Perspektive*, 116.

54. *Anthropology in Theological Perspective*, 119/*Anthropologie in theologischer Perspektive*, 116. Along similar lines Pannenberg asserts that human "eros does need to be liberated from its entanglement with the egoistic striving by reason of which it becomes for human beings an 'instrument of death.' This liberation is achieved only through the new birth in which human beings die to sin and its egoism, as is shown

by the symbolic action of baptism" (*Anthropology in Theological Perspective*, 526/*Anthropologie in theologischer Perspektive*, 511-512).

55. For Pannenberg's teachings on revelation as history I will focus on four sources: (1) the chapter on "Dogmatic Theses on the Doctrine of Revelation," in W. Pannenberg et al., *Revelation as History*, trans. D. Granskou (New York: Macmillan, 1968), 123-158/"Dogmatische Thesen zur Lehre von der Offenbarung," in W. Pannenberg et al., *Offenbarung als Geschichte* (Göttingen: Vandenhoeck & Ruprecht, 1961), 91-114; (2) the third chapter of *Jesus—God and Man*, second edition, trans. L. L. Wilkins and D. A. Priebe (Philadelphia: Westminster, 1977), 53-114/*Grundzüge der Christologie* (Gütersloh: Gütersloher Verlagshaus Gerd Mohn, 1964), 47-112; (3) the essay "How is God Revealed to Us?" in *Faith and Reality*, trans. J. Maxwell (Philadelphia: Westminster, 1977), 50-67/"Wie wird Gott uns offenbar?" in *Glaube und Wirklichkeit* (München: Chr. Kaiser Verlag, 1975), 71-91; and (4) the fourth chapter of *Systematic Theology*, vol. 1, 189-257/*Systematische Theologie*, Band 1, 207-281.

56. *Systematic Theology*, vol. 1, 189/*Systematische Theologie*, Band 1, 207. See also *Systematic Theology*, vol. 1, 4-5/*Systematische Theologie*, Band 1, 14.

57. *Faith and Reality*, 53/*Glaube und Wirklichkeit*, 75.

58. *Systematic Theology*, vol. 1, 257/*Systematische Theologie*, Band 1, 280.

59. *Faith and Reality*, 59-60/*Glaube und Wirklichkeit*, 82.

60. *Faith and Reality*, 60/*Glaube und Wirklichkeit*, 82-83.

61. *Faith and Reality*, 56/*Glaube und Wirklichkeit*, 78.

62. *Systematic Theology*, vol. 1, 244/*Systematische Theologie*, Band 1, 267. See also the related claim that "instead of a direct self-revelation of God, the facts at this point indicate a conception of indirect self-revelation as a reflex of his activity in history" ("Introduction," in *Revelation as History*, 13/"Einführung," in *Offenbarung als Geschichte*, 15).

63. *Faith and Reality*, 56/*Glaube und Wirklichkeit*, 78.

64. *Revelation as History*, 131/*Offenbarung als Geschichte*, 95. See also the related claim in *Systematic Theology*, vol. 1, 257/*Systematische Theologie*, Band 1, 281.

65. *Faith and Reality*, 61-62,/*Glaube und Wirklichkeit*, 84-85, wherein Pannenberg repeatedly appeals to *die Tatsachen selbst*. Pannenberg's monograph *Anthropologie in theologischer Perspektive*, which he describes as a *fundamentaltheologische Anthropologie* (21 in German and English), is aimed at substantiating a parallel argument, namely that "the anthropological datum itself (*den anthropologischen Befunden selbst*) contains a further and theologically relevant dimension" (19 in German, 20 in English).

66. *Revelation as History*, 155/*Offenbarung als Geschichte*, 113-114. Basically the same position is articulated in *Systematic Theology*, vol. 1, 249-250/*Systematische Theologie*, Band 1, 272-273.

67. Pannenberg follows K. Koch in asserting that "the prophetic *dabar* never has the function of subsequently interpreting events" (*Systematic Theology*, vol. 1, 251, note 161/*Systematische Theologie*, Band 1, 274, note 165). Rather, it is the case that "the prophetic *dabar* shows itself to be God's Word only by its historical fulfilment" (*Systematic Theology*, vol. 1, 254/*Systematische Theologie*, Band 1, 278).

68. *Faith and Reality*, 65/*Glaube und Wirklichkeit*, 88.

69. *Faith and Reality*, 65/*Glaube und Wirklichkeit*, 88.

70. *Faith and Reality*, 62/*Glaube und Wirklichkeit*, 85.

71. *Jesus—God and Man*, 109, 105/*Grundzüge der Christologie*, 107, 103. On this, see also the argumentation in *Systematic Theology*, vol. 2, 352-363/*Systematische Theologie*, Band 2, 395-405.

72. *Jesus—God and Man*, 99/*Grundzüge der Christologie*, 96-97.

73. *Jesus—God and Man*, 109/*Grundzüge der Christologie*, 107. See also Pannenberg's granting of authority to "historical interpretation alone (*nur durch historische Interpretation*)" in *Systematic Theology*, vol. 1, x/*Systematische Theologie*, Band 1, 7.

74. *Jesus—God and Man*, 67-73/*Grundzüge der Christologie*, 62-68. Pannenberg assumes here that Jesus' Jewish contemporaries and unprejudiced historians today understand Jesus' resurrection within its traditio-historical context. As Pannenberg puts it, "the events of history speak their own language, the language of facts; however, this language is understandable only in the context of the traditions and the expectations in which the given events occur" (*Revelation as History*, 152-153/*Offenbarung als Geschichte*, 112).

75. *Systematic Theology*, vol. 2, 345, note 59/*Systematische Theologie*, Band 2, 386, note 59.

76. *Revelation as History*, 135/*Offenbarung als Geschichte*, 98). Later in his *Systematic Theology* (vol. 1, 250)/*Systematische Theologie* (Band 1, 273-274), Pannenberg acknowledged that this thesis did not deal adequately with "the Not Yet of the Christian life" which "implies a brokenness of the knowledge of revelation in the context of ongoing debatability and of the power of doubt that constantly assails believers."

77. Placher, "Revealed to Reason: Theology as 'Normal Science,'" 194.

78. *Systematic Theology*, vol. 1, 128/*Systematische Theologie*, Band 1, 143.

79. D. Holwerda, "Faith, Reason, and the Resurrection," in A. Plantinga and N. Wolterstorff (eds.), *Faith and Rationality* (Notre Dame: University of Notre Dame Press, 1983), 304.

80. "Insight and Faith," 34/"Einsicht und Glaube," 231.

81. On this, see the conspicuous absence of sin in Pannenberg's analysis in *Systematic Theology*, vol. 1, 54-55/*Systematische Theologie*, Band 1, 64-65.

82. On this, see the exegetical reflections in *Systematic Theology*, vol. 1, 73-76, 107-118/*Systematische Theologie*, Band 1, 83-86, 121-132.

83. The only exceptions which I found were four isolated sentences buried in other argumentation in *Systematic Theology*, vol. 1, 118, 190 /*Systematische Theologie*, Band 1, 132, 208 and in *Systematic Theology*, vol. 2, 196, 227/*Systematische Theologie*, Band 2, 225-226, 261. In my view, given Pannenberg's extensive treatment of other aspects of Paul's argument in Romans 1:18ff., these few exceptions in no way undermine my argument that Pannenberg does not account adequately for the noetic effects of sin.

84. *Systematic Theology*, vol. 1, 20/*Systematische Theologie*, Band 1, 30.

85. *Systematic Theology*, vol. 1, 40/*Systematische Theologie*, Band 1, 50.

86. *Systematic Theology*, vol. 1, 94/*Systematische Theologie*, Band 1, 106.

87. *Systematic Theology*, vol. 1, 51/*Systematische Theologie*, Band 1, 61.

88. At one point in his discussion of "the varied ways in which reason is defined and understood," Pannenberg makes reference to "the basic principles of identity and contradiction (*der Grundsätze von Identität und Widerspruch*)" (*Systematic Theology*, vol. 1, 21/*Systematische Theologie*, Band 1, 31). However, as he uses the term

elsewhere, "reason" certainly encompasses much more than the claims that "A equals A" and "A does not equal not A."

89. Pannenberg's occasional use of the phrases "natural reason (*die natürliche Vernunft*)" and "true reason (*der wahren Vernunft*)" (*Systematic Theology*, vol. 1, 341, 348, 442/*Systematische Theologie*, Band 1, 369, 377, 477) implies the possible existence of "supernatural reason" and "false reason." However, to my knowledge, Pannenberg never speaks of these entities, and in the main, he speaks simply of "reason."

90. "What is Truth?" in *Basic Questions in Theology*, vol. 2, trans. G. H. Kehm (Philadelphia: Fortress Press, 1971), 17/"Was ist Wahrheit?" in *Grundfragen systematischer Theologie*, Dritte Auflage (Göttingen: Vandenhoeck & Ruprecht, 1967/1979), 215. See also Pannenberg's related argument (following Herder) that humans need to be educated to be themselves, including being "educated to reason" (*Anthropology in Theological Perspective*, 70/*Anthropologie in theologischer Perspektive*, 67).

91. "What is Truth?" 17/"Was ist Wahrheit?" 215.

92. "Faith and Reason," 54/"Glaube und Vernunft," 243. It is precisely Pannenberg's rejection of a monolithic entity known as "the modern reason" which leads him to distinguish between a priori reason, receiving reason, and his preferred historical reason ("Faith and Reason," 54-64/"Glaube und Vernunft," 244-251).

93. "Faith and Reason," 54/"Glaube und Vernunft," 243-244.

94. In support of the latter point, see Pannenberg's use of the term "reason" in his treatment of the personal unity of body and soul (*Systematic Theology*, vol. 2, 181-202/*Systematische Theologie*, Band 2, 209-232).

95. In speaking of Luther, as of Calvin, I employ the term "reason" as they did, while recognizing that in many cases what they meant to denote by the term was a concrete instance of human reasoning or thinking.

96. *Systematic Theology*, vol. 1, 109/*Systematische Theologie*, Band 1, 122. Indeed, as Pannenberg recognizes, for Luther, "the turning to idolatry goes hand in hand with the false conclusions which reason draws from the inextinguishable (*inobscurabilis*) knowledge of God in the heart" (*Systematic Theology*, vol. 1, 109/*Systematische Theologie*, Band 1, 122). See also Pannenberg's statement that, according to Luther, "blinded reason (*die verblendete Vernunft*)" misses that which "may be generally perceived" (*Systematic Theology*, vol. 2, 252, note 259/*Systematische Theologie*, Band 2, 289, note 259).

97. *Systematic Theology*, vol. 1, 20/*Systematische Theologie*, Band 1, 30.

98. *Systematic Theology*, vol. 1, 21/*Systematische Theologie*, Band 1, 30-31.

99. While Pannenberg does not analyze how people's spiritual state influences their thinking, Holwerda suggests that Pannenberg's own case is characterized by the "happy fault" that Pannenberg's faith has "in fact subtly or even basically affected the rational weighing of the historical evidence" (304).

100. "Faith and Reason," 56-57/"Glaube und Vernunft," 245.

101. *Anthropology in Theological Perspective*, 119/*Anthropologie in theologischer Perspektive*, 116.

102. *Anthropology in Theological Perspective*, 119/*Anthropologie in theologischer Perspektive*, 116.

103. *Anthropology in Theological Perspective*, 526/*Anthropologie in theologischer Perspektive*, 511-512

104. *Anthropology in Theological Perspective*, 86/*Anthropologie in theologischer Perspektive*, 83.
105. *Anthropology in Theological Perspective*, p. 171, note 33/*Anthropologie in theologischer Perspektive*, p. 165, note 32.
106. *Systematic Theology*, vol. 2, 265/*Systematische Theologie*, Band 2, 304.
107. *Systematic Theology*, vol. 1, 82/*Systematische Theologie*, Band 1, 93.
108. *Systematic Theology*, vol. 2, 275/*Systematische Theologie*, Band 2, 314.
109. *Jesus—God and Man,* 99, 109/*Grundzüge der Christologie*, 96-97, 107.
110. "Faith and Reality," 62/"Glaube und Wirklichkeit," 85.
111. A. Dulles, "Pannenberg on Revelation and Faith," in C. E. Braaten and P. Clayton (eds.), *The Theology of Wolfhart Pannenberg* (Minneapolis: Augsburg Publishing House, 1988), 181.
112. Dulles, "Pannenberg," 181. See also Braaten's (232) question of why most Christian believers, "indeed almost all of them, say that they have been granted a special insight of faith by the Holy Spirit?"
113. "Insight and Faith," 32-33/"Einsicht und Glaube," 226-227.
114. "Insight and Faith," 34/"Einsicht und Glaube," 227.
115. "Insight and Faith," 33/"Einsicht und Glaube," 227.
116. "Insight and Faith," 33/"Einsicht und Glaube," 227.
117. "Insight and Faith," 34/"Einsicht und Glaube," 228.
118. *Jesus—God and Man*, 67-73/*Grundzüge der Christologie*, 62-68.
119. E. Fuchs, "Theologie oder Ideologie?" *Theologische Literaturzeitung* LXXXVIII (1963): 257-260; cited in Braaten, 232.
120. F. Herzog, *Understanding God* (New York: Scribner's, 1966), 62.
121. Pannenberg acknowledges his indebtedness at this point to the Reformation distinction between *fides historica* and *fides salvifica* ("Insight and Faith," 36f./"Einsicht und Glaube," 229f.).
122. "Insight and Faith," 36-37/"Einsicht und Glaube," 229-230.
123. "Insight and Faith," 37/"Einsicht und Glaube," 230. Note that Pannenberg is quick to follow this assertion with the clarifying claim that saving faith presupposes historical knowledge.
124. "Insight and Faith," 40/"Einsicht und Glaube," 232. See also Pannenberg's related observation that "materially and logically impeccable grounding is *one* thing, but the consent of man is very often quite another matter" ("Insight and Faith," 40/"Einsicht und Glaube," 232-233).
125. "Insight and Faith," 40/"Einsicht und Glaube," 232.
126. *Faith and Reality*, 66/*Glaube und Wirklichkeit*, 90.
127. *Revelation as History*, 147/*Offenbarung als Geschichte*, 108.
128. *Revelation as History*, 135/*Offenbarung als Geschichte*, 98.
129. *Revelation as History*, 136-137; *Offenbarung als Geschichte*, 99-100.
130. *Revelation as History,* 136/*Offenbarung als Geschichte*, 99-100.
131. *Revelation as History*, 137/*Offenbarung als Geschichte*, 100.
132. J. R. Ross, "Historical Knowledge as Basis for Faith," *Zygon* 13 (September 1978): 223. Similar criticisms may be found in (1) Holwerda, "Faith, Reason, and the Resurrection," 308; (2) F. H. Klooster, "Aspects of Historical Method in Pannenberg's Theology," in J. T. Bakker et al. (eds.), *Septuagesimo Anno* (Kampen: Kok,

1973), 126; and (3) D. P. Scaer, "Theology of Hope," in S. Gundry and A. F. Johnson (eds.), *Tensions in Contemporary Theology* (Chicago: Moody Press, 1976), 219.

133. *Systematic Theology*, vol. 2, 192/*Systematische Theologie*, Band 2, 221.

134. *Systematic Theology*, vol. 2, 197/*Systematische Theologie*, Band 2, 226.

135. *Revelation as History*, 156, note 12/*Offenbarung als Geschichte*, 99, note 12.

136. As Lesslie Newbigin characterizes it, the gospel of Christ is an "open secret" (L. Newbigin, *The Open Secret* [Grand Rapids: Eerdmans, 1978]).

Chapter 4

Plantinga's and Wolterstorff's Reformed Epistemology

In the past two decades there has been a strong scholarly interest, among philosophers and theologians alike, in what has been dubbed "the new Calvinist epistemology"[1] or, more frequently, "Reformed epistemology."[2] Though there are many contributors to the development of Reformed epistemology, its acknowledged leaders are two prominent contemporary philosophers, Alvin Plantinga and Nicholas Wolterstorff (both of whom were born in 1932).[3] Plantinga is John A. O'Brien Chair of Philosophy at the University of Notre Dame and is a former president of the American Philosophical Association. Wolterstorff is Noah Porter Professor of Philosophical Theology at Yale University. Each of these philosophers has been honored with invitations to deliver the Wilde Lectures at Oxford and the Gifford Lectures in Scotland.[4]

I. Reformed Epistemology and Thomas Reid's Credulity Disposition

In Wolterstorff's writings the key villainous figure representing classical foundationalism and evidentialism is John Locke.[5] Wolterstorff characterizes Locke's epistemological project as follows:

> In effect, what Locke did was take the classical foundationalist demands that Descartes had laid down for scientific belief and lay them down for rational belief in general. If anyone was to believe anything rationally, he had to satisfy the demands of classical foundationalism. Locke noticed that the central claims

of Christianity, and of theism generally, are neither self-evident to us nor incorrigible reports of our states of consciousness. And so he insisted that to be rational in holding them we needed evidence for them.[6]

In Wolterstorff's view, a major problem with Locke and all evidentialists who have followed in his wake is that they assume we must disbelieve or suspend our theistic beliefs until we can provide convincing evidence for them. Belief in God is guilty until proved innocent. Wolterstorff is convinced that Locke's claim here is simply wrong. According to Wolterstorff, "it is *not in general obligatory* for Christian believers to believe the identity-narrative of the gospels for reasons. Christian belief does not have to be rationally grounded."[7]

If Locke is the villainous figure for Wolterstorff, then Thomas Reid is the heroic (though not flawless) figure. Wolterstorff rejects Locke's classical foundationalism and evidentialism, and as an alternative he champions the ideas of Reid.[8] The following passages from Wolterstorff are illustrative.

> [Locke's] classical foundationalism led him to hold that a necessary condition of evidence being satisfactory is that it consist of propositions that one "sees" or remembers having "seen" to be true. . . . Locke is mistaken about central points in this argument. I take one of Thomas Reid's signal contributions to western philosophy to have been his calling to our attention that we are all entitled to a multiplicity of immediate beliefs which we do not "see" or remember having "seen" to be true: perceptual beliefs, believing what people tell us, etc. And I take the discussion of recent years concerning "Reformed epistemology" to have shown that persons are also sometimes entitled to immediate beliefs about God which they do not "see" to be true.[9]

> The project of Reformed epistemology is to answer the evidentialist critique of Christianity. . . . Why should it be assumed, asks the Reformed episte-mologist, that one is responsible in believing things about God only if one holds those beliefs on good evidence? After all, there are lots of things that we believe immediately; we do not believe them on the evidence of other beliefs of ours. . . . Might it not be the case that belief about God is like that—or that at least *some* beliefs about God for *some* people *some* of the time are like that?[10]

To Wolterstorff's thinking, one of the great merits of Reid's view, and that of Reformed epistemologists, is that they reverse Locke's burden of proof, and reestablish the epistemological baseline as one of trusting in the inborn human "credulity disposition." According to Reformed epistemologists, following Reid, people have an innate disposition to believe their memory, their senses, and what they apprehend others as telling them.[11] While this credulity disposition must, admittedly, be modified (and thereby strengthened) according to a person's learning by experience, it should normally be seen as basically a trustworthy epistemic mechanism.[12] Wolterstorff explains it this way:

Thus it is Reid's view that we are *prima facie* justified in accepting the deliverances of the credulity disposition until such a time as we have adequate reason in specific cases to believe the deliverances false, or until such time as we have adequate reason to believe the deliverances unreliable for certain types of cases. Our situation is not that to be rationally justified in accepting the deliverances of the credulity disposition we need evidence in favor of its reliability. Rather, we are rationally justified in accepting its deliverances until such time as we have evidence of its *un*reliability for certain types of cases. The deliverances of our credulity disposition are innocent until proved guilty, not guilty until proved innocent.[13]

Wolterstorff himself clearly follows Reid's lead here, arguing that "our beliefs are rational unless we have reason for refraining; they are not nonrational unless we have reason *for* believing."[14] Wolterstorff does add, however, one exception to this innocent until proved guilty rule, namely, when a belief disposition has been formed or altered for perverse reasons (e.g., disbelieving a person one has no good reason to disbelieve, out of sheer hostility).[15]

For both Wolterstorff and Reid, the credulity disposition may be seen as basically trustworthy because it comes from the hand of a good Creator. According to Reid, a person may "yield to the direction of my senses, not from instinct only, but from confidence and trust in a faithful and beneficent Monitor, grounded upon the experience of his paternal care and goodness."[16] In Wolterstorff's paraphrase, "the person who believes in a good God does, thereby, have a belief from which he can appropriately infer the reliability of his native noetic faculties."[17] Wolterstorff himself directly adopts Reid's outlook in asserting that a Christian has a good reason "for accepting our native and naturally developed noetic dispositions as trustworthy. He believes that we have been made thus by a good Creator."[18]

As mentioned earlier, in Wolterstorff's view although Reid is a heroic figure, he is not without his own flaws. For Wolterstorff, Reid's two chief flaws are his failure to apply his epistemological principles to beliefs about God and his failure to recognize the corrupting influence of sin on our beliefs. In Wolterstorff's estimation, the second flaw is the more serious.

One point to be noted is a matter of omission: Reid never cites any theistic propositions as principles of common sense. And he never explains this omission. One guesses, however, that in his judgment, one could be a well-formed, mature, human being and not believe such propositions. Of course, a Calvinist would respond to this point by saying that sin has introduced a *mal*formation into our existence—one of the results of this malformation being that people resist acknowledging the existence of God. But I know of no passage in which Reid raises this possibility.[19]

I can emphasize my point by saying that Reid nowhere recognizes the ways in which sin inserts itself in the workings of our belief-dispositions. He bases his epistemology on those dispositions with which we have been endowed by our

Creator. He hardly recognizes how those dispositions are now intermingled with all sorts of dispositions that we have by virtue of our fallenness. In this respect, Calvin and Kuyper were more insightful.[20]

Due to these shortcomings, Wolterstorff maintains that we "cannot be simply Reidians."[21] Instead, Wolterstorff proposes that there is a need to supplement Reid's overly optimistic epistemological analysis with the more pessimistic, suspicious analyses of Calvin, Kuyper, Marx, and Freud.

> What we need, then, is a blend between Reid's general framework of belief-dispositions, and Calvin's and Kuyper's vivid awareness of these ignoble belief-dispositions that we now have—we who are not only created but fallen.[22]

> To the belief dispositions of which Reid took note we may add those rather ignoble belief dispositions of which Marx and Freud made so much: our disposition to believe what gives us a sense of security, our disposition to believe what serves to perpetuate our positions of economic privilege, our disposition to adopt clusters of beliefs which function as ideologies and rationalizations to conceal from our conscious awareness the ignobility of those other dispositions, and so on.[23]

Wolterstorff's outlook, then, is a modified form of Reid's view. Wolterstorff refers to his perspective as a "Reidian approach to epistemology,"[24] and he believes that "when regarded from a Reidian perspective," Locke's foundationalism and evidentialism "looks preposterous."[25] Wolterstorff groups himself among those Reformed epistemologists who "have suggested that in certain situations, not at all uncommon, it is entirely proper to believe certain theistic propositions immediately," so that when the dust has settled after the encounter between Reid and Locke, "it is rather Locke's evidentialist demands that ought to be given up for religion as well as for science and other matters."[26]

Plantinga likewise is forthright about his dependence on Reid. Plantinga recognizes that his own "account of warrant is in some ways similar to that of Thomas Reid,"[27] and he acknowledges that he owes Reid an "intellectual debt" insofar as Plantinga's own position is "broadly Reidian."[28] Like Wolterstorff, Plantinga follows Reid's analysis of the credulity principle, which is modified by experience.[29] Plantinga, again like Wolterstorff and Reid, grounds his basic trust in the credulity principle in the belief that God has "created us with cognitive faculties designed to enable us to achieve true beliefs with respect to a wide variety of propositions."[30] Plantinga writes:

> My whole account of positive pistemic status . . . owes much to Thomas Reid with his talk of faculties and their functions and his rejection of the notion (one he attributes to Hume and his predecessors) that self-evident propositions and propositions about one's own immediate experience are the only properly basic propositions.[31]

The point established in this opening section is that both Wolterstorff and Plantinga are self-consciously dependent on Reid for their key epistemological idea that our immediate beliefs about God are to be given the initial status of trustworthy and properly basic beliefs. The next section argues that Wolterstorff and Plantinga have not yet supplemented this Reidian credulity principle with a healthy Christian acknowledgment that that the deliverances of our fallen human thinking are not always to be initially trusted or viewed as warranted beliefs.

II. Reformed Epistemology and John Calvin's Teachings on the Noetic Effects of Sin

John Calvin is typically viewed as the primal source of Reformed thinking. Plantinga explains that "a Reformed thinker or theologian is one whose intellectual sympathies lie with the Protestant tradition going back to John Calvin,"[32] and Plantinga names Calvin as "the *fons et origo* of all things Reformed and thus of Reformed epistemology."[33] Naturally, then, as self-avowed Reformed epistemologists, Plantinga and Wolterstorff refer back to Calvin's teachings on human reason, faith, and knowledge of God.[34] Plantinga sees in Calvin many of the key themes of Reformed epistemology such as the rejection of evidentialism, the rejection of classical foundationalism, and the assertion that belief in God is properly basic.

> Calvin claims the believer does not need argument—does not need it, among other things, for epistemic respectability. We may understand him as holding, I think, that a rational noetic structure may very well contain belief in God among its foundation. . . . Calvin holds that one can *rationally accept* belief in God as basic; he also claims that one can *know* that God exists even if he has no argument, even if he does not believe on the basis of other propositions.[35]

> [O]n the Reformed tradition in question, the proposition that there is such a person as God belongs in the foundational level of knowledge. It is a proposition that believers (many of them, at any rate) know *immediately*. According to this tradition, the most appropriate way to believe in God is not to believe on the basis of evidence or argument from other propositions, but to take this belief—that there is such a person as God—as basic.[36]

It is not at all surprising that Plantinga and Wolterstorff trace Reformed epistemology back to Calvin as the fountainhead of Reformed thought. What is surprising is that Plantinga and Wolterstorff do not attend more carefully to one of Calvin's key teachings, namely, that ever since the fall, human thinking has been distorted by sin. Plantinga alludes to Calvin's view of the noetic effects of sin,[37] but he does not develop it at length.

Westphal suggests that while Reformed epistemology "shows the failure of foundationalism with exceptional clarity, the alternative it proposes does not take advantage of the new opportunity to make sin an essential epistemological category."[38] As Westphal characterizes Reformed epistemology in its present state, "creation does a full day's work, while the fall is only asked to put in a cameo appearance."[39] That is, Reformed epistemology has emphasized the trustworthiness of our belief-forming mechanisms implanted in us by our good Creator, but it has not yet stressed the damage to those mechanisms caused by sin. Beversluis concurs that "Calvin's view of the epistemically incapacitating consequences of sin have much more serious and far-reaching implications than Plantinga's summary suggests."[40] Jeffreys likewise criticizes Plantinga's exegesis of Calvin, and argues that Plantinga "obscures Calvin's brilliant insights into the noetic effects of sin, minimizing the impact of sin on our noetic faculties."[41]

As Westphal puts it, there is a need "for Reformed epistemology to become more authentically Calvinistic by taking more seriously the noetic effects of sin."[42] Dewey Hoitenga makes much the same charge in asserting that "unlike Calvin and Augustine, Plantinga does not, in the development of his theory so far, explore in detail . . . the noetic effects of sin and grace on the proper functioning of human reason and the will with respect to the formation of the belief in God."[43]

To their credit, both Plantinga and Wolterstorff have acknowledged a degree of validity to this charge. Plantinga recognizes that significant questions about the noetic effects of sin remain unanswered by Reformed epistemology. For instance, he states: "Clearly (from a Christian perspective) sin has had an important effect upon the function of our cognitive faculties," which leads him to query, "just how does this work and how does it bear on specific questions about the degree of positive epistemic status enjoyed by various beliefs?"[44] Wolterstorff is even more direct.

> Westphal claims, at the end of his article, that in the epistemology of religious belief that we have developed we have given insufficient attention to sin; though sin does not go unmentioned, its scope and ravages are not fully acknowledged. I think he is right about that.[45]

Both Plantinga and Wolterstorff affirm that the concept of sin's noetic effects is one of the keys to a comprehensive Calvinist or Reformed epistemology. Plantinga has stated that the notion "that sin has had an important effect on our intellectual or noetic condition" is among the "tenets of Reformed epistemology."[46] Wolterstorff has numbered among the theses on rationality, which in his view, have become characteristic of the Calvinist tradition, the idea "that sin has darkened our capacities for acquiring justified beliefs and for acquiring knowledge. Reason is, in this way, not insulated from the devastation which sin has wrought in our existence."[47] Yet neither Plantinga nor

Wolterstorff has devoted concentrated reflection to the workings of the noetic effects of sin.

One of McLeod's central criticisms of Plantinga is that he "needs to explain why we do not all generate the same beliefs, given the same experience." [48] I suggest that an account of the noetic effects of sin may help Plantinga respond to McLeod's "universality challenge."[49] To date, however, Plantinga and Wolterstorff have depended heavily on the commonsense philosophy and credulity principle of Reid. They have not yet responded to Westphal's argument that "the greatest weakness of Reformed epistemology" is that "ironically, it turns out to be insufficiently Calvinistic" in that it does not take seriously enough what Calvin says about the noetic effects of sin.[50]

It is hoped that the exposition in chapter one of this study will provide Reformed epistemologists with a significant body of research for their consideration of Calvin's teachings on the noetic effects of sin. In addition, the critical and constructive work in the second chapter of this book may provide a further stimulus for the thinking of Reformed epistemologists about the noetic effects of sin, as they pursue a more comprehensive account of the actual workings of human thinking.

I am especially optimistic about this prospect given Wolterstorff's indications that "already Reformed epistemology is going beyond, and can be expected to continue going beyond, its original brush-clearing polemic with evidentialism and classical foundationalism, to offer a positive account of the epistemology of religious belief."[51] In each of the first two volumes of his trilogy on warrant, Plantinga issues promissory notes to the effect that in his forthcoming *Warranted Christian Belief* he will explore in some detail Calvin's notion of the *sensus divinitatis*.[52] The preliminary indications, however, are that Plantinga intends to focus on Calvin to argue for the proper basicality or warrantedness of belief in God rather than to focus on Calvin's treatment of the noetic effects of sin.[53] It is hoped that the present study will encourage Plantinga and Wolterstorff to further examine the latter concept as a key component of Calvin's view of human thinking, or barring that, serve as a supplement to the work of these Reformed epistemologists. The final section of this chapter argues that further analysis of the noetic effects of sin is a valuable undertaking.

III. The Objection of Impracticality

A. The Objection Stated

In the last few paragraphs of the previous section it was noted that although Reformed epistemologists have not yet developed constructive analyses of the noetic effects of sin, they have acknowledged the concept as an important component of a Reformed perspective on human thinking. Interestingly, even this mere acknowledgment of the importance of the noetic effects of sin has evoked the objection that this concept is thoroughly impractical. The objection of impracticality may be one reason that Reformed epistemologists thus far have failed to further develop the concept. Of course, there may be many other reasons for this (time constraints, lack of interest, etc.).[54] This final section of the chapter will show that the objection of impracticality, while making some vital points, does not invalidate further exploration of the noetic effects of sin. The objection has been formulated nicely by Jesse de Boer and George Mavrodes, respectively.

> Appeal to sin as a factor in intellectual error is an empty gesture; for sin, I take it, is universal, so that Calvin and I—not to mention Plato and the Buddha—are all of us subject to its insidious power. I am inclined to wonder whether I cannot spot some effects of sin in Calvin's unjust and imprecise comments on Plato (I.v.11) and Aristotle (I.v.5).[55]

> When I think about other people's absurd theories, their failure to recognize plain truths, and so on, then the idea of a noetic effect of sin comes readily to mind. But I don't know how to use this idea in a way that really makes a difference, when I think about *my own* philosophical work—nor, for that matter, in my own theological thinking.
>   How can I tell which part of my own philosophy has been badly warped by sin? Am I supposed to have an undistorted method, a faculty that has itself escaped the ravages of sin, by which I can make this discrimination? Why should we suppose that there is any such undamaged faculty—and even if there is, how should we recognize it? But if every faculty is damaged or if I have no way of knowing which are not, then it would seem that my thinking about the noetic effects of sin is just as likely to be warped as my thinking about anything else. And in that case I can't improve my intellectual life by thinking about the noetic effects of sin.[56]

As I understand these writers, their objection to the concept of the noetic effects of sin may be summarized in two assertions. First, humans are much more inclined to apply the concept to others than to themselves.[57] Second, the concept is impractical because no human exists and indeed no human faculty exists which is exempt from sin's effects, and therefore it is impossible to identify, in a way which is itself undistorted by sin's effects, exactly where the noetic effects of sin are present. Hoitenga sums up the second point nicely by stating that, in Mavrodes' view, there is an "incoherence of supposing we can detect the noetic effects of sin by means of the very noetic faculties that suffer from those effects."[58] In my view, both of these assertions are insightful and valuable, though neither of them establishes the claim that the concept of the noetic effects of sin is inherently impractical.

B. Reply to the Objection

Mavrodes is certainly right that all too often, as Caroline Simon says, we humans will display the tendency "to detect the speck in our colleagues' noetic eyes, but will be blinded by the log in our own."[59] I appreciate the perspective of Søren Kierkegaard, who "lamented that becoming aware of our own sin is like trying to see our own eyeballs."[60] De Boer and Mavrodes also are correct that there is not any human being (Jesus Christ excepted) nor any human faculty which is exempt from sin's effects. However, these valid points do not establish the objection that the concept of the noetic effects of sin is impractical, such that we should despair altogether of exploring it. Rather, it is possible to identify, at least partially, the distortions in our thinking caused by sin—a possibility which may in large measure be realized through being self-critical and open to correction from others.[61] We are able sometimes to detect distortions in our own thinking caused by sin (contrary to the earlier Kierkegaardian quote). While it is true that normally we cannot see our own eyeballs, with the aid of a mirror those of us who are sighted *can* see our eyeballs. For Christians the Word of God serves as a mirror which brings correction by showing us our sinful ways (James 1:21-25; cf. Hebrews 4:12). Though self-critique is severely limited, it is not by any means a fruitless enterprise. Rather, self-criticalness needs to be supplemented with an openness to correction from others. Simon expounds the latter point nicely.

> Isn't one of the ways that we Christian philosophers, theologians, scholars, and preachers at least *should* acknowledge the effects of sin on our theorizing by *attending*, seriously attending, when someone else attributes a part of our theorizing to self-serving distortion? Isn't a good part of the point of subjecting our work to public commentary, debate, review, and revision a practical acknowledgment of our proneness to err? Intellectual errors have both intellectual and moral causes. We have no epistemic faculty that has escaped the ravages of sin; however, by grace we are part of the Body of believers intended to build us up into Christ.[62]

Burwell concurs that "there is a rich tradition in sociology that emphasizes the value of intersubjectivity as an antidote to error and deception."[63] Much the same intersubjective corrective mechanism is found in the requirement of "the scientific method" that experimental results be replicable. Clark and Gaede supply further support for this view.

> The recognition of our limited perspectives and understandings points to the need for a more communal, multiperspectival effort to apprehend truth. By listening to and testing the views of those with different experiences and interests (including the oppressed and marginal), we are more likely to discover errors and omissions in our viewpoint.[64]

The second chapter of this book argued that human thinking is limited by human finitude and is distorted by human sin. According to the model proposed there, these limits and distortions are especially evident in human thinking about God. That is, theology is particularly bounded by human finitude and particularly susceptible to the noetic effects of sin. For these reasons, the model proposed in this study implies that theologians need to be especially self-critical and open to others' corrections. A further implication of the proposed model is the special need for humility among theologians, as articulated by Thomas.

> Theology, like philosophy, is a product of the finite and fallible reason of man. Its understanding of the Christian revelation is never complete, as we saw, and its expression in rational terms of what it does understand is never perfect. Moreover, theology, like philosophy, is the work of men whose reason has been obscured and distorted by sin. It is amusing—and yet tragic—to read denunciations by theologians of philosophy as the work of proud, rebellious reason, and then to witness them display their own pride in defending their positions and their lack of charity in attacking their opponents.[65]

The model of the noetic effects of sin proposed in the present study has important implications for the proper place of humility within and among theologians today.[66] This claim (as indeed this entire book) obviously has important self-referential implications. That is, to the extent that the model proposed in this study is accurate, my own understanding of the noetic effects of sin is limited by my finite perspective and distorted by the individual and corporate sin in which I participate. Here I am dependent on God and others to help me identify the limits and distortions in my own thinking. If we take the noetic effects of sin seriously then we are faced with the humbling prospect that this side of heaven some of our convictions, in particular our beliefs about God, will be erroneous. David Myers puts it this way:

> If falsehoods creep into all domains of human belief, then they are bound to contaminate my ideas and yours, and the next person's, too. Not only is it therefore okay to have doubts, it is silly self-deification not to grant the likelihood of error within our belief system. Each one of us peers at reality through a glass darkly, glimpsing only its shadowy outlines. The belief we can hold with greatest certainty is the humbling conviction that some of our beliefs contain error, which is, of course, only a way of saying that we are finite men and women, not little gods.[67]

The undoubted presence of error in our thought teaches us to be humble, but it need not drive us to agnosticism or to mere silence concerning our Christian convictions. While we must never claim to possess a finished and comprehensive knowledge of God, we must still proclaim to others, as best we understand it, the good news of Christ's finished and comprehensive work on our behalf.[68] De Wolf says:

When we are speaking of God we need to acknowledge humbly that the best of our concepts are bound to be extremely inadequate. Indeed, our best concepts are seriously inadequate to represent any concrete reality. Yet use concepts we must whenever we would speak concerning any object, even when the object is a personal subject, and even when the object is the Subject who is the Author of our being. The alternative to using concepts is an end of speaking (and writing) and likewise an end of discursive thought.[69]

Our finitude and fallenness ought to produce in us epistemic humility. Our knowledge, especially our knowledge of God, is limited and contains distortions. Nonetheless, God's self-revelation to us in this life and the prospect of our future glorification and communion with God in the life to come ought to help us sustain epistemic hope. We do know some truths now and someday we will know fully, even as we are fully known (1 Corinthians 13:12). As Holmes observes, "humility and hope thus combine in a creational view to avoid both the dogmatism of the rationalist and the pessimism of the relativist."[70]

Attempting to identify and combat the noetic effects of sin is a very challenging process, but this does not mean it is inherently futile. The objection of impracticality reminds us to guard against the tendency to exaggerate the noetic effects of sin on others' thinking and to minimize the noetic effects on our own thinking. As Westphal says, "Sin as an epistemological category cannot be . . . merely a device for discrediting one's opponents. To take Paul seriously is to take seriously the universality of sin."[71] I suggest, then, that the noetic effects of sin should be explored further not in order to judge others but to facilitate our own repentance. I concur with Adams that "the purpose of identifying cognitive failures as sins is not to find a stick to beat the sinner, but rather to learn what we have to repent of."[72]

Casserley notes that "rationalization is a process very similar to ideology. To be aware that it happens, and to know how it happens, is to be forewarned and forearmed against it. Not invincibly forearmed, of course, but forearmed with at least tolerable efficiency."[73] Much the same point is made by Ted Peters: "I operate on the premise that even though better understanding may not rid our lives of sin, it will alert us to what is happening and offer insights that can become opportunities."[74] Hoitenga is right that "belief in the noetic effects of sin on their own faculties makes *more* rather than *less* likely that believers will discover their mistakes and be on guard against making them."[75]

In response to the objection of impracticality, I contend that giving heed to the noetic effects of sin is an important step in identifying, confessing, and counteracting (though not altogether eliminating) them. Attending to the noetic effects of sin can play a significant role in the pursuit of noetic sanctification (being transformed by the renewing of our minds) to which Christians are called. To this end, the final two paragraphs of this chapter set forth some brief Scriptural reflections on what the noetic effects of sin imply for the work of Christian scholars.

Since God is known through God's self-revelation and through the illumination of the Spirit, we must be ever vigilant not to confuse worldly wisdom with Spirit-given wisdom, and we must be ever mindful of our humble dependence on God for knowledge of God (1 Corinthians 1:18-2:16). Because our knowledge is limited by our finitude and distorted by our sin, we must display humble charity toward others, not thinking of ourselves more highly than we ought, not being proud or conceited (Romans 12:3, 16). Instead we must attend to both the substance and the manner of our words by speaking the truth as best we understand it in love (Ephesians 4:15). Since God works through the Church corporately, then we must resist the isolation and academic individualism of the ivory tower, and instead humbly exercise the gift of teaching in service to others (Romans 12:6-8; 1 Peter 4:10-11), accept correction from others, and submit ourselves to Church leaders (Hebrews 13:17). Because God is the least comprehensible of all "objects of knowledge" and the "object of knowledge" most prone to be misunderstood due to our sin, we must humbly recognize that our present knowledge of God is only partial, comparable to a poor reflection in a mirror, though we live in the hope of someday knowing God more fully (1 Corinthians 13:12).

Moreover, since the state of our spiritual sanctification really does affect our knowledge of God, Christian theologians must be ever diligent in their pursuit of holiness. As those who admit the need to confess the sin in our lives (1 John 1:8-10), sin which distorts our knowledge of God, we must also admit the need for (and, in fact, welcome) growth in our knowledge of God accompanying our growth in God's grace (2 Peter 3:18). Because we acknowledge that what is socially or culturally accepted as "reasonable" may at times reflect a distorted outlook affected by corporate sin (John 3:19-20, 8:42-47), we must also be careful to examine critically the attitudes, beliefs, and practices of the communities in which we are involved, in pursuit of corporate holiness (1 Peter 1:13-16). Likewise, since we recognize the importance of personal holiness for our proper (though partial) knowledge of God, that it is those who are pure in heart who will see God (Matthew 5:8), we must seek sanctification through the truth of God's word (John 17:17), through the wisdom that God provides in answer to prayer (James 1:5), through partaking of the sacraments (John 6:35-58; Ephesians 5:25-27), and through the other spiritual resources of our particular ecclesial traditions, to the end that we might not be led astray from a sincere and pure devotion to Christ (2 Corinthians 11:3). As those who take seriously the power of sin to distort our knowledge of God, we must intentionally seek to be transformed by the renewing of our minds so that we will then be able to test and approve what is God's good, pleasing, and perfect will (Romans 12:2).

Notes

1. V. M. Cooke, "The New Calvinist Epistemology," *Theological Studies* 47 (1986): 273-285.

2. Early discussion of this topic may be found in J. Van Hook, "Knowledge, Belief, and Reformed Epistemology," *The Reformed Journal* 31 (July 1981): 12-17; A. Plantinga, "On Reformed Epistemology," *The Reformed Journal* 32 (January 1982): 13-17; H. Hart (ed.), *Rationality in the Calvinian Tradition* (Lanham, MD: University Press of America, 1983); and, most significantly, A. Plantinga and N. Wolterstorff (eds.), *Faith and Rationality* (Notre Dame: University of Notre Dame Press, 1983).

More recent overviews may be found in D. J. Hoitenga Jr., *Faith and Reason from Plato to Plantinga: An Introduction to Reformed Epistemology*; M. Westphal, "A Reader's Guide to 'Reformed Epistemology,'" *Perspectives* 7, no. 9 (1992): 10-13; and N. Wolterstorff, "What Reformed Epistemology Is Not," *Perspectives* 7, no. 9 (1992): 14-16.

Plantinga remarks that, "I regret having referred to this project, half in jest, as 'Reformed Epistemology' or 'Calvinist Epistemology'; some didn't realize this was supposed to be just a clever title, not a gauntlet thrown at the feet of Catholic philosophers" (K. J. Clark [ed.], *Philosophers Who Believe* [Downers Grove, IL: InterVarsity Press, 1993], 67).

3. Sometimes William Alston is also grouped with Plantinga and Wolterstorff as a leading "Reformed epistemologist" (A. Plantinga, "Reformed Epistemology," in P. Quinn and C. Taliaferro [eds.], *A Companion to Philosophy of Religion* (Cambridge, MA: Blackwell Publishers, 1997): 383. I will not give detailed attention to Alston, though he too draws on the insights of Thomas Reid (W. P. Alston, "Christian Experience and Christian Belief," in A. Plantinga and N. Wolterstorff (eds.), *Faith and Rationality* (Notre Dame: University of Notre Dame Press, 1983), 119.

4. Further information on Plantinga's and Wolterstorff's intellectual and spiritual development may be found in their respective autobiographical chapters in K. J. Clark (ed.), *Philosophers Who Believe*, 45-82 and 259-275.

5. See, for instance, Wolterstorff's critical treatment of Locke in (1) "Can Belief in God Be Rational if It Has No Foundations?" in A. Plantinga and N. Wolterstorff (eds.), *Faith and Rationality* (Notre Dame: University of Notre Dame Press, 1983), 135-186; (2) "The Assurance of Faith," *Faith and Philosophy* 7 (October 1990): 396-417, (3) "Evidence, Entitled Belief, and the Gospels," *Faith and Philosophy* 6 (October 1989): 429-459, and (4) "The Migration of the Theistic Arguments: From Natural Theology to Evidentialist Apologetics," in R. Audi and W. J. Wainwright (eds.), *Rationality, Religious Belief, and Moral Commitment* (Ithaca, NY: Cornell University Press, 1986), 38-81.

6. Wolterstorff, "Introduction," in A. Plantinga and N. Wolterstorff (eds.), *Faith and Rationality* (Notre Dame: University of Notre Dame Press, 1983): 6.

7. Wolterstorff, "Evidence, Entitled Belief, and the Gospels," 455.

8. Wolterstorff, "Thomas Reid on Rationality," in H. Hart (ed.), *Rationality in the Calvinian Tradition* (Lanham, MD: University Press of America, 1983), 43-69.

9. Wolterstorff, "The Assurance of Faith," 406-407.

10. Wolterstorff, "What Reformed Epistemology Is Not," 15-16.

11. Wolterstorff, "Thomas Reid on Rationality," 47.

12. Wolterstorff, "Can Belief in God Be Rational if It Has No Foundations?" 152, 162-163. See also "Thomas Reid on Rationality," 49-50.

13. Wolterstorff, "Can Belief in God Be Rational if It Has No Foundations?" 163.

14. Wolterstorff, "Can Belief in God Be Rational if It Has No Foundations?" 163.

15. Wolterstorff, "Can Belief in God Be Rational if It Has No Foundations?" 163. See also 164.

16. *An Inquiry into the Human Mind*, VI, 20. Cited in Wolterstorff, "Thomas Reid on Rationality," 57.

17. Wolterstorff, "Thomas Reid on Rationality," 57.

18. Wolterstorff, "Can Belief in God Be Rational if It Has No Foundations?" 174.

19. Wolterstorff, "Thomas Reid on Rationality," 60-61. See also 69, note 6, where Wolterstorff observes that Reid does not, as Calvin does, attribute the origins of idolatry to a sinful resistance to acknowledging God.

20. Wolterstorff, "Thomas Reid on Rationality," 66.

21. Wolterstorff, "Thomas Reid on Rationality," 65.

22. Wolterstorff, "Thomas Reid on Rationality," 66-67.

23. Wolterstorff, "Can Belief in God Be Rational if It Has No Foundations?" 149. See also "Can Belief?," 174 and "Thomas Reid on Rationality," 66.

24. Wolterstorff, "Can Belief in God Be Rational if It Has No Foundations?" 172.

25. Wolterstorff, "Evidence, Entitled Belief, and the Gospels," 451.

26. Wolterstorff, "Locke's Philosophy of Religion," in V. Chappell (ed.), *The Cambridge Companion to Locke* (New York: Cambridge University Press, 1994), 197.

27. Plantinga, *Warrant: The Current Debate* (New York: Oxford University Press, 1993), viii.

28. Plantinga, *Warrant and Proper Function* (New York: Oxford University Press, 1993), x.

29. Plantinga, "Justification and Theism," *Faith and Philosophy* 4 (October 1987): 417.

30. Plantinga, "Justification and Theism," 405.

31. Plantinga, "Justification and Theism," 426, note 12.

32. Plantinga, "Is Belief in God Properly Basic?" in R. D. Geivett and B. Sweetman (eds.), *Contemporary Perspectives on Religious Epistemology* (New York: Oxford University Press, 1992), 141, note 3.

33. Plantinga, "On Reformed Epistemology," 16.

34. See for example: Plantinga, "Reason and Belief in God," 65-67, 70-73, 89-90; Wolterstorff, "The Assurance of Faith," 399-401, 410-413.

35. Plantinga, "Reason and Belief in God," 73.

36. Plantinga, "On Reformed Epistemology," 14.

37. Plantinga, "Reason and Belief in God," 66.

38. Westphal, "Taking St. Paul Seriously: Sin as an Epistemological Category," in T. P. Flint (ed.), *Christian Philosophy* (Notre Dame: University of Notre Dame Press, 1990), 212.

39. Westphal, "Taking St. Paul Seriously: Sin as an Epistemological Category," 215.

40. J. Beversluis, "Reforming the 'Reformed' Objection to Natural Theology," *Faith and Philosophy* 12 (April 1995): 195. See also the contrary argument that "it is not clear that Plantinga has underestimated the noetic effects of sin" (M. C. Sudduth, "Calvin, Plantinga, and the Natural Knowledge of God: A Response to Beversluis," *Faith and Philosophy* 15 [January 1998]: 100).

41. D. S. Jeffreys, "How Reformed Is Reformed Epistemology? Alvin Plantinga and Calvin's 'Sensus Divinitatis,'" *Religious Studies* 33 (1997): 430.

42. Westphal, "A Reader's Guide to 'Reformed Epistemology,'" 13.

43. Hoitenga, *Faith and Reason from Plato to Plantinga*, 202.

44. Plantinga, "Justification and Theism," 425.

45. Wolterstorff, "What Reformed Epistemology Is Not," 14.

46. Plantinga, "On Reformed Epistemology," 14.

47. Wolterstorff, "Introduction," in H. Hart (ed.), *Rationality in the Calvinian Tradition* (Lanham, MD: University Press of America, 1983), vi.

48. M. S. McLeod, *Rationality and Theistic Belief* (Ithaca, NY: Cornell University Press, 1993), 129.

49. Of course, as McLeod (153) points out, invoking the noetic effects of sin does not resolve all problems associated with the universality challenge.

50. Westphal, "A Reader's Guide To 'Reformed Epistemology,'" 13.

51. Wolterstorff, "What Reformed Epistemology Is Not," 16.

52. Plantinga, *Warrant: The Current Debate*, 86, note 27; *Warrant and Proper Function*, 48.

53. Plantinga, *Warrant and Proper Function*, 42, 183.

54. Wolterstorff has "stressed the modesty of the initial project of Reformed epistemology and suggested that some of the criticisms stem from critics not recognizing the modesty of the project," leading to misplaced critiques of Reformed Epistemology's "pinched and narrow and distorted and incomplete offerings" ("What Reformed Epistemology Is Not," 16).

55. J. de Boer, "Reformed Epistemology: Three Replies," *The Reformed Journal* 32 (January 1982): 24-25.

56. G. I. Mavrodes, "A Futile Search for Sin," *Perspectives* 8 (January 1993): 9.

57. Mavrodes confesses to this inclination, while de Boer exemplifies it in focusing on the effects of sin on Calvin's thinking.

58. D. J. Hoitenga, Jr., "A Futile Search for Sin?" *Perspectives* 8 (March 1993): 9.

59. C. J. Simon, "How Opaque Is Sin?" *Perspectives* 8 (February 1993): 8. Cf. the exclamation in Psalm 19:12: "But who can detect their errors? Clear my hidden faults."

60. D. Myers, "Social Psychology," in S. L. Jones (ed.), *Psychology and the Christian Faith* (Grand Rapids: Baker, 1986), 230.

61. On the importance of self-criticalness at both the individual and corporate levels, see the discussion earlier in this book, 40-43.

62. Simon, "How Opaque Is Sin?" 8.

63. R. Burwell, "Epistemic Justification, Cultural Universals, and Revelation: Further Reflections on the Sociology of Knowledge," in H. Heie and D. L. Wolfe (eds.), *The Reality of Christian Learning* (Grand Rapids: Eerdmans, 1987), 96.

64. Clark and Gaede, "Knowing Together," 83. See also Swartley's related comment that "as interpreters listen to and learn from other interpreters—men from women, whites from blacks, western Christians from eastern Christians, the wealthy from the poor (and vice versa)—new discoveries of truth in both the text and the self will emerge" (W. M. Swartley, *Slavery, Sabbath, War, and Women* [Scottdale, PA: Herald Press, 1983], 220).

65. G. F. Thomas, "Theology and Philosophy: A Mediating View," in E. D. Myers (ed.), *Christianity and Reason* (New York: Oxford University Press, 1951), 55. See also the related argument of Mary D. Doss that in the christological and trinitarian controversies of the fourth century, although "real theological issues were at stake and needed to be resolved," in actuality "it was pride and ambition that caused confusion and disintegration within the Church's governing body" (M. D. Doss, "Humility in Theology: The Way of the Cappodocian Fathers," *Epiphany* 7 [1987]: 57).

66. Evans has argued that "the ethic of humility . . . has not been sufficiently taken into account" (C. A. Evans, "Jesus' Ethic of Humility," *Trinity Journal* 13 [1992]: 138).

67. D. Myers, *The Inflated Self* (New York: The Seabury Press, 1980), 117.

68. On this, see L. Newbigin, *The Finality of Christ* (London: SCM, 1969).

69. L. H. DeWolf, "Theological Rejection of Natural Theology: An Evaluation," *Journal of Religious Thought* 15 (1958): 101. See also Stall's related comment that "knowledge kept to its proper sphere as partial and selective is still knowledge" (S. W. Stall, "Sociology of Knowledge, Relativism, and Theology," in B. Hargrove [ed.], *Religion and the Sociology of Knowledge* [New York: The Edwin Mellen Press, 1984], 67).

70. Holmes, *Contours of a World View*, 128. On this, see also R. J. Mouw, "Humility, Hope and Divine Slowness," *Christian Century* 107 (April 11, 1990): 367.

71. Westphal, "Taking St. Paul Seriously: Sin as an Epistemological Category," 216.

72. R. M. Adams, "The Virtue of Faith," *Faith and Philosophy* 1 (1984): 5.

73. J. V. L. Casserley, *Morals and Man in the Social Sciences* (London: Longmans, Green and Co., 1951), 181. See also the related comments of Habermas that "the mind can always reflect back on the interest structure that joins subject and object a priori: this is reserved to self-reflection. If the latter cannot cancel out interest, it can to a certain extent make up for it" (J. Habermas, *Knowledge and Human Interests* [Boston: Beacon Press, 1971], 313-314).

74. T. Peters, *Sin: Radical Evil in Soul and Society* (Grand Rapids: Eerdmans, 1994), 5.

75. Hoitenga, "A Futile Search for Sin?," 9.

Chapter 5

Social Psychology and Christian Theology on Self-Serving Cognitive Distortion

I. Introduction

The two previous chapters explored some ways in which accounting for the noetic effects of sin might inform influential currents of thought in contemporary theology and philosophy. This concluding chapter examines the mutual contributions of theology and psychology to understanding the ways in which sin affects our thinking. When Christians today speak of "psychology," their focus is typically limited to clinical/counseling psychology or, less often, to developmental psychology. This usage is not limited to laypersons, but also may be found among professional psychologists.[1] These two areas have been the main focus of the evangelical integrationist movement,[2] as well as fundamentalist and evangelical critiques of the integrationist enterprise.[3]

This chapter serves as a supplement to the concentrated interest in clinical/counseling psychology by investigating the less frequently explored relationship of theology to social psychology (the subdiscipline within the field of psychology which "seeks to understand how we think about and interact with others"[4]). The dual theses of this chapter are that (1) social psychology has something valuable to offer to Christian theology, and (2) Christian theology has something valuable to offer to social psychology. To illustrate this reciprocal offering, the present chapter examines what these two disciplines contribute to our understanding of self-serving cognitive distortions (the ways in which we think of ourselves more highly than we ought).

Not all cognitive distortions are self-serving. Some common fallacies in human thinking (e.g., denying the antecedent, affirming the consequent, wrongly inferring causation from correlational data, etc.) may simply be instances of logical errors which are not necessarily self-serving. The present essay focuses specifically on the subset of cognitive distortions which are self-serving, and hence are an exemplary manifestation of the noetic effects of sin.

II. What Social Psychology Has to Offer to Theology

The first two chapters and second appendix of this book demonstrate that key figures from church history have acknowledged that sin distorts our thinking. This past investigation into the noetic effects of sin has been conducted almost exclusively by theologians, and it predates the emergence of social psychology as a prominent academic discipline in the past half century, including its fascinating research on social cognition from the past quarter century. Unlike previous thinkers, we are now in a position to interact with the findings of social psychologists on the foibles of human thinking.

Scripture makes it plain that the thinking of unregenerate sinners is fallen (2 Corinthians 4:4; Colossians 1:21) and that even the thinking of Christians needs to be renewed (Romans 12:2; Ephesians 4:23-24). What the Scriptures do not tell us is exactly *how* our thinking is fallen and *where* it is in need of renewal. This situation is analogous to the way in which the Bible acknowledges the presence of physical sickness ever since the fall, but does not explain the medical particulars of how specific illnesses are contracted or where they attack the body.

Section II of this chapter establishes that recent social psychological research represents a tremendous resource available to Christian theology by specifying how and where our thinking is fallen. It is argued that although social psychology is largely untapped by Christians, it offers many helpful insights into how we slip into self-serving cognitive distortions and where they are most commonly manifested in our lives. These insights may be summarized under two main headings: self-serving attributions and self-serving comparisons.[5]

A. Self-Serving Attributions

Social psychologists have found consistently that we attribute our successes mostly to our own effort and ability (internal factors), but we explain our failures as the result of a difficult task or impossible situation (external factors).[6] This attributional pattern is found in both children[7] and adults.[8] Examples of this phenomenon abound. For instance, athletes tend to attribute their victories to ability and internal causes, but not so their failures.[9] Students who do well on an exam attribute their achievement more to ability and effort, but those who do poorly attribute their performance more to test difficulty.[10] Ministers accept more responsibility for positive outcomes, but attribute negative outcomes more to external circumstances.[11] After a divorce *both* partners typically see themselves as less responsible for the breakup than their ex-spouse.[12] When we are members of successful groups, we claim more responsibility for total group performance than when we are members of groups that have failed.[13] This is true even when reports of group success and failure are fictitiously fabricated for experimental purposes.[14]

It appears that both cognitive factors and motivational factors contribute to our attributional biases.[15] Kunda views motivation as "cognitively mediated," with motivation providing "an initial trigger for the operation of cognitive processes that lead to the desired conclusions."[16] In support of this view, there is strong evidence that our very "cognitive-processing mechanisms impose filters on incoming information that distort it in a positive direction."[17]

The accumulated data has seriously altered many social psychologists' views of what the typical human being is actually like, so that "instead of a naive scientist entering the environment in search of the truth, we find rather the unflattering picture of a charlatan trying to make the data come out in a manner most advantageous to his or her already-held theories."[18] In order to support a positive view of ourselves we will not only ignore but also fabricate social reality.[19]

However, we do not always employ this same charitable standard in our attributions toward others. This is not to say that all of our attributions toward others are skewed. Baron and Byrne observe that often attribution "is a highly rational process in which individuals seeking to identify the causes of others' behavior follow orderly cognitive steps." [20] This notwithstanding, most of us consistently demonstrate biases in our attributions toward others, and these biases are the focus of this section of the chapter.

While excusing our own failures as due to situational causes, we typically blame others' failures on their enduring personality traits. This is a manifestation of the fundamental attribution error, defined by Myers as "the tendency for observers to underestimate situational influences and overestimate dispositional influences upon others' behavior."[21] The fundamental attribution error is also known as "correspondence bias" or "dispositionalism," namely, "the tendency to overestimate the extent to which human behavior is governed by and reflective of broad personal dispositions and the corresponding tendency to underappreciate the power and subtlety of situational control."[22] Typically we do not give enough weight to situational constraints on others' behavior.[23] In plain language, when I fail, it is because I was in an impossible situation, but when others fail, it is because that is just the sort of people they are.

The proclivity to attribute the behavior of others to their enduring personal characteristics appears to be especially strong for conservatives,[24] those in relatively privileged social groups,[25] and those reared in more individualistic Western cultures.[26] Zebrowitz-McArthur has suggested that "the bias to perceive behavior as caused by stable [internal] dispositions, which has been called the 'fundamental attribution error' in U.S. research, reflects a culturally transmitted view of people, rather than some fundamental human perceptual or cognitive process."[27] In support of this contention, it has been noted that in some cultures where collective coping is more common, such as Japan, self-serving attributions may be less pronounced.[28] However, in other collectivist cultures, such as India, self-serving attributions are clearly present.[29] Fletcher and Ward's review of the cross-cultural literature led them to conclude that "research has shown a surprising degree of similarity in achievement attributions across cultures."[30]

Clearly there is a need for more cross-cultural research on self-serving attribution. Nevertheless, the studies to date indicate that while perhaps especially prevalent in the more individualistic West, the phenomenon exists also in the more collectivist East. Similarly, while there may be some gender differences, with the self-serving bias surfacing more prominently for males in the area of academic achievement and more prominently for females in the social arena, it is plain that both sexes take more personal responsibility for positive outcomes and less for negative outcomes.[31]

Moreover, our self-serving attributions cannot be explained merely as a matter of public posturing, as though for social purposes we present ourselves as better than we know ourselves to be.[32] It is not just that we present to others a self which is too good to be true, but that we actually believe that we are the too good self.[33] In fact, our attributions given under private conditions actually may be more self-enhancing than those given under public conditions.[34] Our self-serving attributional bias seems to be "at least as much in the service of maintaining private self-regard as it is in the service of one's public image."[35] It appears that "individuals have a need to present a positive image to themselves as well as to others."[36] Put simply, the evidence suggests that in the attributions which we make, we are truly self-deceived.

Some scholars have suggested that really most people suffer from low self-esteem, and their inflated estimates of themselves are merely defense mechanisms to guard them against their deeper feelings of inferiority. Hypothetically this is possible, though this view appears almost ideological in the sense that it does not allow any evidence to count against it. When people are self-denigrating in their attributions or comparisons (as a small minority of people are), this is accepted as face value support for the inferiority hypothesis. When people are self-eulogizing in their attributions or comparisons (as most people are), this is explained as a defense mechanism which still supports the inferiority hypothesis.

Undoubtedly some people suffer from low self-esteem, underestimate their abilities, and fail to realize their value as persons created in God's image. Furthermore, a subset of these persons may display illusions of grandiosity in an effort to compensate for their deeper sense of inadequacy. However, unless it is interpreted through lenses which reverse its straightforward findings, social psychological research indicates that most humans suffer more from pride than from low self-esteem. Section III of this chapter will show that Christian theology offers the same diagnosis of our human condition. That is why the

Bible does not warn us against thinking of ourselves more lowly than we ought, but instead admonishes us not to think of ourselves more highly than we ought.

To summarize, social psychologists have consistently found that we display a strong penchant for attributional egotism, that is, "taking credit for good outcomes and denying blame for bad ones in order to enhance or preserve self-esteem."[37] We are not so charitable in our evaluations of others, however, and are more likely to blame their failures on their enduring personality traits. Our attributions betray a strong self-serving bias. The next subsection demonstrates that the same self-serving bias is present in our comparisons with others.

B. Self-Serving Comparisons

When we compare ourselves with others on socially desirable traits, most of us report that we are better than average (an aggregate statistical impossibility).[38] Of course, it is not the case that all of us always compare ourselves favorably in relation to others. In some social comparisons we find ourselves lacking desired qualities, attributes, or relationships which others possess, and at times this leads to envy.[39] Nonetheless, the data reviewed in this section of the chapter suggest that most of us usually compare ourselves favorably in relation to others. Our self-ratings are especially exaggerated on broad ambiguous traits (e.g., how "sensitive" or "sophisticated" we are), perhaps because in the absence of hard data (e.g., "I scored in the 48th percentile on math achievement") we are more free to use self-serving idiosyncratic criteria to exaggerate our self-assessments.[40] In other words, "people want to see themselves as better than others and use constructive social comparison to do so unless a clear reality makes such self-perceptions dissonant with the facts."[41]

For example, most of us, including Swedes but especially Americans, believe that we are safer and more skillful drivers than others.[42] Business executives consistently report themselves to be more ethical than average.[43] In a college board survey conducted by the Educational Testing Service, in which nearly one million high school students were asked to compare themselves with their peers, "70% rated themselves as above average in leadership ability whereas only 2% judged themselves as below average."[44] Even more amazingly, in the same survey, "when asked to judge their ability to get along with others, all students rated themselves as at least average, 60% placed themselves in the top 10%, and 25% placed themselves in the top first percentile."[45] Lest professors think ourselves exempt from self-serving comparisons, it should be noted that when asked to rate the quality of our teaching, less than 1 percent of us rate our teaching as poor, 1 percent as acceptable, 10 percent as average, 64 percent as above average, and 25 percent as superior.[46] Practically none of us sees our teaching as below average, perhaps 10 percent as average, and approximately 90 percent of us believe our teaching to be above average. One study found that "an amazing 94 percent rate themselves as above-average teachers, and 68 percent rank themselves in the top quarter in teaching performance."[47]

The belief that our performance is above average has been found to exist for a variety of life roles, as exemplified in the following results from a major study of representative Australians, conducted by Headey and Wearing.[48]

Role	% Above Average	% Average	% Below Average
Main Job	85.9	13.1	1.0
Parent	78.3	20.2	1.7
Spouse/Partner	77.9	19.7	3.5
Friend	76.1	22.2	1.7
Money Manager	64.7	26.0	9.3
Keeping Fit and Healthy	56.0	32.5	11.5
Main Spare Time Activity	49.8	43.2	7.0

Very rarely do we perceive ourselves to be below average as workers, parents, spouses, or friends. In fact, very few of us think of ourselves as average, and the vast majority of us believe ourselves to be above average in all these areas of life. Headey and Wearing found that "differences between men and women, young and old, higher and lower status people, were slight," and concluded aptly that "a sense of relative superiority is the usual state for most people."[49]

It should be noted that the "better-than-average effect" is attenuated when we are asked to compare ourselves with specific people with whom we have had personal contact rather than a hypothetical average peer.[50] It may be that "when people are given a vague comparison target, such as the average person or the average student, they are able to engage in downward comparisons, thereby comparing themselves with someone who is worse off and more at risk."[51] Apparently people often "increase their subjective well-being through comparison with a less fortunate other."[52] However, even when we are asked to make comparisons with specific others, we are often still self-congratulatory. After a series of seven experiments which differentiated between "hypothetical" and "real" comparisons, Alicke et al. found that the better-than-average effect "persevered across a wide range of comparison conditions" and may therefore be described as "a pervasive and robust phenomenon."[53]

In order to support our opinions, we frequently overestimate others' agreement with our views (the false consensus effect). That is, "people distort others' opinions in the direction of seeing more agreement with their own than actually exists."[54] For example, we often overestimate the percentage of the general population which agrees with our political views, leading us to predict irrationally favorable outcomes for our preferred political parties.[55] In matters of opinion it appears that consensus is desirable, and others make good company for us, perhaps assuring us that we are right.[56] We also wrongly cling to a false consensus in areas where we are low in ability or performance, viewing our shortcomings as rather commonplace. As Wood and Taylor observe, "when one has an unfavorable characteristic, one may self-enhance by reminding oneself of others who are similarly flawed."[57] Here misery truly does love company.

We seem, however, to prefer less company when our performance or abilities are favorable, so that we overestimate the sui generis character of our virtues (the false uniqueness effect).[58] This tendency to stress the uniqueness of our positive traits has been found in grade school children, high school students, and middle management bankers.[59] As Rosenblatt puts it, "there is an enormous discrepancy between how 'good' Americans think they are personally and how 'bad' they think their countrymen are."[60] Our false sense of moral superiority to others is abundantly clear in the results of a national survey of Americans' estimation of their own and others' compliance with the Ten Commandments.

Who Follows the Ten Commandments?	Americans Who Say They Do	Americans Who Say the Majority of Others Do
Do not curse or use profanity	64%	15%
Go to church, synagogue, or mosque on holy days	64%	22%
Respect your parents	95%	49%
Do not commit murder	91%	71%
If married, don't have a sexual relationship with someone other than your spouse	86%	45%
Do not steal	90%	54%
Do not say things that aren't true about another person	88%	33%
Do not envy the things another person has	76%	23%
Do not covet another person's husband/wife	84%	42%
Worship only the one true God	81%	49%[61]

Furthermore, our predilection for self-serving comparisons is present not only at the individual level, but at the group level as well.[62] We display a strong in-group ("us") favoritism and out-group ("them") discrimination.[63] Researchers have found that, perhaps in order to enhance our self-esteem, "even in the absence of conflict or competition over resources, people are motivated to show ingroup bias in intergroup comparisons."[64] In fact, even in new groups which are formed by random selection and which involve minimal interaction, we tend to view our own groups as better than other groups.[65] Collective pride in our groups is almost instantaneous, and it is manifest in sexism, racism, nationalism, or any time we wrongly perceive our group as superior to others.[66]

We are ingenious in the many ways we bolster ourselves through comparison with others. Selective and revised memories about ourselves help to feed our self-serving comparisons.[67] Moreover, as with self-serving attributions, so also with self-serving comparisons, cognitive distortion appears to be closely tied to biases in our information processing.[68] Such skewed information processing extends to the credence which we give to incoming data. We are more likely to view as valid those sources of information which provide us with flattering feedback than those which provide us with critical feedback. This is true of scientific research[69] as well as tests.[70] It is even true of horoscopes; astrological skeptics who received flattering horoscopes "perceived the descriptions as extremely accurate and, as a result, significantly changed their opinions about astrology in a favorable direction."[71]

Plainly, we think of ourselves as better than others. Perhaps as a corollary, we also construe our futures as better than others', heading into the unknown of tomorrow with unrealistic optimism. New car buyers believe that they are much less likely to be killed or injured in a car crash compared to people similar to themselves.[72] College students "tend to believe that they are more likely than their peers to experience positive events and less likely to experience negative events."[73] Students consistently report that they are more likely than their classmates to enjoy their post graduation job, own their own home, have a high starting salary, and travel to Europe.[74]

Conversely, college students believe they are less likely than their peers to have a drinking problem, attempt suicide, divorce after a few years of marriage, have a heart attack before the age of forty, contract a venereal disease, be fired from a job, contract lung cancer, be sterile, drop out of college, or not find a job for six months.[75] In comparison to the average student or the average person, college students view themselves as less vulnerable to hypertension, cancer, heart attack, drinking problems, divorce, venereal disease, and being mugged.[76] When they compare themselves to same-sex peers at their institution, students believe they are much less at risk for drug addiction, suicide, venereal disease, epilepsy, alcoholism, lung cancer, obesity, hepatitis, kidney infection, multiple sclerosis, and a host of other health problems and causes of death.[77] In short, people consistently display an unrealistic optimism about the future, perhaps because we overestimate our control over it,[78] and/or perhaps due to our egocentric tendency to neglect careful consideration of others' actual circumstances.[79]

Moreover, we consistently exhibit more confidence than accuracy in our prognostications about the future. In fact, it is precisely when we are most confident about our future predictions that the gap between our level of confidence and the accuracy of our predictions is at its greatest.[80] We think that we know much more about what the future holds for ourselves and others than we actually do.[81] The bottom line is that we demonstrate a predisposition to believe, with undue confidence, that bad things will more often happen to others, but good things will more often happen to us. Even when we experience a negative event, such as an earthquake, we maintain our unrealistic optimism concerning our overall health, and we soon see ourselves as less vulnerable than average others to the very disaster we have just encountered.[82] As Taylor and Brown explain, "In effect, most people seem to be saying, 'The future will be great, especially for me.'"[83] It appears that hope does spring eternal in the human heart.

Finally, it should be noted that the predisposition for self-serving bias is not limited to American college students but is widespread across many age groups and cultures. Myers cites research which has found a self-serving bias at work "among Dutch high school university students, Belgian basketball players, Indian Hindus, Japanese drivers, Australian students and workers, Chinese students, and French people of all ages."[84] Put simply, social psychological research has shown that "there exists a pervasive tendency to see the self as better than others."[85] In fact, the self-serving bias extends even to believing that the research on self-serving bias does not apply to us because we are less self-serving than others. Even when we are informed about the pervasiveness of the self-serving bias, we continue to be "conceited in our perceptions of our own humility," in that we "see ourselves as somewhat better than average at not thinking ourselves to be better than average."[86]

In brief, the preceding section has documented recent social psychological research which has uncovered numerous ways in which humans engage in self-serving, erroneous thinking about themselves and others. It is argued that these findings of social psychology can illumine a Christian understanding of the specific cognitive mechanisms by which humans distort their thinking in self-serving ways. Theologians have long recognized that sin has a corrupting influence on our thinking, but social psychologists help theologians to understand some of the particular ways in which the noetic effects of sin are manifested, for instance, through our tendencies to engage in self-serving attributions and self-serving comparisons. Does theology have a reciprocal gift for social psychology? Establishing an affirmative answer to this question will be the task of the next section.

III. What Theology Has to Offer to Social Psychology

Christians have approached the relatively new, popular, and influential discipline of psychology in a variety of ways. John Carter and Bruce Narramore have set forth perhaps the best known typology of Christian responses to psychology, following the general outline proposed in H. Richard Niebuhr's *Christ and Culture*.[87] Carter and Narramore's typology is closely echoed by the typologies set forth by Larry Crabb,[88] and by Stan Jones and Rich Butman.[89] Within these typologies, the two Christian approaches most pertinent to the study of self-serving cognitive distortions are (1) the Parallels model of the Perspectivalists, and (2) the Integrates model of the Christianizers. According to both models, theology has something of value to offer to psychology, but the two models disagree on the exact nature of this offering.

A. The Parallels Model (Perspectivalists)

Carter and Narramore describe the Parallels model as follows:

> Psychology and Christianity are two separate spheres of knowledge. The two spheres have their own sources of truth (scientific method and revelation), their own methods of investigation (experimentation and exegesis), and their own data (psychological principles and facts, and biblical principles and facts). Integration consists of finding the concepts that are parallel (equivalent) in the other discipline (sphere).[90]

> Both Christianity and psychology can be embraced without fear of conflict since they operate in different spheres. Where we do find areas of relationship and overlap, we view these more as interesting parallels than as indicators of a deeper (or broader) unifying set of truths that could conceivably embrace both disciplines.[91]

Crabb refers to this model as the Separate but Equal approach. Jones and Butman call it Perspectivalism, a belief that "scientific/psychological views and religious understandings complement but don't really affect each other."[92] This is the dominant approach of David Myers, arguably the most prominent Christian social psychologist.[93]

Myers has explicitly acknowledged his preference for the Parallels model (Perspectivalism),[94] and it is exemplified in much of his work, perhaps most clearly in his article on "Yin and Yang in Psychological Research and Christian Belief."[95] When Myers applies his Perspectivalism to the area of cognitive distortion, it leads him to find (1) an example of self-justifying bias in the Pharisee of Luke 18:11-12, (2) an assumption of self-serving comparison in Paul's corrective admonishment in Philippians 2:3 to "count others better than yourselves," (3) an assumption of self-love in Paul (Ephesians 5:28-33) and

Jesus (Matthew 22:39),[96] and (4) hope for overcoming our cognitive conceit, as exemplified by the Psalmist (Psalm 131) and Paul (Philippians 3:9).[97]

In addition to the Scriptures cited by Myers, it would be possible for Perspectivalists to illustrate the tendency to engage in self-justification by pointing to the expert in the law of Luke 10:29 and the Pharisees of Luke 16:14-15. It could be argued that 1 Corinthians 3:18 and Galatians 6:3 anticipate the human propensity to deceive ourselves with an inflated self-view, to think of ourselves as wise when we are foolish, or as something when we are nothing. Echoes of our self-serving attributions might also be found in Proverbs 16:2, 21:2, and 30:12, which describe how we deceive ourselves by wrongly thinking that we are pure and innocent.

Based on Myers' claims regarding levels of analysis, it also seems possible for Perspectivalists to argue that psychology is mainly descriptive, while theology is typically prescriptive. It certainly is striking, in reading the social psychological literature on self-serving cognitive distortions, to find such a helpful detailed *description* of the problems in human thinking but very little accompanying *prescription* for the need to overcome these problems or the manner in which to do so. Kauffmann observes that "the research findings of social psychologists are primarily descriptive," and "psychologists engaged in this type of research seldom make connections with prescriptive criteria; that is, they do not presume to indicate what behaviors *should* take place in the particular setting under study."[98] The little empirical evidence we do have suggests that in many cases mere knowledge of cognitive biases does not eliminate these biases.[99] At present, social psychology provides a helpful diagnosis of our cognitive woes, but provides little in the way of cure. In my view, Christian social psychologists should move beyond mere descriptive studies which document noetic errors to creative experimental investigation into the possibilities and mechanisms for guarding against and reducing our self-serving biases. Sappington is right that, "a true understanding of self-deception will involve a challenge that has not been met as yet by mainstream psychology—how can accurate perception be increased?"[100]

In contrast to the social psychological literature, the Christian Scriptures contain many implicit and explicit prescriptions concerning the need to oppose self-serving cognitive distortions. In Matthew 22:39 Jesus stresses the importance of the commandment first found in Leviticus 19:18, that we love our neighbors as ourselves. Certainly an implicit application of this command is that we love our neighbors with our minds as we do ourselves. We should strive to think rightly about our neighbors, and give them a fair shake in our attributions of why they act as they do, rather than applying harsher attributions to them than to ourselves. Along similar lines, in Matthew 7:12 Jesus gives the golden rule that we do to others what we would have them do to us. Again, an implicit application is that we not be lax in our self-attributions while critical toward others, or engage in wrongful self-serving comparisons with others, which we would not wish others to do unto us.

Romans 12:3 is even more explicit in opposing our inflated views of ourselves: "Do not think of yourself more highly than you ought, but rather think of yourself with sober judgment, in accordance with the measure of faith God has given you."[101] Second Timothy 3:1-5 lists improper love of self as a characteristic of the terrible times in the last days, antithetical to authentic Christianity. Romans 2:1-3 warns us against passing judgment on others. Finally, in Matthew 7:1-5 Jesus is unmistakably direct in his prescription against our tendency to look first to the shortcomings of others rather than our own faults, and to judge others with a severe standard.

> Do not judge, or you too will be judged. For in the same way you judge others, you will be judged, and with the measure you use, it will be measured to you. Why do you look at the speck of sawdust in your brother's eye and pay no attention to the plank in your own eye? You hypocrite, first take the plank out of your own eye, and then you will see clearly to remove the speck from your brother's eye.

In sum, according to the Parallels model of Perspectivalists, psychology offers theology parallels, support, reinforcement, echoes, and enlivening modern examples.[102] Theology, in turn, offers religious anticipations, counterparts, and examples of modern psychological principles.[103] According to this view, theology and psychology do not often interact directly. When, however, the two fields do address common subject matter (as with self-serving cognitive distortions), their varying perspectives represent different, complementary levels of analysis, as illustrated by psychological description and theological prescription.

B. The Integrates Model (Christianizers)

Carter and Narramore are appreciative of the Parallels model, but they also believe that it is unduly restricted in its ability to generate a genuine integration of theology and psychology. They put it this way:

> It [the Parallels model] is based on the assumption that we are dealing with two separate entities that can at best be lined up to find common meaning, and this assumption precludes true and comprehensive integration. This is its most basic fault. It cannot produce the broader unifying principles that are necessary for true integration because of its artificial separation of sources of truth.[104]

Due to this limitation of the Parallels model, Carter and Narramore prefer what they call the Integrates model, which they describe as follows:

> Believing in the unity of truth, proponents of the Integrates model do not look at psychological and theological understandings as distinct fields of study that are essentially unrelatable. Instead, they assume that since God is the Author of

all truth, and since He is the Creator of the entire world, there is ultimately only one set of explanatory hypotheses. While the methods and data of psychology are frequently distinct (and the distinctions need to be maintained), followers of the Integrates model are looking for unifying concepts that will broaden the understanding that would come from either psychology or theology in isolation.[105]

Jones and Butman similarly favor the Christianizer approach "that involves the explicit incorporation of religiously based beliefs as the control beliefs that shape the perception of facts, theories and methods in social science."[106] In this outlook, theological and psychological concepts are allowed to interact much more directly than in the Parallels model. The two fields are not conceived as separate but equal, but rather as mutually informative and reciprocally critical. Psychology may at times challenge fallible theological concepts or Scriptural interpretations, and theology may at times correct erroneous psychological claims. The remainder of this chapter illustrates the Integrates model by arguing that theology has important correctives to offer to recent psychological claims concerning self-serving cognitive distortions. First the psychological claims will be set forth; then the theological correctives will be offered.

Earlier in this chapter it was noted that self-serving attributions and self-serving comparisons have been found in a wide spectrum of people: young and old, male and female, low status and high status, Eastern and Western. However, some researchers have found that one group of people does not engage in this sort of self-serving cognitive distortion, at least not to the same degree as the rest of us. This group consists of people who are mildly depressed, and their more sober self-understanding is commonly referred to as depressive realism, as explained by prominent theorist and researcher Shelley Taylor.

> Normal people exaggerate how competent and well liked they are. Depressed people do not. Normal people remember their past behavior with a rosy glow. Depressed people are more evenhanded in recalling their successes and failures. Normal people describe themselves primarily positively. Depressed people describe both their positive and negative qualities. Normal people take credit for successful outcomes and tend to deny responsibility for failure. Depressed people accept responsibility for both success and failure. Normal people exaggerate the control they have over what goes on around them. Depressed people are less vulnerable to the illusion of control. Normal people believe to an unrealistic degree that the future holds a bounty of good things and few bad things. Depressed people are more realistic in their perceptions of the future. In fact, on virtually every point on which normal people show enhanced self-regard, illusions of control, and unrealistic visions of the future, depressed people fail to show the same biases. "Sadder but wiser" does indeed appear to apply to depression.[107]

Taylor's summary may be an oversimplification of the literature on the cognition of depressed persons, as Taylor herself notes.[108] Though some depressives are realists, others display the optimistic positive illusions common to most of us, and still others exhibit the opposite cognitive distortion of pessimistic negative biases.[109] Also, it is not entirely clear whether negative thinking causes depression or results from it.[110] Be this as it may, Taylor and her colleague Jonathon Brown argue that, in conjunction with many other pieces of evidence, the literature on depressive realism raises important questions about the traditional, historically dominant view that an accurate perception of reality is essential to mental health.[111]

Taylor and Brown argue that "the mentally healthy person appears to have the enviable capacity to distort reality in a direction that enhances self-esteem, maintains beliefs in personal efficacy, and promotes an optimistic view of the future."[112] Depressed persons lack precisely this "enviable capacity to distort reality" in self-serving ways. As Baumeister puts it, "seeing self and world too accurately is depressing; indeed, part of the problem in depression may be the loss of one's rose-colored glasses that make things look better than they are."[113]

If the realists are depressed, then perhaps the traditional view is wrong to laud the virtues of an accurate perception of reality.[114] Taylor suggests that "in many ways, the healthy mind is a self-deceptive one."[115] After all, the cognitive distorters are the ones who appear happy, well-adjusted, and normal.[116] So Taylor and Brown argue that certain types of self-serving illusions should actually be viewed as "adaptive for mental health and well-being."[117] Admittedly, major cognitive distortions may be problematic when they collide with reality, resulting in an unpleasant disconfirmation of our illusions.[118] However, mild self-serving distortions do not carry these same risks, leading Baumeister to hypothesize that "it may be most adaptive to hold a view of self that is a little better than the truth—neither too inflated nor too accurate."[119]

According to this view, which is promoted by Taylor and Brown, and echoed by Baumeister, self-serving cognitive distortions are not something to be shunned or overcome; instead, they are to be actively cultivated. Rather than "help people form more realistic judgments about themselves," Taylor suggests that "the goal of therapy might better be to help people develop cognitive illusions so that they can think more positively about themselves, the world, and the future, employing the mildly inflated biases that normal people characteristically use."[120] Taylor and Brown conclude that our self-serving cognitive distortions are not problems to be counteracted, much less sins from which we should repent. They argue just the opposite, that "the capacity to develop and maintain positive illusions may be thought of as a valuable human resource to be nurtured and promoted, rather than an error-prone processing system to be corrected."[121]

Taylor and Brown's proposal has not gone without criticism from fellow psychologists. Colvin and Block have questioned the logic and the empirical evidence which Taylor and Brown adduce in support of their view.[122] Shedler, Mayman, and Manis likewise have offered alternative explanations of the data, arguing that "people who are prone to distort also give distorted responses to mental health scale items, and their scores simply cannot be taken at face value."[123]

These critics, however, see themselves in the minority. They believe that Taylor and Brown's position "has gained currency among academic researchers,"[124] and has met with "seemingly widespread acceptance."[125] Even Myers seems persuaded that "there may be some practical wisdom in self-serving perceptions,"[126] such that in comparison to the depressive explanatory style, "self-serving illusions are adaptive."[127] It is precisely at this point in the debate over cognitive distortions that Christian theology represents a helpful resource. Specifically, Christian theology offers five antidotes which may be beneficial in counteracting our propensity to engage in self-serving cognitive distortions.

First, Christian theology offers a clear corrective to the mistaken notion that self-serving cognitive distortions should actually be encouraged and cultivated. The Christian Scriptures contain repeated implicit and explicit prescriptions concerning the need to oppose self-serving cognitive distortions, as documented earlier in this chapter (section III.A). That is, despite its apparent temporary benefits of "mental health" or "adjustment," Christian theology names cognitive conceit (thinking more highly of ourselves than we ought) as sin which is not acceptable for Christians.[128] For Christians, psychological utility is not the final standard; self-reported happiness is not the ultimate authority. Realistic thinking, like conviction of sin which leads to repentance, may be uncomfortable, even painful or temporarily depressing, though ultimately it is in our best interests (2 Corinthians 7:8-11, cf. James 4:9-10).[129] Taylor and Brown suggest that our tendency to engage in self-serving cognitive distortions is "a valuable human resource to be nurtured and promoted."[130] By contrast, Christian theology teaches us to name our self-serving cognitive distortions as sins—transgressions which should be confessed and opposed through the pursuit of humble, truthful, gospel-enlightened thinking about ourselves and others.

Second, Christian theology offers three means of counteracting our sinful tendency to think of ourselves more highly than we ought. The history of Christian theology contains numerous, though frequently unheeded, admonishments for followers of Christ to be self-critical, open to criticism from others, and humble. Self-critique, illumined by the Holy Spirit and the Word of God, may serve as a helpful starting point for detecting our cognitive distortions.[131] However, our ability to see our own errors is limited, and so we also need to be open to criticism from others.[132] As Proverbs 27:17 puts it, "As iron sharpens iron, so one man sharpens another." Even Peter and Barnabas had to be shown the error of their ways by Paul (Galatians 2:11-14). Theology also reminds us of our need to be humble.[133] When "we see ourselves as gullible creatures who can be seduced readily into accepting social fictions, self-deceptions, and distortions of the truth,"[134] we realize our need for humility. A humble attitude could serve us well within the body of Christ, as well as in our relationships with unbelievers. To the extent that we really "clothe ourselves with humility toward one another" (1 Peter 5:5) and "show true humility toward all people" (Titus 3:2), we will be less prone to engage in all-too-common self-serving attributions and self-serving comparisons.[135]

Third, Christian theology offers us the hope of eternal bliss in heaven, which may reduce our need to seek happiness through an inflated view of our earthly future. We are not called to "adjust" to our culture, or seek our ultimate happiness in this life. Rather, we are commanded to "not conform any longer to the pattern of this world, but be transformed by the renewing of your mind" (Romans 12:2). The Scriptures remind us that this world is not our home, but that we are "aliens and strangers on earth" (Hebrews 11:13), "aliens and strangers in the world" (1 Peter 2:11), whose final citizenship is in heaven (Philippians 3:20). To the extent that we place our ultimate hope in Christ's return and the bliss of eternal fellowship with God, we will have less need to fabricate unrealistically optimistic views of our earthly futures (Luke 12:18-20; James 4:13-16).

Fourth, Christian theology offers us grace, forgiveness, and a new identity in Christ which, if deeply embraced, reduces our need to engage in self-serving attributions and comparisons with others. The gospel teaches that we need not earn our acceptance with God through our performance or superiority to others. Rather, our salvation is the gracious gift of God which we receive by faith in Christ (Ephesians 2:8-9). Everyone who is in Christ is a new creation, reconciled to God and made righteous in God's sight because of Christ's substitutionary atoning death (2 Corinthians 5:17-21). When we meditate on our equality at the foot of the cross (Romans 3:23), and our equality in Christ (Galatians 3:26-28), we may become less prone to self-enhancement through social cannibalism, the practice of building ourselves up by rating ourselves more highly than others. It is noteworthy that the New Testament never encourages downward social comparison (2 Corinthians 10:12; Galatians 6:4-5), but only upward imitation of godly models (Philippians 3:17; Hebrews 13:7) and ultimately of the Lord Jesus himself (1 Corinthians 11:1; 1 Thessalonians 1:6).

Fifth and finally, Christian theology offers us a compelling motivation to strive for holiness in our thinking, to seek what might be called noetic sanctification. The Scriptures repeatedly call us to pursue truthful, wholesome thinking, in accordance with the mind of Christ (Romans 12:3; 2 Peter 3:1). In imitation of the One who called us, Christians are to aspire to be holy in all that we do (1 Peter 1:15-16), and presumably this includes striving for holiness in our thinking about ourselves and others. Non-Christians may not have immediately compelling reasons to abandon self-serving attributions and comparisons. Jesus Christ, however, is full of grace and truth (John 1:14); indeed, he is The Truth (John 14:6), and Christ's followers, who are indwelt by the Spirit of truth (John 14:17), are called to truthful thinking. This, at least in part, is what it means to love the Lord our God with all of our minds (Matthew 22:37).

IV. Concluding Summary

Valuable insights on how sin affects our thinking may be found in the writings of John Calvin (chapter one and appendix one). The ideas of Calvin and later Reformed thinkers, such as Abraham Kuyper and Emil Brunner, may be critically appropriated in the process of constructing a new contemporary model of the noetic effects of sin (chapter two). This model, in turn, may help to supplement and correct blindspots in the rational theology of Wolfhart Pannenberg (chapter three) and the Reformed epistemology of Alvin Plantinga and Nicholas Wolterstorff (chapter four). Social psychology helps to identify some of the specific ways in which sin distorts our thinking, though Christian theology repudiates the mistaken proposal that we should actively cultivate self-deceptions which enhance our lives (chapter five). The fact that sin distorts our thinking has long been recognized in the Christian Tradition and it is taught in the Christian Scriptures (appendix two). It is hoped that this book sheds new light on sin's noetic effects and serves as a catalyst for others' investigation of how sin affects our thinking.

Notes

1. For instance, see J. R. Fleck and J. D. Carter (eds.), *Psychology and Christianity: Integrative Readings* (Nashville: Abingdon, 1981). Its general title notwithstanding, at least thirty-one of the thirty-four chapters (over 90 percent) address some aspect of clinical/counseling or developmental psychology, and a similar percentage of the contributors to the volume report their primary specialization in one of these two areas, with the heaviest emphasis clearly on clinical/counseling psychology.

2. J. D. Carter and B. Narramore, *The Integration of Psychology and Theology* (Grand Rapids, MI: Zondervan, 1979); G. R. Collins, *Christian Counseling*, revised edition (Dallas, TX: Word, 1988); C. S. Evans, *Preserving the Person* (Grand Rapids, MI: Baker, 1977/1982); S. L. Jones and R. E. Butman, *Modern Psychotherapies: A Comprehensive Christian Appraisal* (Downers Grove, IL: InterVarsity, 1991).

3. J. E. Adams, *Competent to Counsel* (Grand Rapids, MI: Baker, 1970); D. Hunt and T. McMahon, *The Seduction of Christianity* (Eugene, OR: Harvest House, 1985); M. Bobgan and D. Bobgan, *Psychoheresy: The Psychological Seduction of Christianity* (Santa Barbara, CA: Eastgate, 1987); J. MacArthur, *Our Sufficiency in Christ* (Dallas, TX: Word, 1991).

4. R. A. Baron and D. Byrne, *Social Psychology*, seventh edition (Boston: Allyn and Bacon, 1994), 8.

5. Though I find this two-fold schema to be heuristically valuable, I acknowledge that "any taxonomy of illusions is, to some extent, arbitrary" (S. E. Taylor and J. D. Brown, "Illusion and Well-being: A Social Psychological Perspective on Mental Health," *Psychological Bulletin* 103 [1988]: 194). My initial acquaintance with

much of this literature came through selected references scattered throughout chapters 2 and 3 of D. G. Myers, *Social Psychology*, fifth edition (New York: McGraw-Hill, 1996).

6. J. E. R. Luginbuhl, D. H. Crowe, and J. P. Kahan, "Causal Attributions for Success and Failure," *Journal of Personality and Social Psychology* 31 (1975): 86-93.

7. B. F. Whitley and I. H. Frieze, "Children's Causal Attributions for Success and Failure in Achievement Settings: A Meta-Analysis," *Journal of Educational Psychology* 77 (1985): 608-616.

8. B. F. Whitley and I. H. Frieze, "Measuring Causal Attributions for Success and Failure: A Meta-Analysis of the Effects of Question-Wording Style," *Basic and Applied Social Psychology* 7 (1986): 35-51.

9. B. Mullen and C. A. Riordan, "Self-Serving Attributions for Performance in Naturalistic Settings: A Meta-Analytic Review," *Journal of Applied Social Psychology* 18 (1988): 3-22.

10. M. H. Davis and W. G. Stephan, "Attributions for Exam Performance," *Journal of Applied Social Psychology* 10 (1980): 235-248.

11. R. Nauta, "Task Performance and Attributional Biases in the Ministry," *Journal for the Scientific Study of Religion* 27 (1988): 609-620.

12. J. D. Gray and R. C. Silver, "Opposite Sides of the Same Coin: Former Spouses' Divergent Perspectives in Coping with their Divorce," *Journal of Personality and Social Psychology* 59 (1990): 1185.

13. B. R. Schlenker, "Group Members' Attributions of Responsibility for Prior Group Performance," *Representative Research in Social Psychology* 6 (1975): 96-108.

14. B. R. Schlenker, "Group Members' Attributions of Responsibility for Prior Group Performance," 96-108. See also B. R. Schlenker and R. S. Miller, "Egocentrism in Groups: Self-Serving Biases or Logical Information Processing?" *Journal of Personality and Social Psychology* 35 (1977): 755-764.

15. R. M. Sorrentino and E. T. Higgins, "Motivation and Cognition: Warming Up to the Synergism," in R. M. Sorrentino and E. T. Higgins (eds.), *Handbook of Motivation and Cognition* (New York: The Guilford Press, 1986), 3-19. See also P. E. Tetlock and A. Levi, "Attributional Bias: On the Inconclusiveness of the Cognition-Motivation Debate," *Journal of Experimental Social Psychology* 18 (1982): 68-88.

16. Z. Kunda, "The Case for Motivated Reasoning," *Psychological Bulletin* 108 (1990): 480, 493.

17. Taylor and Brown, "Illusion and Well-Being: A Social Psychological Perspective on Mental Health," 193.

18. S. T. Fiske and S. E. Taylor, *Social Cognition* (Reading, MA: Addison-Wesley, 1984), 88.

19. G. R. Goethals, "Fabricating and Ignoring Social Reality: Self-Serving Estimates of Consensus," in J. M. Olson, C. P. Herman, and M. P. Zanna (eds.), *Relative Deprivation and Social Comparison: The Ontario Symposium*, vol. 4 (Hillsdale, NJ: Erlbaum, 1986), 135-157.

20. Baron and Byrne, *Social Psychology*, 63.

21. Myers, *Social Psychology*, 80.

22. D. Dunning, D. W. Griffin, J. D. Milojkovic, and L. Ross, "The Overconfidence Effect in Social Prediction," *Journal of Personality and Social Psychology* 58 (1990): 569.

23. E. E. Jones and V. A. Harris, "The Attribution of Attitudes," *Journal of Experimental Social Psychology* 3 (1967): 1-24. Note, however, the exception that, "people in happier relationships blame outside forces or unusual circumstances, not their spouse" (J. C. Pearson, "Positive Distortion: 'The Most Beautiful Woman in the World,'" in K. M Galvin and P. Cooper [eds.], *Making Connections* [Los Angeles: Roxbury, 1996], 176).

24. G. S. Zucker and B. Weiner, "Conservatism and Perceptions of Poverty: An Attributional Analysis," *Journal of Applied Social Psychology* 23 (1993): 925-943.

25. J. L. Beauvois and N. Dubois, "The Norm of Internality in the Explanation of Psychological Events," *European Journal of Social Psychology* 18 (1988): 299-316.

26. J. G. Miller, "Cultural Influences on the Development of Conceptual Differentiation in Person Description," *British Journal of Developmental Psychology* 5 (1987): 309-319. See also L. S. Newman, "How Individualists Interpret Behavior: Idiocentrism and Spontaneous Trait Inference," *Social Cognition* 11 (1993): 243-269.

27. L. Zebrowitz-McArthur, "Person Perception in Cross-Cultural Perspective," in M. H. Bond (ed.), *The Cross-Cultural Challenge to Social Psychology* (Newbury Park, CA: Sage, 1988), 254.

28. Y. Kashima and H. C. Triandis, "The Self-Serving Bias in Attributions as a Coping Strategy: A Cross-Cultural Study," *Journal of Cross-Cultural Psychology* 17 (1986): 83-97.

29. T. A. Chandler, D. D. Sharma, F. M. Wolf, and S. K. Planchard, "Multiattributional Causality: A Five Cross-National Samples Study," *Journal of Cross-Cultural Psychology* 12, (1981): 207-221.

30. G. J. O. Fletcher and C. Ward, "Attribution Theory and Processes: A Cross-Cultural Perspective," in M. H. Bond (ed.), *The Cross-Cultural Challenge to Social Psychology* (Newbury Park, CA: Sage, 1988), 235.

31. H. L. Mirels, "The Avowal of Responsibility for Good and Bad Outcomes: The Effects of Generalized Self-Serving Biases," *Personality and Social Psychology Bulletin* 6 (1980): 299-306.

32. J. Greenberg, T. Pyszczynski, and S. Solomon, "The Self-Serving Attributional Bias: Beyond Self-Presentation," *Journal of Experimental Social Psychology* 18 (1982): 56-67. See also D. Frey, "Reactions to Success and Failure in Public and Private Conditions," *Journal of Experimental Social Psychology* 14 (1978): 172-179.

33. A. G. Greenwald and S. J. Breckler, "To Whom Is the Self Presented?" in B. Schlenker (ed.), *The Self and Social Life* (New York: McGraw-Hill, 1985), 126-145.

34. G. Weary, J. H. Harvey, P. Schwieger, C. T. Olson, R. Perloff, and S. Pritchard, "Self-Presentation and the Moderation of Self-Serving Attributional Biases," *Social Cognition* 1 (1982): 140-159. See also B. R. Schlenker, J. R. Hallam, and N. E. McCown, "Motives and Social Evaluation: Actor-Observer Differences in the Delineation of Motives for a Beneficial Act," *Journal of Experimental Social Psychology* 19 (1983): 254-273.

35. Greenwald and Breckler, "To Whom Is the Self Presented?" 129.

36. J. Greenberg, T. Pyszczynski, and S. Solomon, "The Causes and Consequences of a Need for Self-Esteem: A Terror Management Theory," in R. F. Baumeister (ed.), *Public Self and Private Life* (New York: Springer-Verlag, 1986), 195.

37. M. L. Snyder, W. G. Stephan, and D. Rosenfield, "Attributional Egotism." In J. H. Harvey, W. J. Ickes, and R. F. Kidd (eds.), *New Directions in Attribution Research*, vol. 2 (Hillsdale, NJ: Erlbaum, 1978), 113.

38. D. G. Myers and J. Ridl, "Can We All Be Better Than Average?" *Psychology Today* (August 1979): 89-98.

39. P. Salovey, "Social Comparison Processes in Envy and Jealousy," in J. Suls and T. A. Wills (eds.), *Social Comparison Research: Contemporary Theory and Research* (Hillsdale, NJ: Erlbaum, 1991), 261-285.

40. D. Dunning, J. A. Meyerowitz, and A. D. Holzberg, "Ambiguity and Self-Evaluation," *Journal of Personality and Social Psychology* 57 (1989): 1082-1090.

41. G. R. Goethals, D. M. Messick, and S. T. Allison, "The Uniqueness Bias: Studies of Constructive Social Comparison," in J. Suls and T. A. Wills (eds.), *Social Comparison Research: Contemporary Theory and Research* (Hillsdale, NJ: Erlbaum, 1991), 172.

42. O. Svenson, "Are We All Less Risky and More Skillful Than Our Fellow Drivers?" *Acta Psychologica* 47 (1981): 143-148.

43. S. N. Brenner and E. A. Molander, "Is the Ethics of Business Changing?" *Harvard Business Review* (January-February 1977): 64-66.

44. Dunning, Meyerowitz, and Holzberg, "Ambiguity and Self-Evaluation," 1082. Original results reported in College Board, *Student Descriptive Questionnaire* (Princeton, NJ: Educational Testing Service, 1976-1977).

45. Dunning, Meyerowitz, and Holzberg, "Ambiguity and Self-Evaluation," 1082.

46. R. T. Blackburn, G. R. Pellino, A. Boberg, and C. O'Connell, "Are Instructional Improvement Programs Off-Target?" *Current Issues in Higher Education* 1 (1980): 37.

47. K. P. Cross, "Not *Can* but *Will* College Teachers be Improved?" *New Directions for Higher Education* 17 (Spring 1977): 10.

48. B. Headey and A. Wearing, "The Sense of Relative Superiority—Central to Well-Being," *Social Indicators Research* 20 (1988): 503. I am uncertain why the data on the role of spouse/partner total 101.1 percent.

49. B. Headey and A. Wearing, "The Sense of Relative Superiority," 497, 499.

50. M. D. Alicke, M. L. Klotz, D. L. Breitenbecher, T. J. Yurak, and D. S. Vrendenburg, "Personal Contact, Individuation and Better Than Average Effect," *Journal of Personality and Social Psychology* 68 (1995): 804-825.

51. L. S. Perloff and B. K. Fetzer, "Self-Other Judgments and Perceived Vulnerability to Victimization," *Journal of Personality and Social Psychology* 50 (1986): 505.

52. T. A. Wills, "Downward Comparison Principles in Social Psychology," *Psychological Bulletin* 90 (1981): 245. See also the literature review by T. A. Wills, "Similarity and Self-Esteem in Downward Comparison," in J. Suls and T. Wills (eds.) *Social Comparison: Contemporary Theory and Research* (Hillsdale, NJ: Erlbaum, 1991), 51-78. Though downward comparison may make us feel better about ourselves, upward comparison may actually help us make positive concrete changes in our lives (P. Brickman and R. J. Bulman, "Pleasure and Pain in Social Comparison," in J. M. Suls and R. L. Miller [eds.], *Social Comparison Processes: Theoretical and Empirical Perspectives* [Washington, DC: Hemisphere, 1977], 149-186).

53. M. D. Alicke, M. L. Klotz, D. L. Breitenbecher, T. J. Yurak, and D. S. Vrendenburg, "Personal Contact, Individuation and Better Than Average Effect," 822.

54. J. D. Campbell, "Similarity and Uniqueness: The Effects of Attribute Type, Relevance, and Individual Differences in Self-Esteem and Depression," *Journal of Personality and Social Psychology* 50 (1986): 281.

55. E. Babad, M. Hills, and M. O'Driscoll, "Factors Influencing Wishful Thinking and Predictions of Election Outcomes," *Basic and Applied Social Psychology* 13 (1992): 461-476. See also D. Granberg and S. Holmberg, *The Political System Matters: Social Psychology and Voting Behavior in Sweden and the United States* (Cambridge: Cambridge University Press, 1988).

56. G. Marks, "Thinking One's Abilities Are Unique and One's Opinions Are Common," *Personality and Social Psychology Bulletin* 10 (1984): 203-208.

57. J. V. Wood and K. L. Taylor, "Serving Self-Relevant Goals through Social Comparison," in J. Suls and T. Wills (eds.), *Social Comparison: Contemporary Theory and Research* (Hillsdale, NJ: Erlbaum, 1991), 31.

58. Marks, "Thinking One's Abilities Are Unique," 203-208.

59. Goethals, Messick, and Allison, "The Uniqueness Bias," 149-176, especially 166-168. Interestingly, these researchers found that "men consistently think that they are smarter than their peers," but women "claim more for themselves than men in the moral domain" (169).

60. R. Rosenblatt, "The 11th Commandment," *Family Circle* (December 21, 1993): 30.

61. Rosenblatt, "The 11th Commandment," 30. Note the paraphrasing (e.g., mosque attendance qualifies as keeping the Sabbath day holy). Note also that in Myers' summary of Rosenblatt's data more than half of the reported figures are erroneous (*Social Psychology*, fifth edition, 58).

62. R. Luhtanen and J. Crocker, "Self-Esteem and Intergroup Comparisons: Toward a Theory of Collective Self-Esteem," in J. Suls and T. Wills (eds.), *Social Comparison: Contemporary Theory and Research* (Hillsdale, NJ: Erlbaum, 1991), 211-234.

63. M. B. Brewer, "Ingroup Bias in the Minimal Intergroup Situation: A Cognitive-Motivational Analysis," *Psychological Bulletin* 86 (1979): 307-324. See also S. Hinkle and J. Schopler, "Bias in the Evaluation of In-Group and Out-Group Performance," in S. Worchel and W. G. Austin (eds.), *Psychology of Intergroup Relations*, 2nd edition (Chicago: Nelson-Hall, 1986), 196-212.

64. Luhtanen and Crocker, "Self-Esteem," 214.

65. Luhtanen and Crocker, "Self-Esteem," 214. See also H. Tajfel and J. C. Turner, "The Social Identity Theory of Intergroup Behavior," in S. Worchel and W. G. Austin (eds.), *Psychology of Intergroup Relations*, 2nd edition (Chicago: Nelson-Hall, 1986), 7-24.

66. D. Myers, *The Inflated Self* (New York: The Seabury Press, 1980), 37.

67. W. Klein and Z. Kunda, "Maintaining Self-Serving Social Comparisons: Biased Reconstruction of One's Past Behaviors," *Personality and Social Psychology Bulletin* 19 (1993): 732-739. Klein and Kunda conclude that "people may convince themselves that they are superior to others either by biasing their beliefs about others or by biasing their beliefs about themselves" (737).

68. N. A. Kuiper, L. J. Olinger, M. R. MacDonald, and B. F. Shaw, "Self-Schema Processing of Depressed and Nondepressed Content: The Effects of Vulnerability to Depression," *Social Cognition* 3 (1985): 77-93.

69. Kunda, "The Case for Motivated Reasoning," 489-490.

70. T. Pyszczynski, J. Greenberg, and K. Holt, "Maintaining Consistency Between Self-serving Beliefs and Available Data: A Bias in Information Evaluation," *Personality and Social Psychology Bulletin* 11 (1985): 179-190.

71. P. Glick, D. Gottesman, and J. Jolton, "The Fault Is Not in the Stars: Susceptibility of Skeptics and Believers in Astrology to the Barnum Effect," *Personality and Social Psychology Bulletin* 15 (1989): 580.

72. L. S. Robertson, "Car Crashes: Perceived Vulnerability and Willingness to Pay for Crash Protection," *Journal of Community Health* 3 (1977): 136-141.

73. N. D. Weinstein, "Unrealistic Optimism about Future Life Events," *Journal of Personality and Social Psychology* 39 (1980): 818.

74. Weinstein, "Unrealistic Optimism about Future Life Events," 810.

75. Weinstein, "Unrealistic Optimism about Future Life Events," 810.

76. Perloff and Fetzer, "Self-Other Judgments," 504. Interestingly, the "illusions of unique invulnerability were primarily observed when subjects rated themselves and the average person or the average college student. These illusions largely disappeared when subjects rated themselves and their friends or family" (504).

77. N. D. Weinstein, "Unrealistic Optimism about Susceptibility to Health Problems," *Journal of Behavioral Medicine* 5 (1982): 447.

78. Weinstein, "Unrealistic Optimism about Susceptibility to Health Problems," 441-460.

79. N. D. Weinstein and E. Lachendro, "Egocentrism as a Source of Unrealistic Optimism," *Personality and Social Psychology Bulletin* 8 (1982): 195-200.

80. Dunning, Griffin, Milojkovic, and Ross, "The Overconfidence Effect," 572-576. For those predictions of which subjects were 100 percent confident, less than 80 percent were true (574).

81. R. Vallone, D. Griffin, S. Lin, and L. Ross, "Overconfident Prediction of Future Actions and Outcomes by Self and Others," *Journal of Personality and Social Psychology* 58 (1990): 582-592.

82. J. M. Burger and M. L. Palmer, "Changes in and Generalization of Unrealistic Optimism Following Experiences with Stressful Events: Reactions to the 1989 California Earthquake," *Personality and Social Psychology Bulletin* 18 (1992): 39-43.

83. Taylor and Brown, "Illusion and Well-Being: A Social Psychological Perspective on Mental Health," 197.

84. Myers, *Social Psychology*, 69.

85. Taylor and Brown, "Illusion and Well-Being: A Social Psychological Perspective on Mental Health," 195.

86. J. Friedrich, "On Seeing Oneself as Less Self-Serving Than Others: The Ultimate Self-Serving Bias?" *Teaching of Psychology* 23 (April 1996): 107.

87. H. R. Niebuhr, *Christ and Culture* (New York: Harper and Row, 1951). Explicit acknowledgment of this dependence on Niebuhr is found in Carter and Narramore, 72, note 2. Because my focus here is on Christian responses to psychology,

my comments will center on the "sacred" versions of the models proffered by Carter and Narramore.

It should be noted that two of Carter and Narramore's approaches, the Against model and the Of model, are more relevant to the arena of psychotherapy than to the field of social psychology. I am unaware of Christians who reduce Scripture to social psychology or press all Scripture into the cookie-cutter mold of social psychology (the "Of" model). Similarly, proponents of the Against model have typically aimed their criticisms at what they understand to be anti-Christian speculations of secular therapists (Freud, Rogers, etc.), not social psychologists per se. Moreover, the entire argument of section two of this chapter has been that social psychology has valuable insights to offer to Christian theology. So, neither of these two models will be discussed in further detail in the present work.

88. L. J. Crabb Jr. "Biblical Counseling: A Basic View," *CAPS Bulletin* 4 (1978): 1-6. In my view, Crabb's categories of (1) Separate but Equal, (2) Spoiling the Egyptians, (3) Nothing Butterists, and (4) Tossed Salad roughly correspond to Carter and Narramore's (1) Parallels, (2) Integrates, (3) Against, and (4) Of models. For reasons explained in the previous note, the latter two categories will not be explored in detail in the present work.

89. Jones and Butman, *Modern Psychotherapies*, 17-38. In my view, what Jones and Butman label (1) "perspectival integration" and (2) "humanizer or Christianizer of science" are essentially equivalent to Carter and Narramore's (1) Parallels model and (2) Integrates model, respectively. Jones and Butman's third category of ethical integration (e.g., practicing high Christian moral standards as a psychologist) is not directly relevant to the questions raised in this section of the paper and so it will not be discussed in further detail here.

90. Carter and Narramore, *The Integration of Psychology and Theology*, 99.

91. Carter and Narramore, *The Integration of Psychology and Theology*, 98.

92. Jones and Butman, *Modern Psychotherapies*, 20.

93. See (1) Myers, *Social Psychology*, 7; and (2) D. G. Myers and M. A. Jeeves, *Psychology Through the Eyes of Faith* (San Francisco: Harper and Row, 1987), 9.

94. Myers and Jeeves, *Psychology Through the Eyes of Faith*, 17.

95. D. G. Myers, "Yin and Yang in Psychological Research and Christian Belief," *Perspectives on Science and Christian Faith* 39 (1987): 128-139. It should be noted, however, that portions of Myers' *The Inflated Self* and Myers and Jeeves' *Psychology Through the Eyes of Faith* move beyond the Parallels model to more interactive, integrative work.

96. Myers and Jeeves, *Psychology Through the Eyes of Faith*, 134-135. The same Scriptures are alluded to, with the addition of Psalm 19:12, in Myers, "Yin and Yang in Psychological Research and Christian Belief," 137.

97. Myers, "Yin and Yang in Psychological Research and Christian Belief," 137-138.

98. D. Kauffmann, "Belief and Behavior: Social Psychology and Christian Living," *Journal of Psychology and Christianity* 15 (1996): 47.

99. On this, see the following studies: (1) J. S. Croxton and N. Morrow, "What Does It Take to Reduce Observer Bias?" *Psychological Reports* 55 (1984): 135-138; (2) J. T. Johnson, J. B. Jemmot III, and T. F. Pettigrew, "Causal Attribution and Dispositional Inference: Evidence of Inconsistent Judgments," *Journal of Experimental*

Social Psychology 20 (1984): 567-585; (3) J. S. Croxton and A. G. Miller, "Behavioral Disconfirmation and the Observer Bias," *Journal of Social Behavior and Personality* 2 (1987): 145-152; (4) G. D. Reeder, G. J. O. Fletcher, and K. Furman, "The Role of Observers' Expectations in Attitude Attribution," *Journal of Experimental Social Psychology* 25 (1989): 168-188; (5) J. Krueger and R. Clement, "The Truly False Consensus Effect: An Ineradicable and Egocentric Bias in Social Perception," *Journal of Personality and Social Psychology* 67 (1994): 596-610; and (6) J. Friedrich, "On Seeing Oneself as Less Self-serving Than Others: The Ultimate Self-Serving Bias?" *Teaching of Psychology* 23 (April 1996): 107-109.

100. A. A. Sappington, "Psychology for the Practice of the Presence of God: Putting Psychology at the Service of the Church," *Journal of Psychology and Christianity* 13 (1994): 8

101. All quotations from the New International Version.

102. Myers, "Yin and Yang in Psychological Research and Christian Belief," 135-139.

103. Myers, "Yin and Yang in Psychological Research and Christian Belief," 138-139.

104. Carter and Narramore, *The Integration of Psychology and Theology*, 100.

105. Carter and Narramore, *The Integration of Psychology and Theology*, 104.

106. Jones and Butman, *Modern Psychotherapies*, 20.

107. S. E. Taylor, *Positive Illusions: Creative Self-Deception and the Healthy Mind*. New York: Basic Books, 1989, 214. In the final sentence Taylor is referring to a phrase coined in the pioneering study by L. B. Alloy and L. Y. Abramson, "Judgment of Contingency in Depressed and Nondepressed Students: Sadder but Wiser?" *Journal of Experimental Psychology: General*, 108 (1979): 441-485.

108. Taylor, *Positive Illusions*, 215. See also S. E. Taylor and J. D. Brown, "Positive Illusions and Well-Being Revisited: Separating Fact from Fiction," *Psychological Bulletin* 116 (1994): 22.

109. See (1) K. Dobson and R. Franche, "A Conceptual and Empirical Review of the Depressive Realism Hypothesis," *Canadian Journal of Behavioural Science* 21 (1989): 419-433; (2) D. Dunning and A. L. Story, "Depression, Realism, and the Overconfidence Effect: Are the Sadder Wiser When Predicting Future Actions and Events?" *Journal of Personality and Social Psychology* 61 (1991): 521-532; and (3) R. Ackerman and R. J. DeRubeis, "Is Depressive Realism Real?" *Clinical Psychology Review* 11 (1991): 565-584.

110. See the literature review and argument for bi-directional causation in Myers, *Social Psychology*, 174-177.

111. Taylor and Brown, "Illusion and Well-Being: A Social Psychological Perspective on Mental Health," 197.

112. Taylor and Brown, "Illusion and Well-Being: A Social Psychological Perspective on Mental Health," 204.

113. R. F. Baumeister, "The Optimal Margin of Illusion," *Journal of Social and Clinical Psychology* 8 (1989): 184.

114. Taylor, *Positive Illusions*, 46.

115. Taylor, *Positive Illusions*, ix.

116. Taylor, *Positive Illusions*, 49.

117. Taylor and Brown, "Illusion and Well-Being: A Social Psychological Perspective on Mental Health," 193.

118. Taylor and Brown, "Illusion and Well-Being: A Social Psychological Perspective on Mental Health," 204. See also Baumeister, "The Optimal Margin of Illusion," 177-181.

119. Baumeister, "The Optimal Margin of Illusion," 184. See also Taylor, *Positive Illusions*, 244.

120. Taylor, *Positive Illusions*, 220.

121. Taylor and Brown, "Illusion and Well-Being: A Social Psychological Perspective on Mental Health," 205.

122. C. R. Colvin and J. Block, "Do Positive Illusions Foster Mental Health? An Examination of the Taylor and Brown Formulation," *Psychological Bulletin* 116 (1994): 3-20. See also the response and rejoinder which follow immediately in the same issue: S. E. Taylor and J. D. Brown, "Positive Illusions and Well-Being Revisited: Separating Fact from Fiction," *Psychological Bulletin* 116 (1994): 21-27; J. Block and C. R. Colvin, "Positive Illusions and Well-Being Revisited: Separating Fiction from Fact," *Psychological Bulletin* 116 (1994): 28.

123. J. Shedler, M. Mayman, and M. Manis, "The *Illusion* of Mental Health," *American Psychologist* 48 (November 1993): 1128. See also the response and rejoinders appearing one year later: S. E. Taylor and J. D. Brown, "'Illusion' of Mental Health Does Not Explain Positive Illusions," *American Psychologist* 49 (1994): 972-973; J. Shedler, M. Mayman, and M. Manis, "More Illusions," *American Psychologist* 49 (1994): 974-976.

124. Shedler, Mayman, and Manis, "The *Illusion* of Mental Health," 1128.

125. Colvin and Block, "Do Positive Illusions Foster Mental Health?" 4.

126. Myers, *Social Psychology*, 62.

127. Myers, *Social Psychology*, 174. See also Myers' (70) annotation on Taylor's *Positive Illusions*: "The ancient wisdom to 'know thyself' notwithstanding, mental health may instead reflect the art of being well deceived."

128. Myers and Jeeves observe correctly that "for the heroes of the Bible, good adjustment—thinking well of oneself and feeling positive about the world—was not the aim of life" (148).

129. Thanks to Dr. Mark McMinn (personal correspondence, 7/10/97) for raising an important question about whether the call for Christians to think accurately about themselves is "a life sentence for depression." Dr. McMinn speculates that perhaps "Christians who understand grace can afford to think of themselves realistically without depression," so that we need not conclude "that the best Christians are inevitably depressed." Dr. McMinn's suggestions, which are closely related to my third and fourth "antidotes" may find some support in research which has found a positive correlation between religious commitment and happiness (see D. Myers, *The Pursuit of Happiness* [New York: William Morrow, 1992], especially 183, 261).

Beyond this empirical literature, there are numerous Scriptural indications that God's people will experience joy not only in the life to come, but often in this life as well (1 Kings 1:40; 1 Chronicles 12:40; 2 Chronicles 30:26; Ezra 6:22; Nehemiah 12:43; Esther 8:16-17; Psalm 16:11; John 15:11; Acts 13:52; Romans 15:13; 1 Thessalonians 3:9; 1 Peter 1:8-9). In fact, the Bible teaches that joy is to be part of the "normal" Christian experience of the fruit of the Spirit (Galatians 5:22-23), which is possible even in the midst of troubles in this life (Luke 6:20-23; Romans 5:3-5; 1 Corinthians 8:2; 1 Thessalonians 1:6; James 1:2-4; 1 Peter 1:6-7). Within a single chapter of Scripture, Paul indicates that, by God's grace, Christians can both "think of themselves with sober judgment" (Romans 12:3) and "be joyful" (Romans 12:12 and 12:15).

130. Taylor and Brown, "Illusion and Well-Being: A Social Psychological Perspective on Mental Health," 205.

131. S. Kierkegaard, *Attack upon "Christendom"* (Princeton, NJ: Princeton University Press, 1855/1968); R. Montgomery, "Bias in Interpreting Social Facts: Is It a Sin?" *Journal for the Scientific Study of Religion* 23 (1984): 278-291; S. Mott, "Biblical Faith and the Reality of Social Evil," *Christian Scholar's Review* 9 (1980): 225-240.

132. Clarke and Gaede, "Knowing Together," 55-86. W. Swartley, *Slavery, Sabbath, War, and Women* (Scottdale, PA: Herald Press, 1983).

133. M. D. Doss, "Humility in Theology: The Way of the Cappodocian Fathers," *Epiphany* 7 (1987): 57-62.

134. Clark and Gaede, "Knowing Together," 80.

135. Thanks to a Christian friend from the Orthodox tradition for suggesting that in addition to my scriptural reflections, a further antidote to self-serving cognitive distortions may be found in the practice of Christian liturgy. For instance, humility may be inculcated in us through repeating the prayer, "Lord have mercy on me a sinner," or through examining ourselves as part of participating in the Lord's Supper/Eucharist (1 Corinthians 11:27-29).

Appendix 1

Calvin's Psychology

The first chapter of this book provides an exposition of Calvin's teachings on human reason at creation, after the fall, and after redemption. In order to position the function of reason in relationship to other human capacities, this appendix expounds Calvin's teachings on the relations of body, soul, and spirit, as well as his view of the relation between reason and will.[1] Notes in the appendix also contribute to scholarly debates, including discussions about Calvin's alleged dualism (note 2) and the question of whether Calvin was a voluntarist or intellectualist (note 33).

I. Relations of Body, Soul, and Spirit

Calvin followed prior thinkers (most notably, Plato) in his assumption that humans consist of body and soul (or its synonym, spirit), with the latter being the nobler and principal part of humanity. In my view, Calvin was a "dichotomist," in the sense that he believed that humans were composed of two elements, the material body and the more important immaterial soul or spirit. In my judgment, however, Calvin was not a "dualist," in the sense of believing that the separation of body and soul/spirit was the desired condition of humanity. Calvin did not substitute belief in the immortality of the soul for belief in the resurrection of the body, and in this respect he clearly differentiated himself from Plato.[2] It should also be noted that within his dichotomism, Calvin took pains to emphasize the unity of the one person who was made up of body and soul, stating for example, "that there is one person in man composed of two elements joined together, and that there are two diverse underlying natures that make up this person."[3] The following statement is typical of Calvin's thought.

Furthermore, that man consists of a soul and a body ought to be beyond
controversy. Now I understand by the term 'soul' an immortal yet created
essence, which is his noblest part. Sometimes it is called 'spirit.' For even when
these terms are joined together, they differ from one another in meaning; yet
when the word 'spirit' is used by itself, it means the same thing as soul.[4]

Against the Anabaptists, Calvin eagerly affirmed the soul as an immortal
essence, and against Plato and the Libertines, Calvin eagerly affirmed the soul as
a created essence, thus denying the eternity of the soul.[5] Hence, Calvin
distinguished himself from several groups simultaneously when he defined the
soul as "an immortal yet created essence."[6] In his psychology Calvin understood
himself to be following the plain teaching of the Christian Scriptures.

Now unless the soul were something essential, separate from the body,
Scripture would not teach that we dwell in houses of clay (Job 4:19) and at
death leave the tabernacle of the flesh, putting off what is corruptible so that at
the Last Day we may finally receive our reward, according as each of us has
done in the body. For surely these passages and similar ones that occur
repeatedly not only clearly distinguish the soul from the body, but by
transferring to it the name 'man' indicate it to be the principal part.[7]

In Calvin's understanding of Paul, the soul was of preeminent importance
because it had to do with humanity's spiritual life and the kingdom of God,
whereas the body had to do with this present world.[8] Calvin repeatedly referred
to the body as an "earthly prison" (*carcer terrenus*)[9] or a "prison house of the
flesh" (*carnis ergastulum*),[10] and he spoke of souls being "freed from the prison
houses of their bodies" (*corporum ergastulis solutae*).[11] Indeed, Calvin asked
rhetorically, "if to be freed from the body is to be released into perfect freedom,
what else is the body but a prison" (*quid aliud est corpus quam carcer*)?[12]

The soul, on the other hand, is the dwelling place of the *imago dei*,
according to Calvin. Calvin maintained that "although God's glory shines forth
in the outer man, yet there is no doubt that the proper seat of his image is in the
soul."[13] More specifically, Calvin claimed that "the chief seat of the divine
image was in his [Adam's] mind and heart."[14] And more specifically still,
Calvin asserted that "the mind of man is the true image of him [God]."[15]

These last three quotations from Calvin claim, respectively, that the *imago
dei* resides in humanity's soul, in humanity's mind and heart, and in humanity's
mind. This raises the thorny question as to the relations between soul (*anima*),
heart (*cor*), mind (*mens*), and other psychological terms in Calvin's thought. At
times Calvin used heart (*cor*) and mind (*mens*) as synonyms.[16] Calvin argued
that both heart (*cor*) and mind (*mens*) were necessary to proper knowledge of
God, though the heart presents more difficult barriers than the mind in this
enterprise.[17] At times Calvin also employed heart (*cor*) and understanding
(*intelligentia*) as synonyms.[18] Calvin further used reason (*ratio*) and
understanding (*intelligentia*) interchangeably.[19] Synonymous uses of heart (*cor*)
and soul (*anima*) may also be found in Calvin's writings.[20] Calvin saw close
interconnections between spirit, mind, and soul (*spiritus*, *mens*, and *anima*),[21] as

also between spirit, reason, mind, and judgment (*spiritus, ratio, mens,* and *iudicium*).[22]

As a biblical exegete, Calvin believed that his usage of these psychological terms had Scriptural precedent, which he attempted to follow.

> As by the word heart (*cor*) he [Ezekiel] means affections (*affectus*), so also by the spirit (*spiritus*) he signifies the mind itself and all its thoughts (*mentem ipsam et omnes cogitationes*). The spirit (*spiritus*) of a man is often taken for the whole soul (*tota anima*), and then it comprehends also all the affections (*omnes affectus*). But where the two are joined together, as the heart (*cor*) and spirit (*spiritus*), the heart is called the seat of all the affections (*cor vocatur sedes omnium affectuum*), it is in truth the very will of man (*denique est ipsa voluntas hominis*), while the spirit is the faculty of intelligence (*spiritus autem est facultas intelligendi*).[23]

Calvin's varied terminology has led some scholars to despair over ever discerning a precise, consistent psychology in his writings.[24] I do not think the situation is entirely hopeless. Two statements aptly summarize the findings of this appendix thus far. (1) Calvin clearly gave much higher standing to the soul than to the body. (2) Within Calvin's subdivision of the soul, both "mind" and "heart" were important in attaining the knowledge of God. As will be evident in the next section of the appendix, Calvin typically employed the term soul (*anima*) as the overarching concept which included, among other faculties, mind (*mens*) and heart (*cor*).

II. Relation of Reason and Will

In the same way that Calvin followed prior thinkers in his body/soul dichotomy, he also followed prior thinkers (notably, Aristotle and Aristotelians) in his faculty psychology, which divided the human soul into reason and will. Synonyms for reason (*ratio*) include understanding (*intelligentia*) and mind (*mens*).[25] Heart (*cor*) was occasionally used interchangeably with will (*voluntas*).[26] Whatever terms were employed in any given statement, Calvin consistently upheld the basic bipartite structure of the human soul. He wrote:

> Scripture is accustomed to divide the soul of man, as to its faculties, into two parts, the mind and the heart. The mind means the understanding, while the heart denotes all the dispositions or wills. These two terms, therefore, include the entire soul.[27]

> Thus let us, therefore, hold—as indeed is suitable to our present purpose—that the human soul consists of two faculties, understanding and will. Let the office, moreover, of understanding be to distinguish between objects, as each seems worthy of approval or disapproval; while that of the will, to choose and follow what the understanding pronounces good, but to reject and flee what it disapproves.[28]

Calvin posited a theoretical unity of the soul, according to which "the understanding is, as it were, the leader and governor of the soul; and that the will is always mindful of the bidding of the understanding, and in its own desires awaits the judgment of the understanding."[29] Ideally, for Calvin, the will would simply "strive after what understanding and reason present."[30] Calvin believed that in prelapsarian Adam "the will [was] completely amenable to the guidance of the reason."[31]

In postlapsarian humans, however, Calvin claimed that such a unity of reason and will is not always present, so that for fallen humans, knowledge does not always lead to concomitant action.

> Sometimes the shamefulness of evil-doing presses upon the conscience so that one, imposing upon himself no false image of the good, knowingly and willingly rushes headlong into wickedness. Out of such a disposition of mind come statements like this: "I see what is better and approve it, but I follow the worse."[32]

In my view, the failure to attend to Calvin's distinctions between prelapsarian humans, postlapsarian humans, and redeemed humans (once again, the creation-fall-redemption schema) has contributed to confusion about whether Calvin's teaching was "intellectualist," in stressing the primacy of reason or "voluntarist" in stressing the primacy of will. For the most part, those who view Calvin as an "intellectualist" stress his teachings on prelapsarian and redeemed humans, whereas those who view Calvin as a "voluntarist" stress his teachings on fallen, unredeemed humans.[33]

My research leads to the following three conclusions. (1) Calvin taught the primacy of reason in prelapsarian Adam.[34] (2) Calvin taught that in fallen humans, reason which "holds primacy in the life of man" is vain,[35] and the will does not always follow it.[36] Calvin also taught that in fallen humans, the will is the chief seat of sin,[37] so that the power of right thinking is a lesser power than the power of right willing.[38] (3) Calvin taught that in redeemed humans, reason is progressively restored to its position as governor of the soul, so that as the will obeys it, the will becomes increasingly free.[39]

Thus, according to Calvin, one problem with fallen humans is that their wills do not always follow the leading of their minds. But, in Calvin's view, perhaps a greater problem still is that even when a person's will does carry out the bidding of his or her mind, that bidding is often a sinful one, because it is the product of a sinful mind.[40] Hence Calvin's paraphrase of Matthew 6:23: "See that your mind, which should shine as a lantern to guide your actions, does not throw a shadow and a perversion across your whole life."[41]

In his psychology, Calvin sometimes used words as tight, technical terms with specific denotations (for example, contrasting *anima* and *spiritus*; *cor* and *voluntas*; *mens*, *ratio*, and *intelligentia*). At other times Calvin used these same words as loose, general terms with significantly overlapping connotations. This produces some difficulties in understanding "Calvin's psychology," as Prins has aptly observed.

> Calvin's inconsistencies, ambiguities, and contradictions are traceable to four sources: (1) the difficulty of maintaining consistency and focus throughout a corpus of some fifty collected volumes; (2) imprecision or incompleteness within his thought; (3) unawareness of conflicts within his thought or reluctance to face those conflicts; (4) the possibility that Calvin's inconsistencies reflect those of the Bible.[42]

An additional difficulty in expounding "Calvin's psychology" is that in his commentaries Calvin frequently explicates his understanding of the "psychology" of the various biblical writers (e.g., Ezekiel and Paul) without indicating clearly whether his own usage of these terms always follows their precise distinctions. Moreover, even when Calvin did attempt to follow Scriptural distinctions he found that "the usage of Scripture is different (*alius est scripturae usus*)."[43] Because Calvin's use of psychological terms varies, it is difficult to paint a firm picture of "Calvin's psychology." Nonetheless, it is possible to deduce from Calvin's writings a general schema like the one developed in the following diagram.[44] This understanding of "Calvin's psychology" is assumed in the discussion of Calvin in chapter one, unless otherwise noted.

Humanity (*Homo*)
/ \
Body (*Corpus*) Spirit (*Spiritus*)/Soul (*Anima*)
/ \
Reason/Understanding/Mind → ideally → Will/Heart
(*Ratio/Intelligentia/Mens*) → governs → (*Voluntas/Cor*)
(includes *sensus* and *cogitatio*)   (includes *affectus* and *appetitus*)

Notes

1. This appendix is restricted, by and large, to the sources listed in the final paragraph on page 2 of the text. For an analysis of Calvin's psychology as it appeared in his early works, the *Commentary on Seneca's 'De Clementia'* (1532) and the *Psychopannychia* (1534), see M. L. Monheit, "Passion and Order in the Formation of Calvin's Sense of Religious Authority" (Ph.D. diss., Princeton University, 1988), especially 66-99, 242-336.

2. See, for instance, *A Harmony of the Gospels*, Matthew 22:23 (*CO* XLV: 604-605): "I grant that philosophers who knew nothing of the resurrection of the flesh have discussed at length the immortal nature of the soul: but it is such foolish talk on the nature of the life to come that their opinions have no weight. Scripture informs us that the life of the spirit depends on the hope of resurrection, and to this souls released from the

body look with expectancy. Whoever destroys the resurrection is also depriving souls of immortality."

My study of Calvin on this issue calls seriously into question the reading of Battenhouse who claims, in his widely cited article, that "both the Neoplatonists and Calvin base their thinking about man on the premise of a dualism between soul and body. The soul is associated with the body yet ideally detached" (R. W. Battenhouse, "The Doctrine of Man in Calvin and in Renaissance Platonism," *The Journal of the History of Ideas* 9 [1948]: 468). Rather, I concur with Engel that, "while Calvin does elevate the soul over the body and show a clear preference for the soul throughout his work (spiritualism), he does not denigrate, reject, or finally separate the soul from the body in his work (dualism)" (M. P. Engel, *John Calvin's Perspectival Anthropology* [Atlanta: Scholars Press, 1985]: 169.)

3. *Institutes*, II. xiv. 1; *OS* III: 458-459, where Calvin drew an analogy to the two natures in the one person of Jesus Christ. As Partee notes, Calvin's eschatology contains "a distinction between soul and body without a final division" (C. Partee, "The Soul in Plato, Platonism, and Calvin," *Scottish Journal of Theology* 22 [1969]: 294).

4. *Institutes*, I. xv. 2; *OS* III: 174. See also *A Harmony of the Gospels*, Luke 1:46; *CO* XLV: 37, where Calvin commented that "the terms *soul* and *spirit* are taken variously in Scripture, but taken together apply in particular to two aspects of the soul (*animus*). The spirit (*spiritus*) is used for the intelligence (*intelligentia*), the soul (*animus*) for the seat of the affections, desires (*affectuum*)."

5. *Institutes*, I. xv. 2; *OS* III: 174.

6. *Institutes*, I. xv. 2; *OS* III: 174 (*essentiam immortalem, creatam*).

7. *Institutes*, I. xv. 2; *OS* III: 176. Calvin did grant clear priority to the soul over the body, a point emphasized in M. Miles, "Theology, Anthropology, and the Human Body in Calvin's *Institutes*," *Harvard Theological Review* 74 (1981): 303-323. But Calvin (*Institutes*, I. xv. 3; *OS* III: 178) was also clear in affirming that by itself, "the soul is not man" (*anima non sit homo*).

8. *Commentary on Ephesians*, 3:16; *CO* LI: 186. However, that there were "bodily aspects" to Calvin's soteriology is established by T. J. Davis, "Not 'Hidden and Far Off': The Bodily Aspect of Salvation and Its Implications for Understanding the Body in Calvin's Theology," *Calvin Theological Journal* 29 (1994): 406-418.

9. *Institutes*, III. vi. 5; *OS* IV: 150. See also *Institutes*, III. ii. 19; *OS* IV: 30.

10. *Institutes*, I. xv. 2; *OS* III: 175 and *Institutes* III. xxv. 1; *OS* IV: 432. See also *Institutes*, IV. xvi. 19; *OS* V: 323, where Calvin spoke of being taken *ex carnis ergastulo*.

11. *Institutes*, I. xv. 2; *OS* III: 176. See also *Institutes*, II. vii. 13; *OS* III: 339 and III. iii. 20; *OS* IV: 78. Calvin used such language of Christ in *Institutes*, IV. xvii. 30; *OS* V: 389, though he qualified it with the so-called extra-Calvinisticum, as in *Institutes*, II. xiii. 4; *OS* III: 458.

12. *Institutes*, III. ix. 4; *OS* IV: 174. See also *Institutes*, IV. xv. 11; *OS* V: 293, where Calvin spoke of being "cooped up in this prison of our body" (*carcere corporis nostri clausi degemus*).

13. *Institutes*, I. xv. 3; *OS* III: 176.

14. *Commentary on Genesis*, 1:26; *CO* XXIII: 26. Note, however, that Calvin concluded this sentence with the concession that there was "no part of him [Adam] in which some scintillations of it [the *imago dei*] did not shine forth." See also *Institutes*, I. xv. 3; *OS* III: 177-78, where Calvin allowed that "the image of God" is "seen or glows in

these outward marks," and where Calvin asserted that "although the primary seat of the divine image was in the mind and heart, or in the soul and its powers, yet there was no part of man, not even the body itself, in which some sparks did not glow." In my view, such statements count against Fowler's claim that, according to Calvin, "man's body does not bear the image of God" (S. Fowler, "The Persistent Dualism in Calvin's Thought," in T. Van der Walt [ed.], *Our Reformational Tradition: A Rich Heritage and Lasting Vocation* [Potchefstroom: Institute for Reformational Studies, 1984], 342).

15. *Commentary on Acts*, 17:22; *CO* XLVIII: 408.

16. *A Harmony of the Last Four Books of Moses*, Deuteronomy 29:4; *CO* XXIV: 243; *Commentary on Jeremiah*, 4:9, 5:20-21; *CO* XXXVII: 582, 630; and *Commentary on Acts*, 16:14; *CO* XLVIII: 377.

17. *Institutes* III. ii. 36; *OS* IV: 46-47. See also *Institutes* III. ii. 33; *OS* IV: 44 and *Institutes* III. vi. 4; *OS* IV: 149.

18. *Commentary on Jeremiah*, 4:9; *CO* XXXVII: 582 and *Commentary on Jeremiah*, 5:20-21; *CO* XXXVII: 630.

19. *Institutes*, I. xv. 3; *OS* III: 178; *Commentary on Romans*, 8:6; *CO* XLIX: 142; *Commentary on Ezekiel*, 11:19-20; *CO* XL: 243; and *Commentary on Jeremiah*, 24:7; *CO* XXXVIII: 462; though note the distinction in *Institutes*, I. xv. 6; *OS* III: 183, where Calvin gave hesitant approval to the Platonic scheme of the three cognitive faculties of the soul in which *phantasiam* "distinguishes those things which have been apprehended by common sense," *ratio* "embraces universal judgment," and *intelligentia* "in intent and quiet study contemplates what *ratio* discursively ponders."

20. *Commentary on Jeremiah*, 24:7; *CO* XXXVIII: 462 and *Institutes*, III. ii. 36; *OS* IV: 46-47.

21. *Commentary on John*, 13:21; *CO* XLVII: 314.

22. *Commentary on Isaiah*, 40:13; *CO* XXXVII: 16.

23. *Commentary on Ezekiel*, 11:19-20; *CO* XL: 243. Contrast this with the statement found in Calvin's *Commentary on John*, 12:40; *CO* XLVII: 298: "In Scripture *the heart* is sometimes taken as the seat of the affections. But here, as in many other places, it means the so-called intellectual part of the soul."

24. See Stuermann (*A Critical Study*, 86, 391), as well as J. J. Denniston III, "An Examination of Calvin's Theory of Knowledge in His Theology and Exegesis," (Ph.D. diss., Fordham University, 1991), 109.

25. For synonymous uses of *ratio* and *intelligentia* see *Institutes*, I. xv. 3; *OS* III: 78; *Commentary on Romans*, 8:6; *CO* XLIX: 142; *Commentary on Ezekiel*, 11:19-20; *CO* XL: 243; and *Commentary on Jeremiah*, 24:7; *CO* XXXVIII: 462. For a synonymous use of *ratio* and *mens* see *Institutes*, I. xv. 8; *OS* III: 185-186, though note the remark in the *Commentary on Ephesians*, 2:3; *CO* LI: that, "'the mind' includes reason (*mens porro rationem comprehendit*)." For synonymous uses of *mens* and *intelligentia* see *Commentary on Ezekiel*, 11:19-20; *CO* XL: 243; and *Institutes*, IV. x. 3; *OS*: V: 166.

26. For synonymous uses of *cor* and *voluntas* and see *Commentary on Ezekiel*, 11:19-20; *CO* XL: 243; *Institutes*, II. ii. 27; *OS* III: 271; and *Institutes*, II. iii. 6; *OS* III: 279-280. On the view that Calvin saw the heart as an aspect of the will, see (1) A. N. S. Lane, "Calvin's Doctrine of Assurance," *Vox Evangelica* 11 (1979): 42 and (2) R. A. Muller, "*Fides* and *Cognitio* in Relation to the Problem of Intellect and Will in Calvin," *Calvin Theological Journal* 25 (1990): 217ff.

27. *Commentary on Philippians*, 4:7; *CO* LII: 61-62.

28. *Institutes*, I. xv. 7; *OS* III: 184-185. A few sentences later in this same section Calvin insisted that "no power can be found in the soul that does not duly have reference to one or the other of these members [*intellectus* and *voluntas*]."

29. *Institutes*, I. xv. 7; *OS* III: 185.

30. *Institutes*, I. xv. 6; *OS* III: 183.

31. *Institutes*, I. xv. 8; *OS* III: 185-186.

32. *Institutes*, II. ii. 23; *OS* III: 265-266. J. M. Jones observes that "although he [Calvin] formally admits the unity of the soul, he puts a chasm between the reason and the will in the [fallen] soul's functioning" (240).

33. On the one side, Fowler asserts that Calvin "subordinates the will to the intellect" ("Faith and Reason in the Period of the Reformation," in T. Van der Walt [ed.], *Our Reformational Tradition: A Rich Heritage and Lasting Vocation* [Potchefstroom: Institute for Reformational Studies, 1984]: 73); Torrance maintains that "Calvin held to the primacy of the intellect over the will" ("Knowledge of God and Speech about Him, According to John Calvin," 410); and Lane declares that Calvin "taught the primacy of the intellect over the will in that the will follows the mind" ("Calvin's Doctrine of Assurance," 42).

On the other side, J. M. Jones concludes that "both in his conception of God and of man, Calvin regarded the will as primary" (210), and that "voluntarism pervades all his thinking" (134); Nixon asserts that "common to Augustine, Luther, and Calvin is the emphasis upon the primacy of the will" (11); and Muller (223) argues vigorously "against the tendency of some recent scholarship to identify Calvin's definition of faith as *cognitio* with a purely 'intellectualist' position," instead concluding that "Calvin's theology falls, in its basic attitude toward the problems of human knowing and willing in their relation to the temporal working out of salvation, into a voluntarist rather than an intellectualist pattern."

34. *Institutes*, I. xv. 7; *OS* III: 184-185.

35. *Commentary on Ephesians*, 4:17; *CO* LI: 204.

36. *Institutes*, I. xv. 7; *OS* III: 185 and *Institutes*, II. ii. 23; *OS* III: 265-266.

37. *Institutes*, II. ii. 27; *OS* III: 271.

38. *Commentary on II Corinthians*, 3:5; *CO* L: 38.

39. *Commentary on Ezekiel*, 11:19-20; *CO* XL: 242-250. On this last point, see Schreiner (159), who concludes that "in the process of sanctification, the renewed will gradually becomes subject to the dictates of reason which are, in turn, subject to God. This process is the restoration of order within the soul, definitive of the image of God."

40. See *Institutes*, I. xv. 6; *OS* III: 183, *Commentary on II Corinthians*, 3:5; *CO* L: 38, and *Commentary on Ezekiel*, 11:19-20; *CO* XL: 242-250, where Calvin made the similar point that possessing a right reason/heart is prerequisite to possessing a truly free will. Muller (216) notes correctly that, according to Calvin, in fallen humans "reason has become a weak guide and the will, in any case, is no longer inclined to follow reason." Likewise, Leithart observes that, in Calvin's view, "sin brings disorder to the soul both by filling the mind with evil thoughts and by weakening the reason, rendering the latter incapable of exercising its hegemony over the other faculties" (P. J. Leithart, "Stoic Elements in Calvin's Doctrine of the Christian Life," *Westminster Theological Journal* 55 [1993]: 45).

41. *A Harmony of the Gospels*, Matthew 6:23; *CO* XLV: 207. Conversely, for Calvin, "the whole economy of a good and righteous life depends upon our being governed and directed by the light of understanding" and "the commencement of

integrity and uprightness of life consists in an enlightened and sound mind" (*Commentary on Psalms*, 14:2; *CO* XXXI: 137).

42. R. Prins, "The Image of God in Adam and the Restoration of Man in Jesus Christ: A Study in Calvin," *Scottish Journal of Theology* 25 (1972): 33, note 1.

43. *Commentary on I Thessalonians*, 5:23; *CO* LII: 179. Cf. Prins's fourth point in the preceding quote.

44. For a succinct statement of Calvin's general schema, see his *Commentary on I Thessalonians*, 5:23; *CO* LII: 179, where he divided humanity into body and soul/spirit and divided soul/spirit into will and understanding.

Appendix 2

Representative Teachings on the Noetic Effects of Sin in Christian Tradition and Christian Scripture

The notion that sin has noetic effects is sometimes thought to be a notion peculiar to the Reformed tradition. Certainly it is true that, as the present study has shown, Reformed thinkers like Calvin, Kuyper, and Brunner have written extensively on the subject of how sin affects human thinking. However, I share Merold Westphal's optimism about an "ecumenical approach to the notion of sin as an epistemological category."[1] I share Westphal's ecumenical optimism because I believe that the notion that sin has noetic effects is grounded in the Christian Tradition and the Christian Scriptures. This appendix attempts to substantiate this claim.

I. The Noetic Effects of Sin in Christian Tradition

The Christian Tradition repeatedly acknowledges that sin can have noetic effects. An exhaustive investigation of the Christian Tradition is beyond the scope of this present study. In this appendix, attention will be given to representative figures from various periods of church history.

Augustine of Hippo, arguably the most influential theologian in the early church, taught that humanity possessed a natural knowledge of God, but this knowledge could be corrupted by error. Thus Augustine advised those persons who were entrapped by the illusions of Manicheeism to fall back on "the natural conviction of every human mind, unless it is corrupted by error, of the perfect unchangeableness and incorruptibility of the nature and substance of God."[2]

The corruption of human knowledge of God, in turn, could be traced to human sin, especially human pride, according to Augustine. Pertinent here is Augustine's autobiographical self-analysis, recorded in his *Confessions*.

Sweet Truth, although I was straining to catch the sound of your secret melody,
I deafened the ears of my heart by allowing my mind to twist and turn among
these material inventions of my imagination. As I pondered over beauty and
proportion, all the time I wanted to stand still and listen to you and rejoice at
hearing the bridegroom's voice, the voice of the Bridegroom of my soul; but
this I could not do, because the voice of my own error called me away from
him and I was dragged down and down by the weight of my own pride (*quia
vocibus erroris mei rapiebar foras, et pondere superbiae meae inima
decidebam*).[3]

Augustine freely admitted that during his Manichaean period pride obscured
his vision of God.[4] Augustine described the Manichees in similarly unflattering
terms.

[They] want to be light, not in the Lord, but in themselves, because they think
that the nature of the soul is the same as God. In this way their darkness
becomes denser still, because in their abominable arrogance (*horrenda
arrogantia*) they have separated themselves still further from you, who are the
true Light which enlightens every soul born into the world.[5]

According to Augustine, sinful seeking of human applause is "apt to
produce in the soul what may be likened to a dangerous swelling, beneath which
lurk the germs of decay, and by it the eye of the mind becomes suffused, so that
it cannot discern the riches of truth."[6] Until people were redeemed from their
sin, argued Augustine, their minds would remain unhealed and they would
continue to suffer the noetic effects of sin.[7] For Augustine, the mind which has
been crippled by sin must be healed; it must be purified by faith.[8] Augustine
taught that whereas the sin of unbelief closes the door to right knowledge of
God, faith opens this door and provides the understanding with access to right
knowledge of God.[9]

Hence the famous Augustinian slogan that "understanding is the reward of
faith. Therefore, seek not to understand that thou mayest believe, but believe
that thou mayest understand." Later Anselm would follow the Augustinian
dictum in his claim that "I do not seek to understand in order to believe, but I
believe in order to understand." Significantly, Anselm's statement follows
immediately after his confession that the image of God in him "is so effaced and
worn away by my faults, it is so obscured by the smoke of my sins, that it cannot
do what it was made to do [think of God and love God], unless thou renew and
reform it."[10] Clearly, both Augustine and Anselm were keenly aware of the fact
that sin distorted their thinking and regeneration included the redemption of
their minds.

Thomas Aquinas, arguably the most influential theologian in the late
medieval church, also acknowledged that sin has noetic effects. The argument
here stands in opposition to Hoffecker's claim that "Aquinas exalted our rational
capacity and implicitly affirmed that sin has virtually no effect on one important
area of man's life, his knowledge. The Thomist method denies any noetic effect
of sin."[11] Likewise, the understanding of this study conflicts with Rushdoony's

view that according to Aquinas "a man is able to reason and to know reality without reference to his ethical status, i.e., whether or not he is a sinner. . . . [For Aquinas] the domain of mind is untouched by the fall and still operative on the same basis as in Eden when properly instructed."[12]

Aquinas stated plainly that "reason is dulled by sin," and by "sin" he meant both the "original sin" of the first human pair and the "actual sin" of their progeny. Aquinas describes the change in "reason" after the fall:

> Through original justice reason had perfect control over the inferior powers of the soul, and reason itself was perfected by God and subject to God. But original justice was lost through the sin of the first parents, as has been said [in Q. 81, Art. 2]. As a result, all powers of the soul have been left to some extent destitute of their proper order, by which they are naturally inclined to virtue, and this destitution is called the 'wounding of nature.'. . . But all four [wounds inflicted on the whole of human nature by the sin of our first parents] are also caused by other sins, since the inclination to virtue is diminished in every one of us by actual sin [*per peccatum actuale*] as has been said [in Arts. 1 and 2]. Reason is dulled by sin, especially in moral decisions [*per peccatum et ratio hebetatur præcipue in agendis*].[13]

According to Aquinas, chief among the spiritual penalties for original sin was "the frailty of human reason: from this it happens that man with difficulty arrives at knowledge of the truth; that with ease he falls into error; and that he cannot entirely overcome his beastly appetites, but is over and over again beclouded by them."[14] In terms of "actual sin" Aquinas believed that concupiscence and other passions could hinder the proper operation of human reason. He observed that natural law may be "blotted out in the case of a particular action when reason is hindered [*ratio impeditur*], because of concupiscence or some other passion, in applying a general principle to a particular action."[15] Similarly, Aquinas recognized that "emotional pressure could be so intense that a man is completely deprived of the use of reason, for many men are completely carried out of their minds [*in insaniam conversi*] by excessive wrath or love."[16]

Aquinas maintained that "in divine matters the natural reason has its failings."[17] In fact, Aquinas' belief that "human reason is very defective in divine things [*ratio enim humana in rebus divinis est multum deficiens*]," was one of the reasons that he was convinced that "it is necessary for people to accept by way of faith not only such things as are beyond reason [*supra rationem*], but also such things as reason can know [*rationem cognosci possunt*]."[18]

Martin Luther, widely viewed as the key catalyst of the Protestant Reformation, also believed that sin had noetic effects. Luther, like Calvin after him, argued that natural human reason is blinded when it comes to divine things (*res coelestes*). In his work *On the Bondage of the Will* Luther wrote: "It is therefore not astonishing that in divine things men of outstanding talent through so many centuries have been blind. In human things it would be astonishing. In divine things the wonder is rather if there are one or two who are not blind, but it is no wonder if all without exception are blind."[19] Luther makes much the same argument in his *Postil for Ephiphany*, on Isaiah 60:1-6:

> In temporal affairs and those which have to do with men, the rational man is self-sufficient: here he needs no other light than reason's. Therefore, God does not teach us in the Scriptures how to build houses, make clothing, marry, wage war, navigate, and the like. For here the light of nature is sufficient. But in godly affairs, that is, in those which have to do with God, where man must do what is acceptable with God and be saved thereby—here, however, nature is absolutely stone-blind, so that it cannot even catch a glimpse of what those things are.[20]

While natural human reason is adequate to guide us in temporal, earthly matters, Luther maintained that when it comes to "the depth of divine wisdom and of the divine purpose, the profundity of God's grace and mercy, and what eternal life is like," reason speaks "with the same authority with which a blind man discusses color."[21] As documented in the first chapter of this book, John Calvin also propounded a very strong doctrine of the noetic effects of sin. So, as with the early church and the medieval church, key theologians from the Reformation church acknowledged the negative influence of sin on human thinking.

Likewise, Jonathan Edwards, an influential early American theologian, taught, in no uncertain terms, that sin distorts humanity's thinking, particularly in religious matters. This is abundantly clear in Edwards' sermon entitled, pointedly, "Man's Natural Blindness in the Things of Religion."[22]

> That is the woeful tendency of the mind of man since the fall, notwithstanding his noble powers and faculties; even to sink down into a kind of brutality, to lose and extinguish all useful light, and to sink lower and lower into darkness.[23]

> It [humanity's blindness] appears, in that they are so blind in those *same things* in religious matters, which they are sufficiently sensible of in other matters. In temporal things they are very sensible that it is a point of prudence to improve the first opportunity in things of great importance. But in matters of religion, which are of infinitely the greatest importance, they have not this discernment. In temporal matters they are sensible that it is great folly to delay and put off, when life is in danger, and all depends upon it. But in the concerns of their souls, they are insensible of this truth. So in the concerns of this world, they are sensible it is prudence to improve times of special advantage, and to embrace a good offer when made them. They are sensible that things of long continuance are of greater importance, than those of short duration; yet in religious concerns, none of these things are sensibly discerned. In temporal things they are sufficiently sensible, that it is a point of prudence to lay up for hereafter, in summer to lay up for winter, and to lay up for their families, after they are dead; but men do not generally discern the prudence of making proper provision for a future state. In matters of importance in this world, they are sensible of the wisdom of taking thorough care to be on sure grounds; but in their soul's concerns, they see nothing of this.[24]

As documented in the second chapter of this book, the prominent nineteenth century theologian Abraham Kuyper and the important twentieth century theologian Emil Brunner also upheld a firm doctrine of the noetic effects of sin. So, representative figures from the early church (Augustine), the medieval church (Aquinas), the Reformation church (Luther and Calvin), the eighteenth century American church (Edwards), and the nineteenth and twentieth century European church (Kuyper and Brunner) have all acknowledged that sin has noetic effects. As Clark and Gaede state, "though church traditions differ regarding the extent to which sin distorts human reason, there is general agreement that our ability to discover and understand God's truth is influenced to some degree by sin."[25] Westphal observes similarly that while the notion that sin has noetic effects "may be distinctive of Calvinism, it is by no means unique to that tradition."[26] This evidence substantiates the claim that the concept of the noetic effects of sin is acknowledged in the Christian Tradition. The second half the appendix aims to substantiate the claim that the concept of the noetic effects of sin is likewise taught in the Christian Scriptures.

II. The Noetic Effects of Sin in Christian Scripture

An exhaustive investigation of the Christian Scriptures is beyond the scope of this present study. In this final section of the appendix, attention will be focused on the gospel of John. If this one gospel acknowledges the noetic effects of sin, then this establishes the claim that the Christian Scriptures do. Additional key passages of Scripture pertaining to the noetic effects of sin are found on pages 2, 84, 98-100, 103-104, and throughout the book.[27]

As with the synoptic gospels, the gospel of John makes frequent reference to people's failure to truly understand who Jesus was. John 1:5 states simply that "the light shines in the darkness, but the darkness has not understood it."[28] John 1:10-11 declares that the true light "was in the world, and the world came into being through him; yet the world did not know him. He came to what was his own, and his own did not accept him." As C.K. Barrett remarks, "the world neither recognized nor responded to him."[29] In John 3:32, John the Baptist proclaims, of Jesus, that "he testifies to what he has seen and heard, yet no one accepts his testimony." In John 6:36 Jesus tells a crowd simply that "you have seen me and yet do not believe." In brief, John makes repeated reference to people having a problem in recognizing and accepting Jesus for who he truly was: the Son of God sent by the heavenly Father above, the Messiah, the very light of the world.

Why did so many people not understand Jesus as the light of the world? John 3:19-20 explains that "this is the judgment, that the light has come into the world, and people loved darkness rather than light because their deeds were evil. For all who do evil hate the light and do not come to the light, so that their deeds may not be exposed." Clearly John connects people's sin (doing evil deeds and loving darkness) with their failure to rightly understand and accept Jesus. Leon

Morris comments succinctly that "there is a moral basis behind much unbelief."[30]

The moral dimension to human knowledge of God is also highlighted in John 5:39-44, wherein Jesus is reported as saying the following to a group of Jews who persecuted him.

> You search the scriptures because you think that in them you have eternal life; and it is they that testify on my behalf. Yet you refuse to come to me to have life. I do not accept glory from human beings. But I know that you do not have the love of God in you. I have come in my Father's name, and you do not accept me; if another comes in his own name, you will accept him. How can you believe when you accept glory from one another and do not seek the glory that comes from the one who alone is God?

In this passage it is those who "do not have the love of God in them" who refuse to recognize Jesus as the promised Messiah who gives life. F.F. Bruce maintains that, "had there been any love for God in their hearts, it would have manifested itself by their acceptance of the one who came to them in the name of God."[31] Moreover, a sinful communal influence was obviously at work in those who sought praise and glory from other humans, rather than from God, and were thereby hindered from believing in Jesus. John 12:42-44 speaks similarly of a sinful communal influence, which prevented outward confessions of faith among those who "loved human glory more than the glory that comes from God."

The connection between loving God, obeying God, and knowing God is also explicit elsewhere in John's gospel.[32] For instance, in John 14:21 and 23, Jesus makes the following statement.

> They who have my commandments and keep them are those who love me; and those who love me will be loved by my Father, and I will love them and reveal myself to them. . . . Those who love me will keep my word, and my Father will love them, and we will come to them and make our home with them.

Here, obedience to God, love of God, and knowledge of God are intimately related. Bruce observes that "where love and obedience are shown, the presence of God and of Christ is realized. . . . No such revelation is possible where love and obedience are absent."[33] As Jesus put it in John 7:17: "Anyone who resolves to do the will of God will know whether the teaching is from God or whether I am speaking on my own." Raymond Brown notes that "we are told that anyone who does God's will will recognize that Jesus' doctrine comes from the Father. These requirements are simply variants of the fundamental requirement—being attuned to God's voice in order to recognize one who speaks for God."[34]

The noetic effects of sin are also highlighted in John 8:42-47.

> Jesus said to them, "If God were your Father, you would love me, for I came from God and now I am here. I did not come on my own, but he sent me. Why do you not understand what I say? It is because you cannot accept my word.

You are from your father the devil, and you choose to do your father's desires. He was a murderer from the beginning and does not stand in the truth, because there is no truth in him. When he lies, he speaks according to his own nature, for he is a liar and the father of lies. But because I tell the truth, you do not believe me. Which of you convicts me of sin? If I tell the truth, why do you not believe me? Whoever is from God hears the words of God. The reason you do not hear them is that you are not from God."

This passage teaches that the people in Jesus' audience did not understand (ου γινωσκετε) what Jesus said because they were unable (ου δυνασθε) to accept Jesus' word, which in turn was related to their choice to carry out their father's (the devil's) desires. Rudolph Bultmann comments: "If the revelation consists in a calling into question of the natural man, then it will be unintelligible to a man who is not aware of his own questionableness." [35] They do not hear Jesus' words as the words of God because they do not belong to God. A similar point is made in John 10:22-30, which teaches that certain Jews did not believe that Jesus was the Messiah because they were not Jesus' sheep, having not been given to Jesus by the Father. Those who belong to God hear the words of God. As Jesus said to Pilate in John 18:37, "everyone who belongs to the truth listens to my voice." The clarity with which people hear Jesus' words as God's words may be very much related to their own spiritual state. In sum, the notion that sin affects our thinking is a repeated theme in the Gospel of John, as throughout the other sixty-five books of the Christian Scriptures. [36]

Notes

1. M. Westphal, "Taking St. Paul Seriously: Sin as an Epistemological Category," 202.

2. Augustine, *Contra Faustum Manichæum*, book XXXIII, chapter 9; in P. Schaff (ed.) *Nicene and Post-Nicene Fathers*, series 1, vol. 4 (Grand Rapids: Eerdmans, 1956), 345.

3. Book IV, 15; Latin text in *St. Augustine's Confessions*, vol. 1, Loeb Classical Library (London: William Heinemann, 1960), 194.

4. *Confessions*, Book VII, 7; Latin text, 362 ("*tumore meo separabar abs te, et nimis inflata facies claudebat oculos meos*").

5. *Confessions*, Book VIII, 10; Latin text, 450.

6. Augustine, *Letters*, CXVIII, chapter 1, section 5; in *Nicene and Post-Nicene Fathers*, series 1, vol. 1, 440.

7. *Soliliquies*, book I, chapter 6, section 12; in *Nicene and Post-Nicene Fathers*, series 1, vol. 7, 541.

8. "Sed quia ipsa mens, cui ratio et intellegentia naturaliter inest, vitiis quibusdam tenebrosis et veteribus invalida est non solum ad inhaerendum fruendo, verum etiam ad perferendum incommutabile lumen, donec de die in diem renovata atque sanata fiat tantae felicitatis capax, fide primum fuerat inbuenda atque purganda" (*City of God*, XI, 2; Latin text in *The City of God against the Pagans*, vol. 3, Loeb Classical Library [London: William Heinemann, 1968], 430).

9. *Letters*, CXXXVII, chapter IV, section 15; in *Nicene and Post-Nicene Fathers*, series 1, vol. 1, 479.

10. Anselm, *Proslogion*, chapter 1, in E. R. Fairweather (ed. and trans.), *A Scholastic Miscellany: Anselm to Ockham* (Philadelphia: Westminster Press, 1956), 73.

11. Hoffecker, "Augustine, Aquinas, and the Reformers," 250-251.

12. R. J. Rushdoony, "The Quest for Common Ground," in Gary North (ed.), *Foundations of Christian Scholarship: Essays in the Van Til Perspective* (Vallecito, CA: Ross House Books, 1976), 29.

13. Aquinas, *Summa Theologiæ*, I-II, Question 85, Article 3. Latin text from the Blackfriars edition published in conjunction with Eyre and Spottiswoode and McGraw-Hill, 1964-1976.

14. "Inter spirituales autem est potissima debilitas rationis, ex qua contingit quod homo difficulter pervenit ad veri cognitionem, et de facili labitur in errorem; et appetitus bestiales omnino superare non potest, sed multoties obnubilatur ab eis." *Summa Contra Gentiles*, book IV, chapter 52, section 1. Latin text from the Editio Leonina Manualis published by Apud Sedem Commissionis Leoninae in Rome in 1934.

15. *Summa Theologiæ*, I-II, Question 94, Article 6.

16. *Summa Theologiæ*, I-II, Question 77, Article 2.

17. *Summa Contra Gentiles*, book I, chapter 2, section 3. Along similar lines, Bonaventure argued that people's doubts about God's existence came "from a defect in the knower rather than from a deficiency in the object known" (*Disputed Questions on the Mystery of the Trinity*, trans. Zachary Hayes [St. Bonaventure, NY: The Franciscan Institute, 1979], Question I, Article 1, 118).

18. *Summa Theologiæ*, II-II, Question 2, Article 4. Note that in this section Aquinas refers to the sin of intellectual laziness as a hindrance to the knowledge attainable by reason. See also the related argument at the very beginning of the *Summa Theologiæ* that "it is necessary that people should be instructed by divine revelation even in such things concerning God as human reason could discover. For such truth about God as could be discovered by reason would be known only by the few, and that after a long time, and mixed with many errors [*cum admixtione multorum errorrum*]" (Part I, Question 1, Article 1). Aquinas makes the same point in *Summa Contra Gentiles*, book I, chapter 4.

19. *LW* 33:98; *WA* 18:659.

20. *WA*[1,1] 531; translation taken from B. Gerrish, *Grace and Reason* (New York: Oxford University Press, 1962), 12.

21. *LW* 22:153.

22. J. Edwards, "Man's Natural Blindness in the Things of Religion," in *The Works of President Edwards*, vol. 7 (New York: S. Converse, 1829), 3-30.

23. Edwards, "Man's Natural Blindness," 12.

24. Edwards, "Man's Natural Blindness," 20.

25. Clark and Gaede, "Knowing Together," 77. The church's acknowledgment of the noetic effects of sin has some interesting secular parallels, especially in scientific methodology. On this, see Westphal, "Taking St. Paul Seriously: Sin as an Epistemological Category," and Montgomery.

26. Westphal, "Taking St. Paul Seriously: Sin as an Epistemological Category," 202.

27. For a study of Paul's view of the noetic effects of sin, see Theo J. W. Kunst, "The Implications of Pauline Theology of the Mind for the Work of the Theologian" (Th.D. diss., Dallas Theological Seminary, 1979), especially chapter 3.

28. Here I prefer the rendering of κατελαβεν as "understood" (NIV) rather than as "overcome" (NRSV). Bruce prefers "overcome" (F. F. Bruce, *The Gospel of John* [Grand Rapids: Eerdmans, 1983], 34). Bultmann and Schnackenburg prefer "understood" in the sense of "grasp," "comprehend," or "embrace with mind and will" (R. Bultmann, *The Gospel of John* [Philadelphia: Westminster Press, 1971], 48; R. Schnackenburg, *The Gospel According to John*, vol. 1 [New York: Herder and Herder, 1968], 246). Barrett argues that the evangelist is intentionally "playing on the two meanings" (C. K. Barrett, *The Gospel According to St. John*, Second Edition [Philadelphia: Westminster Press, 1978], 158). A helpful discussion of the translation options may be found in R. E. Brown, *The Gospel According to John* (Garden City, NY: Doubleday, 1966), 8. Unless otherwise indicated, as here, in this appendix the NRSV translation is employed.

29. Barrett, *The Gospel According to St. John*, 162.

30. L. Morris, *The Gospel According to John* (Grand Rapids: Eerdmans, 1971), 234.

31. Bruce, *The Gospel of John*, 137. See also Bruce's argument that "by 'the love of God' here is most probably meant their love for God; the genitive 'of God' in other words, is objective" (137).

32. More recently Hans Urs von Balthasar has argued for an intimate connection between love and knowledge, stating "that the meaning of being lies in love and that knowledge is only explainable through love and for love. The will which exists in the object to open itself and the will which exists in the knowing subject to open itself in receptivity are the double form of the surrender which manifests itself in these two ways. From this follows the insight, that love is never separable from truth (*die Liebe von der Wahrheit nicht trennbar ist*)" (*Theologik I, Wahrheit der Welt* [Einsiedeln: Johannes Verlag, 1985], 118).

33. Bruce, *The Gospel of John*, 304.

34. Brown, *The Gospel According to John*, 316. On the connection between obedience and the knowledge of God, see also Psalm 111:10: "The fear of the Lord is the beginning of wisdom; all those who practice it have a good understanding."

35. Bultmann, *The Gospel of John*, 317.

36. Zemek's investigation of noetic terms in the Bible led him to conclude that "the noetic effects of the Fall are attested on nearly every page of the Holy Scriptures" (G. J. Zemek, "Aiming the Mind: A Key to Godly Living," *Grace Theological Journal* 5 [1984]: 205).

Works Cited

Ackerman, R., and R. J. DeRubeis. "Is Depressive Realism Real?" *Clinical Psychology Review* 11 (1991): 565-584.

Adams, J. E. *Competent to Counsel*. Grand Rapids: Baker, 1970.

Adams, R. M. "The Virtue of Faith." *Faith and Philosophy* 1 (1984): 3-15.

Alicke, M. D., M. L. Klotz, D. L. Breitenbecher, T. J. Yurak, and D. S. Vredenburg. "Personal Contact, Individuation and Better than Average Effect." *Journal of Personality and Social Psychology* 68 (1995): 804-825.

Alloy, L. B., and L. Y. Abramson. "Judgment of Contingency in Depressed and Nondepressed Students: Sadder but Wiser?" *Journal of Experimental Psychology: General* 108 (1979): 441-485.

Alston, W. P. "Christian Experience and Christian Belief." In A. Plantinga and N. Wolterstorff (eds.), *Faith and Rationality*. Notre Dame: University of Notre Dame Press, 1983, 103-134.

Anderson, A. L. "Calvin's Conception of Sin and Guilt." Master of theology thesis, Union Theological Seminary, 1947.

Anselm. *Proslogion*. In E. R. Fairweather (ed.), *A Scholastic Miscellany: Anselm to Ockham*. Philadelphia: Westminster Press, 1956.

Aquinas, T. *Summa Contra Gentiles*, Editio Leonina Manualis. Rome: Apud Sedem Commissionis Leoninae, 1934.

___. *Summa Theologiæ*, Blackfriars edition. New York: McGraw-Hill, 1964-1976.

Archiv für Reformationsgeschichte, Beiheft, Literaturbericht. Jahrgang 1 (1972), and successive years through 1998.

Augustine, A. *St. Augustine's Confessions*. Vol. I. Loeb Classical Library. London: William Heinemann, 1960.

___. *The City of God against the Pagans*. Vol. III. Loeb Classical Library. London: William Heinemann, 1968.

Ayers, R. H. "Language, Logic and Reason in Calvin's *Institutes*." *Religious Studies* 16 (1980): 283-298.

Babad, E., M. Hills, and M. O'Driscoll. "Factors Influencing Wishful Thinking and Predictions of Election Outcomes." *Basic and Applied Social Psychology* 13 (1992): 461-476.

Baillie, J. *Our Knowledge of God*. New York: Charles Scribner's Sons, 1959.

Bainton, R., and E. W. Gritsch. *Bibliography of the Continental Reformation*, second edition. Hamden, CT: Archon Books, 1972, 161-181.

Balthasar, H. U. von. *Theologik I, Wahrheit der Welt*. Einsiedeln: Johannes Verlag, 1985.

Baron, R. A., and D. Byrne. *Social Psychology*, 7th edition. Boston: Allyn and Bacon, 1994.

Barrett, C. K. *The Gospel According to St. John*, 2nd edition. Philadelphia: Westminster Press, 1978.

Battenhouse, R. W. "The Doctrine of Man in Calvin and in Renaissance Platonism." *The Journal of the History of Ideas* 9 (1948): 447-471.

Baumeister, R. F. "The Optimal Margin of Illusion." *Journal of Social and Clinical Psychology* 8 (1989): 176-189.

Beauvois, J. L., and N. Dubois. "The Norm of Internality in the Explanation of Psychological Events." *European Journal of Social Psychology* 18 (1988): 299-316.

Belford, L. A. "Foreword." In L. Nixon, *John Calvin's Teachings on Human Reason*. New York: Exposition Press, 1963, v-vii.

Berkvall, A. "Reason in Luther, Calvin, and Sidney." *Sixteenth Century Journal* 23 (1992): 115-127.

Beversluis, J. "Reforming the 'Reformed' Objection to Natural Theology." *Faith and Philosophy* 12 (1995): 189-206.

Blackburn, R. T., G. R. Pellino, A. Boberg, and C. O'Connell. "Are Instructional Improvement Programs Off-Target?" *Current Issues in Higher Education* 1 (1980): 32-48.

Block, J., and C. R. Colvin. "Positive Illusions and Well-Being Revisited: Separating Fiction from Fact," *Psychological Bulletin* 116 (1994): 28.

Bobgan, M., and D. Bobgan. *Psychoheresy: The Psychological Seduction of Christianity*. Santa Barbara, CA: Eastgate, 1987.

Bonaventure. *Disputed Questions on the Mystery of the Trinity*. Translated by Z. Hayes. St. Bonaventure, NY: The Franciscan Institute, 1979.

Bouwsma, W. J. "Calvin and the Renaissance Crisis of Knowing." *Calvin Theological Journal* 17 (1982): 190-211.

Braaten, C. "The Current Controversy in Revelation: Pannenberg and His Critics." *Journal of Religion* 45 (1965): 225-237.

Breen, Q. *John Calvin: A Study in French Humanism*, 2nd edition. Hamden, CT: Archon Books, 1968. (Originally published by Eerdmans in 1931.)

Brenner, S. N. and Molander, E. A. "Is the Ethics of Business Changing?" *Harvard Business Review* (January-February 1977): 57-71.

Brewer, M. B. "Ingroup Bias in the Minimal Intergroup Situation: A Cognitive-Motivational Analysis." *Psychological Bulletin* 86 (1979): 307-324.

Brickman, P., and R. J. Bulman. "Pleasure and Pain in Social Comparison." In J. M. Suls and R. L. Miller (eds.), *Social Comparison Processes: Theoretical and Empirical Perspectives.* Washington, DC: Hemisphere, 1977, 149-186.

Brown, R. E. *The Gospel According to John.* Garden City, NY: Doubleday, 1966.

Bruce, F. F. *The Gospel of John.* Grand Rapids: Eerdmans, 1983.

Brunner, E. *The Christian Doctrine of Creation and Redemption*, Dogmatics Volume II. Philadelphia: Westminster, 1952.

___. *Die christliche Lehre von Schöpfung und Erlösung.* Dogmatik Band II. Zürich: Zwingli-Verlag, 1950.

___. *Man in Revolt.* Philadelphia: Westminster, 1939.

___. *Der Mensch im Widerspruch.* Berlin: Furche-Verlag, 1937.

___. *Offenbarung und Vernunft.* Zürich: Zwingli-Verlag, 1941.

___. *Revelation and Reason.* Philadelphia: Westminster, 1946.

Buber, M. *I and Thou.* New York: Scribner, 1937.

Bultmann, R. *The Gospel of John.* Philadelphia: Westminster Press, 1971.

Burger, J. M., and M. L. Palmer. "Changes in and Generalization of Unreal-istic Optimism Following Experiences with Stressful Events: Reactions to the 1989 California Earthquake." *Personality and Social Psychology Bulletin* 18 (1992): 39-43.

Burwell, R. "Epistemic Justification, Cultural Universals, and Revelation: Further Reflections on the Sociology of Knowledge." In H. Heie and D. L. Wolfe (eds.), *The Reality of Christian Learning.* Grand Rapids: Eerdmans, 1987, 87-100.

Calvin, J. *Calvin's Commentaries [Old Testament]*, 45 vols. Translated by The Calvin Translation Society, 1843-1855. Reprint edition. Grand Rapids: Eerdmans, 1948-1950.

___. *Calvin's New Testament Commentaries*, 12 vols. Edited by D. W. Torrance and T. F. Torrance. Various translators. Grand Rapids: Eerdmans, 1959-1972.

___. *Calvin's Tracts and Treatises.* Reprint edition. 3 vols. Translated by H. Beveridge. Grand Rapids: Eerdmans, 1958.

___. *Concerning Scandals.* Translated by J. W. Fraser. Grand Rapids: Eerdmans, 1978.

___. *Institutes of the Christian Religion*, 2 vols. Translated by F. L. Battles. Edited by J. T. McNeill. Philadelphia: Westminster Press, 1960.

___. *Instruction in Faith.* Translated by P. T. Fuhrmann. Philadelphia: Westminster Press, 1949.

___. *Ioannis Calvini opera quae supersunt omnia.* 59 vols. *Corpus Reformatorum*, vols. 29-87. Edited by G. Baum, E. Cunitz, and E. Reuss. Brunsvigae: A. Schwetschke et Filium, 1863-1900. (*CO*)

___. *Johannis Calvini opera selecta*, 5 vols. Edited by P. Barth and W. Niesel. Munich: Chr. Kaiser Verlag, 1926-1952. (*OS*)

___. *The Mystery of Godliness and Other Selected Sermons*. Grand Rapids: Eerdmans, 1950.

___. *Treatises against the Anabaptists and the Libertines*. Edited and translated by B. W. Farley. Grand Rapids: Baker, 1982.

Casserley, J. V. L. *Morals and Man in the Social Sciences*. London: Longmans, Green and Co., 1951.

Campbell, J. D. "Similarity and Uniqueness: The Effects of Attribute Type, Relevance, and Individual Differences in Self-Esteem and Depression." *Journal of Personality and Social Psychology* 50 (1986): 281-294.

Carter, J., and Narramore, B. *The Integration of Psychology and Theology*. Grand Rapids: Zondervan, 1979.

Chandler, T. A., D. D. Sharma, F. M. Wolf, and S. K. Planchard. "Multiattributional Causality: A Five Cross-National Samples Study." *Journal of Cross-Cultural Psychology* 12 (1981): 207-221.

Clark, K. J., ed. *Philosophers Who Believe*. Downers Grove, IL: InterVarsity Press, 1993.

Clark, R. A., and S. D. Gaede. "Knowing Together: Reflections on a Holistic Sociology of Knowledge." In H. Heie and D. L. Wolfe (eds.), *The Reality of Christian Learning*. Grand Rapids: Eerdmans, 1987, 55-86.

College Board. *Student Descriptive Questionnaire*. Princeton, NJ: Educational Testing Service, 1976-1977.

Collins, G. R. *Christian Counseling*, revised edition. Dallas, TX: Word, 1988.

Colvin, C. R., and J. Block. "Do Positive Illusions Foster Mental Health? An Examination of the Taylor and Brown Formulation." *Psychological Bulletin* 116 (1994): 3-20.

Commission internationale d'histoire ecclésiastique comparée. *Bibliographie de la Réforme, 1450-1648, Ouvrages parus de 1940 à 1955*, Premier Fascicule. Leiden: E. J. Brill, 1958. Also Deuxième Fascicule–1960, Quatrième Fascicule—1963, Sixième Fascicule—1967.

Conn, H. M. "The Concept of Reason in the Theology of John Calvin." Master of theology thesis, Westminster Theological Seminary, 1958.

Cooke, V. M. "The New Calvinist Epistemology." *Theological Studies* 47 (1986): 273-285.

Cooper, J. "Agreeing to Disagree." *The Reformed Journal* 31 (1981): 12-13.

Crabb, L. "Biblical Counseling: A Basic View." *The CAPS Bulletin* 4 (1978): 1-6.

Cross, K. P. "Not *Can* but *Will* College Teaching Be Improved?" *New Directions for Higher Education* 17 (Spring 1977): 1-15.

Croxton, J. S., and A. G. Miller. "Behavioral Disconfirmation and the Observer Bias." *Journal of Social Behavior and Personality* 2 (1987): 145-152.

Croxton, J. S., and N. Morrow. "What Does It Take to Reduce Observer Bias?" *Psychological Reports* 55 (1984): 135-138.

Cuneo, T. D. "Combating the Noetic Effects of Sin: Pascal's Strategy for Natural Theology." *Faith and Philosophy* 11 (1994): 645-662.

Davis, M. H., and W. G. Stephan. "Attributions for Exam Performance." *Journal of Applied Social Psychology* 10 (1980): 235-248.

Davis, T. J. "Not 'Hidden and Far Off': The Bodily Aspect of Salvation and Its Implications for Understanding the Body in Calvin's Theology." *Calvin Theological Journal* 29 (1994): 406-418.

De Boer, J. "Reformed Epistemology: Three Replies." *The Reformed Journal* 32 (January 1982): 24-25.

DeKlerk, P. "Calvin Bibliography 1972." *Calvin Theological Journal* 8 (1973): 221-250, and successive years through 1998.

Demarest, B. A. *General Revelation*. Grand Rapids: Zondervan, 1982.

Denniston, J. J., III. "An Examination of Calvin's Theory of Knowledge in His Theology and Exegesis." Ph.D. diss., Fordham University, 1991.

DeWolf, L. H. "Theological Rejection of Natural Theology: An Evaluation." *Journal of Religious Thought* 15 (1958): 91-106.

Dobson, K., and R. Franche. "A Conceptual and Empirical Review of the Depressive Realism Hypothesis." *Canadian Journal of Behavioural Science* 21 (1989): 419-433.

Doss, M. D. "Humility in Theology: The Way of the Cappodocian Fathers." *Epiphany* 7 (1987): 57-62.

Dowey, E. A., Jr. *The Knowledge of God in Calvin's Theology*. New York: Columbia University Press, 1952.

___. "Survey—Continental Reformation: Works of General Interest. Studies in Calvin since 1948." *Church History* 24 (1955): 360-367.

___. "Survey—Continental Reformation: Works of General Interest. Studies in Calvin since 1955." *Church History* 29 (1960): 187-204.

Dufour, A. "Bibliographie calvinienne en 1959." *Bibliothèque d'Humanisme et Renaissance* 21 (1959): 619-642.

Dulles, A. "Pannenberg on Revelation and Faith." In C. E. Braaten and P. Clayton (eds.), *The Theology of Wolfhart Pannenberg*. Minneapolis: Augsburg Publishing House, 1988, 169-187.

Dunning, D., D. W. Griffin, J. D. Milojkovic, and L. Ross. "The Overconfidence Effect in Social Prediction." *Journal of Personality and Social Psychology*, 58 (1990): 568-581.

Dunning, D., J. A. Meyerowitz, and A. D. Holzberg. "Ambiguity and Self-Evaluation." *Journal of Personality and Social Psychology* 57 (1989): 1082-1090.

Dunning, D., and A. L. Story. "Depression, Realism, and the Overconfidence Effect: Are the Sadder Wiser When Predicting Future Actions and Events?" *Journal of Personality and Social Psychology* 61 (1991): 521-532.

Edwards, J. "Man's Natural Blindness in the Things of Religion." In *The Works of President Edwards*. Vol. VII. New York: S. Converse, 1829, 3-30.

Engel, M. P. *John Calvin's Perspectival Anthropology*. Atlanta: Scholars Press, 1985.

Erichson, A. *Bibliographia Calviniana*. Nieuwkoop: B. De Graaf, 1955. (Originally published in Berlin in 1900.)

Evans, C. A. "Jesus' Ethic of Humility." *Trinity Journal* 13 (1992): 127-138.

Evans, C. S. *Preserving the Person*. Grand Rapids: Baker, 1977/1982.

Ferré, N. F. S. *Faith and Reason*. New York: Harper and Brothers, 1946.

Fiske, S. T., and S. E. Taylor. *Social Cognition*. Reading, MA: Addison-Wesley, 1984.

Fleck, J. R., and J. D. Carter (eds.). *Psychology and Christianity: Integrative Readings*. Nashville, TN: Abingdon, 1981.

Fletcher, G. J. O., and C. Ward. "Attribution Theory and Processes: A Cross-Cultural Perspective." In M. H. Bond (ed.), *The Cross-Cultural Challenge to Social Psychology*. Newbury Park, CA: Sage, 1988, 230-244.

Fowler, S. "Faith and Reason in the Period of the Reformation." In T. Van der Walt (ed.), *Our Reformational Tradition: A Rich Heritage and Lasting Vocation*. Potchefstroom: Institute for Reformational Studies, 1984, 61-85.

___. "Martin Luther: Faith Beyond Reason." In T. Van der Walt (ed.), *Our Reformational Tradition: A Rich Heritage and Lasting Vocation*. Potchefstroom: Institute for Reformational Studies, 1984, 98-112.

___. "The Persistent Dualism in Calvin's Thought." In T. Van der Walt (ed.), *Our Reformational Tradition: A Rich Heritage and Lasting Vocation*. Potchefstroom: Institute for Reformational Studies, 1984, 339-352.

Fraenkel, P. "Petit Supplément aux bibliographies calviniennes, 1901-1963." *Bibliothèque d'Humanisme et Renaissance* 33 (1971): 385-413.

Frame, J. M. *The Doctrine of the Knowledge of God*. Phillipsburg, NJ: Presbyterian and Reformed, 1987.

___. "Rationality and Scripture." In H. Hart (ed.) *Rationality in the Calvinian Tradition*. Lanham, MD: University Press of America, 293-318.

___. "Van Til and the Ligonier Apologetic." *Westminster Theological Journal* 47 (1985): 279-299.

Frey, D. "Reactions to Success and Failure in Public and Private Conditions." *Journal of Experimental Social Psychology* 14 (1978): 172-179.

Friedrich, J. "On Seeing Oneself as Less Self-Serving than Others: The Ultimate Self-Serving Bias?" *Teaching of Psychology* 23 (1996): 107-109.

Fuchs, E. "Theologie oder Ideologie?" *Theologische Literaturzeitung* LXXXVIII (1963): 257-260.

Fuller, D. P. "The Holy Spirit's Role in Biblical Interpretation." In W. W. Gasque and W. S. LaSor (eds.), *Scripture, Tradition, and Interpretation*. Grand Rapids: Eerdmans, 1978, 189-198.

Gamble, R. C. (ed). *Articles on Calvin and Calvinism*, 14 vols. New York: Garland Publishing, 1992.

Gerrish, B. *Grace and Reason*. New York: Oxford University Press, 1962.

Glick, P., D. Gottesman, and J. Jolton. "The Fault is Not in the Stars: Susceptibility of Skeptics and Believers in Astrology to the Barnum Effect." *Personality and Social Psychology Bulletin* 15 (1989): 572-583.

Goethals, G. R. "Fabricating and Ignoring Social Reality: Self-Serving Estimates of Consensus." In J. M. Olson, C. P. Herman, and M. P. Zanna (eds.), *Relative Deprivation and Social Comparison: The Ontario Symposium*, vol. 4. Hillsdale, NJ: Erlbaum, 1986, 135-157.

Goethals, G., D. Messick, and S. Allison. "The Uniqueness Bias: Studies of Constructive Social Comparison." In J. Suls and T. A. Wills (eds.), *Social Comparison: Contemporary Theory and Research*. Hillsdale, NJ: Erlbaum, 1991, 149-176.

Granberg, D., and S. Holmberg. *The Political System Matters: Social Psychology and Voting Behavior in Sweden and the United States.* Cambridge: Cambridge University Press, 1988.

Gray, J. D., and R. C. Silver. "Opposite Sides of the Same Coin: Former Spouses' Divergent Perspectives in Coping with Their Divorce." *Journal of Personality and Social Psychology* 59 (1990): 1180-1191.

Greenberg, J., T. Pyszczynski, and S. Solomon. "The Causes and Consequences of a Need for Self-Esteem: A Terror Management Theory." In R. F. Baumeister (ed.). *Public Self and Private Life.* New York: Springer-Verlag, 1986, 189-212.

Greenberg, J., T. Pyszczynski, and S. Solomon. "The Self-Serving Attributional Bias: Beyond Self-Presentation," *Journal of Experimental Social Psychology* 18 (1982): 56-67.

Greene, B. "Women, Men, and Corporate Sin." *Daughters of Sarah* 4, no. 3 (May 1978): 5-6; and 4, no. 4 (July 1978): 5-7.

Greenwald, A. G., and S. J. Breckler. "To Whom Is the Self Presented?" In B. Schlenker (ed.). *The Self and Social Life.* New York: McGraw-Hill, 1985, 126-145.

Grenz, S. J. "The Appraisal of Pannenberg: A Survey of the Literature." In C. E. Braaten and P. Clayton (eds.), *The Theology of Wolfhart Pannenberg.* Minneapolis: Augsburg Publishing House, 1988, 19-52.

___. *Reason for Hope.* New York: Oxford University Press, 1990.

Habermas, J. *Knowledge and Human Interests.* Boston: Beacon Press, 1971.

Hart, H., ed. *Rationality in the Calvinian Tradition.* Lanham, MD: University Press of America, 1983.

Headey, B., and A. Wearing. "The Sense of Relative Superiority—Central to Well-Being." *Social Indicators Research* 20 (1988): 497-516.

Heideman, E. P. *The Relation of Revelation and Reason in E. Brunner and H. Bavinck.* Assen, Netherlands: Van Gorcum, 1959.

Helm, P. "John Calvin the *Sensus Divinitatis*, and the Noetic Effects of Sin." *International Journal for Philosophy of Religion* 43 (1998): 87-107.

Herzog, F. *Understanding God.* New York: Scribner's, 1966.

Hinkle, S., and J. Schopler. "Bias in the Evaluation of In-Group and Out-Group Performance." In S. Worchel and W. G. Austin (eds.), *Psychology of Intergroup Relations*, 2nd edition. Chicago: Nelson-Hall, 1986, 196-212.

Hodges, B. "Perception, Relativity, and Knowing and Doing the Truth." In S. L. Jones (ed.), *Psychology and the Christian Faith*. Grand Rapids: Baker, 1986, 51-77.

Hoffecker, W. A. "Augustine, Aquinas, and the Reformers." In W. A. Hoffecker (ed.), *Building a Christian World View*. Vol. 1. Phillipsburg, NJ: Presbyterian and Reformed, 1986, 235-258.

Hoitenga, D. J., Jr. *Faith and Reason from Plato to Plantinga: An Introduction to Reformed Epistemology*. Albany: State University of New York Press, 1991.

___. "Faith and Reason in Calvin's Doctrine of the Knowledge of God." In H. Hart (ed.) *Rationality in the Calvinian Tradition*. Lanham, MD: University Press of America, 1983, 17-39.

___. "A Futile Search for Sin?" *Perspectives* 8 (March 1993): 8-9.

___. *John Calvin and the Will: A Critique and Corrective*. Grand Rapids: Baker, 1997.

Holmes, A. *All Truth Is God's Truth*. Grand Rapids: Eerdmans, 1977.

___. *Contours of a World View*. Grand Rapids: Eerdmans, 1983.

Holwerda, D. "Faith, Reason, and the Resurrection." In A. Plantinga and N. Wolterstorff (eds.), *Faith and Rationality*. Notre Dame: University of Notre Dame Press, 1983, 265-316.

Hunt, D., and T. McMahon. *The Seduction of Christianity*. Eugene, OR: Harvest House, 1985.

Jeffreys, D. S. "How Reformed Is Reformed Epistemology? Alvin Plantinga and Calvin's 'Sensus Divinitatis.'" *Religious Studies* 33 (1997): 419-431.

Johnson, J. T., J. B. Jemmot III, and T. F. Pettigrew. "Causal Attribution and Dispositional Inference: Evidence of Inconsistent Judgments." *Journal of Experimental Social Psychology* 20 (1984): 567-585.

Jones, E. E., and V. A. Harris. "The Attribution of Attitudes." *Journal of Experimental Social Psychology* 3 (1967): 1-24.

Jones, J. M. "The Problem of Faith and Reason in the Thought of John Calvin." Ph.D. diss., Duke University, 1942.

Jones, S. L., and R. E. Butman. *Modern Psychotherapies: A Comprehensive Christian Appraisal*. Downers Grove, IL: InterVarsity, 1991.

Kashima, Y., and H. C. Triandis. "The Self-Serving Bias in Attributions as a Coping Strategy: A Cross-Cultural Study." *Journal of Cross-Cultural Psychology* 17 (1986): 83-97.

Kauffmann, D. "Belief and Behavior: Social Psychology and Christian Living." *Journal of Psychology and Christianity* 15 (1996): 46-57.

Kempff, D. *A Bibliography of Calviniana, 1959-1974*. Leiden: E. J. Brill, 1975.

Kierkegaard, S. *Attack upon "Christendom."* Princeton, NJ: Princeton University Press, 1855/1968.

Kim, Y. I. "Luther and Calvin on Human Reason." S.T.M. thesis, Concordia Seminary (St. Louis), 1971.

Klapwijk, J. "Rationality in the Dutch Neo-Calvinist Tradition." In H. Hart (ed.), *Rationality in the Calvinian Tradition*. Lanham, MD: University Press of America, 1983, 93-111.

Klein, W., and Z. Kunda. "Maintaining Self-Serving Social Comparisons: Biased Reconstruction of One's Past Behaviors." *Personality and Social Psychology Bulletin* 19 (1993): 732-739.

Klooster, F. H. "Aspects of Historical Method in Pannenberg's Theology." In J. T. Bakker et al. (eds.), *Septuagesimo Anno*. Kampen: Kok, 1973, 112-127.

Krueger, J., and R. Clement. "The Truly False Consensus Effect: An Ineradicable and Egocentric Bias in Social Perception." *Journal of Personality and Social Psychology* 67 (1994): 596-610.

Kuiper, N. A., L. J. Olinger, M. R. MacDonald, and B. F. Shaw. "Self-Schema Processing of Depressed and Nondepressed Content: The Effects of Vulnerability to Depression." *Social Cognition* 3 (1985): 77-93.

Kuhn, T. *The Structure of Scientific Revolutions*. Chicago: University of Chicago Press, 1962.

Kunda, Z. "The Case for Motivated Reasoning." *Psychological Bulletin* 108 (1990): 480-493.

Kunst, T. J. W. "The Implications of Pauline Theology of the Mind for the Work of the Theologian." Th.D. diss., Dallas Theological Seminary, 1979.

Kuyper, A. *Lectures on Calvinism*. Grand Rapids: Eerdmans, 1931. (Originally delivered as the Stone Lectures at Princeton University in 1898.)

___. *Principles of Sacred Theology*. Translated by J. H. De Vries. Grand Rapids: Eerdmans, 1954. (Originally published in Dutch in 1894.)

Lane, A. N. S. "Calvin's Doctrine of Assurance." *Vox Evangelica* 11 (1979): 32-54.

Lang, A. "Recent German Books on Calvin." *Evangelical Quarterly* 6 (1934): 64-81.

Leith, J. H. "Calvin's Theological Method and the Ambiguity of His Theology." In F. H. Littell (ed.), *Reformation Studies: Essays in Honor of Roland H. Bainton*. Richmond: John Knox, 1962, 106-116.

Leithart, P. J. "Stoic Elements in Calvin's Doctrine of the Christian Life." *Westminster Theological Journal* 55 (1993): 31-54.

Lobstein, P. "La connaissance religieuse d'après Calvin." *Revue de Théologie et de Philosophie* 42 (1909): 53-110.

Luginbuhl, J. E. R., D. H. Crowe, and J. P. Kahan. "Causal Attributions for Success and Failure." *Journal of Personality and Social Psychology* 31 (1975): 86-93.

Luhtanen, R., and J. Crocker. "Self-Esteem and Intergroup Comparisons: Toward a Theory of Collective Self-Esteem." In J. Suls and T. Wills (eds.), *Social Comparison: Contemporary Theory and Research*. Hillsdale, NJ: Erlbaum, 1991, 211-234.

Luther, M. *Luther's Works.* American edition. Volumes 1-30, edited by J. Pelikan. St. Louis: Concordia Publishing House, 1956 ff. Volumes 31-55 edited by H. T. Lehmann. Philadelphia: Muhlenberg Press, 1956 ff. (*LW*)

___. *Martin Luthers Werke: Kritische Gesamtausgabe.* Weimar: H. Böhlaus Nachfolger, 1883 ff. (*WA*)

MacArthur, J. *Our Sufficiency in Christ.* Dallas, TX: Word, 1991.

MacIntyre, A. *Whose Justice? Which Rationality?* Notre Dame: University of Notre Dame Press, 1988.

Marks, G. "Thinking One's Abilities Are Unique and One's Opinions Are Common." *Personality and Social Psychology Bulletin* 10 (1984): 203-208.

Marsden, G. "The Collapse of American Evangelical Academia." In A. Plantinga and N. Wolterstorff (eds.), *Faith and Rationality*. Notre Dame: University of Notre Dame Press, 1983, 219-264.

Matheson, P., ed. *The Third Reich and the Christian Churches.* Grand Rapids: Eerdmans, 1981.

Mavrodes, G. I. "A Futile Search for Sin." *Perspectives* 8 (January 1993): 9.

McLeod, M. S. *Rationality and Theistic Belief: An Essay on Reformed Epistemology.* Ithaca, NY: Cornell University Press, 1993.

McNeill, J. T. "Thirty Years of Calvin Study." *Church History* 17 (1948): 207-240; and "Addendum." *Church History* 18 (1949): 241.

___., ed. *Institutes of the Christian Religion.* Philadelphia: Westminster Press, 1960.

Menninger, K. *Whatever Became of Sin?* New York: Hawthorne Books, 1973.

Miles, M. "Theology, Anthropology, and the Human Body in Calvin's *Institutes*." *Harvard Theological Review* 74 (1981): 303-323.

Miller, J. G. "Cultural Influences on the Development of Conceptual Differentiation in Person Description." *British Journal of Developmental Psychology* 5 (1987): 309-319.

Miller, P. D. *Sin and Judgment in the Prophets.* Chico, CA: Scholars Press, 1982.

Mirels, H. L. "The Avowal of Responsibility for Good and Bad Outcomes: The Effects of Generalized Self-Serving Biases." *Personality and Social Psychology Bulletin* 6 (1980): 299-306.

Monheit, M. L. "Passion and Order in the Formation of Calvin's Sense of Religious Authority." Ph.D. diss., Princeton University, 1988.

Montgomery, R. L. "Bias in Interpreting Social Facts: Is It a Sin?" *Journal for the Scientific Study of Religion* 23 (1984): 278-291.

Morris, L. *The Gospel According to John.* Grand Rapids: Eerdmans, 1971.

Mott, S. C. "Biblical Faith and the Reality of Social Evil." *Christian Scholar's Review* 9 (1980): 225-240.

Mouw, R. J. "Humility, Hope, and the Divine Slowness." *The Christian Century* 107 (April 11, 1990): 364-368.

Mullen, B., and C. Riordan. "Self-Serving Attributions for Performance in Naturalistic Setting: A Meta-Analytic Review." *Journal of Applied Social Psychology* 18 (1988): 3-22.

Muller, R. A. "*Fides* and *Cognitio* in Relation to the Problem of Intellect and Will in Calvin." *Calvin Theological Journal* 25 (1990): 207-224.

Myers, D.G. *The Inflated Self.* New York: The Seabury Press, 1980.

___. *The Pursuit of Happiness.* New York: William Morrow, 1992.

___. *Social Psychology*, fifth edition. New York: McGraw-Hill. 1996.

___. "Social Psychology." In S. L. Jones (ed.), *Psychology and the Christian Faith.* Grand Rapids: Baker, 1986, 217-239.

___. "Yin and Yang in Psychological Research and Christian Belief." *Perspectives on Science and Christian Faith* 39 (1987): 128-139.

Myers, D. G., and M. A. Jeeves. *Psychology through the Eyes of Faith.* San Francisco: Harper and Row, 1987.

Myers, D. G., and J. Ridl. "Can we all be Better Than Average?" *Psychology Today* (August 1979): 89-98.

Nauta, R. "Task Performance and Attributional Biases in the Ministry." *Journal for the Scientific Study of Religion* 27 (1988): 609-620.

Newbigin, L. *The Finality of Christ.* London: SCM, 1969.

___. *The Open Secret.* Grand Rapids: Eerdmans, 1978.

Newman, L. S. "How Individualists Interpret Behavior: Idiocentrism and Spontaneous Trait Inference." *Social Cognition* 11 (1993): 243-269.

Niebuhr, H. R. *Christ and Culture.* New York: Harper and Row, 1951.

Niesel, W. *Calvin-Bibliographie, 1901-1959.* München: Kaiser, 1961.

Nixon, Leroy. *John Calvin's Teachings on Human Reason.* New York: Exposition Press, 1963.

___. "John Calvin's Teachings on Human Reason and Their Implications for Theory of Reformed Protestant Christian Education: A Problem in Philosophy of Religion Studied for Its Possible Implications for Theory of Religious Education." Ph.D. diss., School of Education of New York University, 1960.

Pannenberg, W. *Anthropologie in Theologischer Perspektive.* Göttingen: Vandenhoeck & Ruprecht, 1983.

___. *Anthropology in Theological Perspective.* Translated by M. J. O'Connell. Philadelphia: Westminster, 1985.

___. "An Autobiographical Sketch." In C. E. Braaten and P. Clayton (eds.), *The Theology of Wolfhart Pannenberg.* Minneapolis: Augsburg Publishing House, 1988, 11-18.

___. "Dogmatic Theses on the Doctrine of Revelation." In W. Pannenberg et al., *Revelation as History.* Translated by D. Granskou. New York: Macmillan, 1968, 123-158.

___. "Dogmatische Thesen zur Lehre von der Offenbarung." In W. Pannenberg et al., *Offenbarung als Geschichte.* Göttingen: Vandenhoeck & Ruprecht, 1961, 91-114.

___. "Einführung." In W. Pannenberg et al., *Offenbarung als Geschichte*. Göttingen: Vandenhoeck & Ruprecht, 1961, 7-20.

___. "Einsicht und Glaube." In *Grundfragen systematischer Theologie*, Dritte Auflage. Göttingen: Vandenhoeck & Ruprecht, 1967/1979, 223-236.

___. "Faith and Reason." In *Basic Questions in Theology*. Vol. II. Translated by G. H. Kehm. Philadelphia: Fortress Press, 1971, 46-64.

___. "Glaube und Vernunft." In *Grundfragen systematischer Theologie*, Dritte Auflage. Göttingen: Vandenhoeck & Ruprecht, 1967/1979, 237-251.

___. "God's Presence in History." *The Christian Century* 98 (March 11, 1981): 260-263.

___. *Grundzüge der Christologie*. Gütersloh: Gütersloher Verlagshaus Gerd Mohn, 1964.

___. "How Is God Revealed to Us?" In *Faith and Reality*. Translated by J. Maxwell. Philadelphia: Westminster, 1977, 50-67.

___. "Insight and Faith." In *Basic Questions in Theology*. Vol. II. Translated by G. H. Kehm. Philadelphia: Fortress Press, 1971, 28-45.

___. "Introduction." In W. Pannenberg et al., *Revelation as History*. Translated by D. Granskou. New York: Macmillan, 1968, 1-21.

___. *Jesus—God and Man*, second edition. Translated by L. L. Wilkins and D. A. Priebe. Philadelphia: Westminster, 1977.

___. "Response to the Discussion." In J. M. Robinson and J. B. Cobb Jr. (eds.), *Theology as History*. New York: Harper and Row, 1967, 221-276.

___. *Systematic Theology*. Vol. 1. Translated by G. W. Bromiley. Grand Rapids: Eerdmans, 1991.

___. *Systematic Theology*. Vol. 2. Translated by G. W. Bromiley. Grand Rapids: Eerdmans, 1994.

___. *Systematische Theologie*, band 1. Göttingen: Vandenhoeck & Ruprecht, 1988.

___. *Systematische Theologie*, band 2. Göttingen: Vandenhoeck & Ruprecht, 1991.

___. *Was ist der Mensch?* Göttingen: Vandenhoeck & Ruprecht, 1962.

___. "Was ist Wahrheit?" In *Grundfragen systematischer Theologie*, Dritte Auflage. Göttingen: Vandenhoeck & Ruprecht, 1967/1979, 202-222.

___. *What Is Man?* Translated by D. A. Priebe. Philadelphia: Fortress Press, 1970.

___. "What Is Truth?" In *Basic Questions in Theology*. Vol. II. Translated by G. H. Kehm. Philadelphia: Fortress Press, 1971, 1-27.

___. "Wie wird Gott uns offenbar?" In *Glaube und Wirklichkeit*. München: Chr. Kaiser Verlag, 1975, 71-91.

Parker, T. H. L. "A Bibliography and Survey of the British Study of Calvin, 1900-1940." *Evangelical Quarterly* 18 (1946): 123-131.

___. *Calvin's Doctrine of the Knowledge of God*, second edition. Edinburgh: Oliver and Boyd, 1969. (Originally published by Oliver and Boyd in 1952.)

Partee, C. "Calvin, Calvinism, and Rationality." In H. Hart (ed.), *Rationality in the Calvinian Tradition.* Lanham, MD: University Press of America, 1983, 1-15.

___. "The Soul in Plato, Platonism, and Calvin." *Scottish Journal of Theology* 22 (1969): 278-296.

Pazmiño, R. *By What Authority Do We Teach?* Grand Rapids: Baker, 1994.

___. *Principles and Practices of Christian Education.* Grand Rapids: Baker, 1992.

Pearson, J. C. "Positive Distortion: 'The Most Beautiful Woman in the World.'" In K. M. Galvin and P. Cooper (eds.), *Making Connections.* Los Angeles: Roxbury, 1996, 175-181.

Perloff, L. S., and B. K. Fetzer. "Self-Other Judgments and Perceived Vulnerability to Victimization." *Journal of Personality and Social Psychology* 50 (1986): 502-510.

Peters, T. *Sin: Radical Evil in Soul and Society.* Grand Rapids: Eerdmans, 1994.

Placher, W. C. "Revealed to Reason: Theology as 'Normal Science.'" *The Christian Century* 109 (February 19, 1992): 192-195.

___. "Review of *Anthropology in Theological Perspective* by Wolfhart Pannenberg." *Encounter* 47 (1986): 172-173.

Plantinga, A. "Is Belief in God Properly Basic?" In R. D. Geivett and B. Sweetman (eds.), *Contemporary Perspectives on Religious Epistemology.* New York: Oxford University Press, 1992, 133-141.

___. "Justification and Theism." *Faith and Philosophy* 4 (October 1987): 403-426.

___. "On Reformed Epistemology." *The Reformed Journal* 32 (January 1982): 13-17.

___. *Warrant and Proper Function.* New York: Oxford University Press, 1993.

___. *Warrant: The Current Debate.* New York: Oxford University Press, 1993.

Plantinga, A., and N. Wolterstorff, eds., *Faith and Rationality.* Notre Dame: University of Notre Dame Press, 1983.

Plantinga, C., Jr. *Not the Way It's Supposed To Be: A Breviary of Sin.* Grand Rapids: Eerdmans, 1995.

___. "Not the Way It's S'pposed to Be: A Breviary of Sin." *Theology Today* 50 (July 1993): 179-192.

Polanyi, M. *Personal Knowledge.* Chicago: University of Chicago Press, 1958.

Poling, J. N. *Deliver Us from Evil.* Minneapolis: Augsburg Fortress, 1996.

Prins, R. "The Image of God in Adam and the Restoration of Man in Jesus Christ: A Study in Calvin." *Scottish Journal of Theology* 25 (1972): 32-44.

Pyszczynski, T., J. Greenberg, and K. Holt. "Maintaining Consistency between Self-Serving Beliefs and Available Data: A Bias in Information Evaluation." *Personality and Social Psychology Bulletin* 11 (1985): 179-190.

Ratzsch, D. "Abraham Kuyper's Philosophy of Science." *Calvin Theological Journal* 27 (1992): 277-303.

Reeder, G. D., G. J. O. Fletcher, and K. Furman. "The Role of Observers' Expectations in Attitude Attribution." *Journal of Experimental Social Psychology*, 25 (1989): 168-188.

Robertson, L. S. "Car Crashes: Perceived Vulnerability and Willingness to Pay for Crash Protection." *Journal of Community Health* 3 (1977): 136-141.

Rosenblatt, R. "The 11th Commandment." *Family Circle* (December 21, 1993): 30-32, 45.

Ross, J. R. "Historical Knowledge as Basis for Faith." *Zygon* 13 (September 1978): 209-224.

Rowe, K. E. *Calvin Bibliography*. Madison, NJ: Drew University, 1967.

Rueckert, H. "Calvin-Literatur seit 1945." *Archiv für Reformationsgeschichte* 50 (1959): 64-74.

Rushdoony, R. J. "The Quest for Common Ground." In G. North (ed.), *Foundations of Christian Scholarship: Essays in the Van Til Perspective*. Vallecito, CA: Ross House Books, 1976, 27-38.

Salovey, P. "Social Comparison Processes in Envy and Jealousy." In J. Suls and T. A. Wills (eds.), *Social Comparison Research: Contemporary Theory and Research*. Hillsdale, NJ: Erlbaum, 1991, 261-285.

Sappington, A. A. "Psychology for the Practice of the Presence of God: Putting Psychology at the Service of the Church." *Journal of Psychology and Christianity* 13 (1994): 5-16.

Scaer, D. P. "Theology of Hope." In S. Gundry and A. F. Johnson (eds.), *Tensions in Contemporary Theology*. Chicago: Moody Press, 1976, 197-234.

Schaff, P., ed. *Nicene and Post-Nicene Fathers*. Series 1. Grand Rapids: Eerdmans, 1956.

Schlenker, B. R. "Group Members' Attributions of Responsibility for Prior Group Performance." *Representative Research in Social Psychology* 6 (1975): 96-108.

Schlenker, B. R., J. R. Hallam, and N. E. McCown. "Motives and Social Evaluation: Actor-Observer Differences in the Delineation of Motives for a Beneficial Act." *Journal of Experimental Social Psychology* 19 (1983): 254-273.

Schlenker, B. R., and R. S. Miller. "Egocentrism in Groups: Self-Serving Biases or Logical Information Processing?" *Journal of Personality and Social Psychology* 35 (1977): 755-764.

Schmidt, E. "In Candid Conversation: Theology and Sociology of Knowledge." In B. Hargrove (ed.), *Religion and the Sociology of Knowledge*. New York: Edwin Mellen Press, 1984, 15-32.

Schnackenburg, R. *The Gospel According to John*. Vol. 1. New York: Herder and Herder, 1968.

Schreiner, S. "The Theater of His Glory: Nature and the Natural Order in the Thought of John Calvin." Ph.D. diss., Duke University, 1983.

Shedler, J., M. Mayman, and M. Manis. "The *Illusion* of Mental Health." *American Psychologist* 48 (November 1993): 1117-1131.

___. "More Illusions." *American Psychologist* 49 (1994): 974-976.

Shepherd, V. A. *The Nature and Function of Faith in the Theology of John Calvin.* Macon, GA: Mercer University Press, 1983.

Simon, C. J. "How Opaque Is Sin?" *Perspectives* 8 (February 1993): 8.

Snyder, M. L., W. G. Stephan, and D. Rosenfield. "Attributional Egotism." In J. H. Harvey, W. J. Ickes, and R. F. Kidd (eds.), *New Directions in Attribution Research.* Vol. 2. Hillsdale, NJ: Erlbaum, 1978, 91-117.

Sobrino, J. "500 Years: Structural Sin and Structural Grace." *SEDOS Bulletin* 24 (May 15, 1992): 151-156.

Sorrentino, R. M., and E. T. Higgins. "Motivation and Cognition: Warming Up to the Synergism." In R. M. Sorrentino and E. T. Higgins (eds.), *Handbook of Motivation and Cognition.* New York: The Guilford Press, 1986, 3-19.

Stall, S. W. "Sociology of Knowledge, Relativism, and Theology." In B. Hargrove (ed.), *Religion and the Sociology of Knowledge.* New York: The Edwin Mellen Press, 1984, 61-78.

Steinmetz, D. C. "Calvin and the Natural Knowledge of God." In H. A. Oberman and F. A. James III (eds.), *Via Augustini.* Leiden: E. J. Brill, 1991, 142-156.

___. "The Theology of Calvin and Calvinism." In S. Ozment (ed.), *Reformation Europe: A Guide to Research.* St. Louis: Center for Reformation Research, 1982, 211-232.

Stinson, C. H. "Reason and Sin According to Calvin and Aquinas." Master of arts thesis, The Catholic University of America, 1966.

Stuermann, W. E. *A Critical Study of John Calvin's Concept of Faith.* Tulsa: University of Tulsa Press, 1952.

Sudduth, M. C. "Calvin, Plantinga, and the Natural Knowledge of God: A Response to Beversluis." *Faith and Philosophy* 15 (1998): 92-103.

Svenson, O. "Are We All Less Risky and More Skillful than Our Fellow Drivers?" *Acta Psychologica* 47 (1981): 143-148.

Swartley, W. M. *Slavery, Sabbath, War, and Women.* Scottdale, PA: Herald Press, 1983.

Tajfel, H., and J. C. Turner. "The Social Identity Theory of Intergroup Behavior." In S. Worchel and W. G. Austin (eds.), *Psychology of Intergroup Relations*, 2nd edition. Chicago: Nelson-Hall, 1986, 7-24.

Talbot, M. "Is It Natural to Believe in God?" *Faith and Philosophy* 6 (1989): 155-171.

Taylor, S. E. *Positive Illusions: Creative Self-Deception and the Healthy Mind.* New York: Basic Books, 1989.

Taylor, S. E., and J. D. Brown. "Illusion and Well-Being: A Social Psychological Perspective on Mental Health." *Psychological Bulletin* 103 (1988): 193-210.

___. "'Illusion' of Mental Health Does Not Explain Positive Illusions." *American Psychologist* 49 (1994): 972-973.

___. "Positive Illusions and Well-Being Revisited: Separating Fact from Fiction." *Psychological Bulletin* 116 (1994): 21-27.

Tetlock, P. E., and A. Levi. "Attributional Bias: On the Inconclusiveness of the Cognition-Motivation Debate," *Journal of Experimental Social Psychology* 18 (1982): 68-88.

Thomas, G. F. "Theology and Philosophy: A Mediating View." In E. D. Myers (ed.), *Christianity and Reason*. New York: Oxford University Press, 1951, 36-56.

Torrance, T. F. *Calvin's Doctrine of Man*. Westport, CT: Greenwood Press, 1977. (Originally published by Eerdmans in 1957.)

___. "Knowledge of God and Speech about Him, According to John Calvin." *Revue d'Histoire et de Philosophie Religieuses* 44 (1964): 402-422.

Trinkaus, C. E. "Renaissance Problems in Calvin's Theology." *Studies in the Renaissance* 1 (1954): 59-80.

Tylenda, J. N. "Calvin Bibliography, 1960-1970." *Calvin Theological Journal* 6 (1971): 156-193.

Vallone, R., D. Griffin, S. Lin, and L. Ross. "Overconfident Prediction of Future Actions and Outcomes by Self and Others." *Journal of Personality and Social Psychology* 58 (1990): 582-592.

Van Hook, J. "Knowledge, Belief, and Reformed Epistemology." *The Reformed Journal* 31 (July 1981): 12-17.

Van Til, C. "Antitheses in Education." In L. Berkhof and C. Van Til, *Foundations of Christian Education*. Phillipsburg, NJ: Presbyterian and Reformed, 1990, 3-24.

Vidal, M. "Structural Sin: A New Category in Moral Theology?" In R. Gallagher and B. McConvery (eds.), *History and Conscience*. Dublin: Gill and MacMillan, 1989, 181-198.

Vogelsanger, P. "Neuere Calvin-Literatur." *Reformatio* 8 (1959): 362-366.

Walsh, B. J. "A Critical Review of *Anthropology in Theological Perspective*." *Christian Scholar's Review* 15 (1986): 247-259.

Walty, J. N. "Calvin et le calvinisme." *Revue des Sciences Philosophiques et Théologiques* 49 (1965): 245-287.

Weary, G., J. H. Harvey, P. Schwieger, C. T. Olson, R. Perloff, and S. Pritchard. "Self-Presentation and the Moderation of Self-Serving Attributional Biases." *Social Cognition*, 1 (1982): 140-159.

Weber, H. J. "The Formal Dialectical Rationalism of Calvin." *Papers of the American Church History Society* series 2, vol. 8 (1928): 19-41.

Weinstein, N. D. "Unrealistic Optimism about Future Life Events." *Journal of Personality and Social Psychology* 39 (1980): 806-820.

___. "Unrealistic Optimism about Susceptibility to Health Problems." *Journal of Behavioral Medicine* 5 (1982): 441-460.

Weinstein, N. D., and E. Lachendro. "Egocentrism as a Source of Unrealistic Optimism." *Personality and Social Psychology Bulletin* 8 (1982): 195-200.

Westphal, M. "Hegel, Pannenberg, and Hermeneutics." *Man and World* 4 (1971): 276-293.

___. "A Reader's Guide to 'Reformed Epistemology.'" *Perspectives* 7, no. 9 (1992): 10-13.

___. *Suspicion and Faith: The Religious Uses of Modern Atheism*. Grand Rapids: Eerdmans, 1993.

___. "Taking St. Paul Seriously: Sin as an Epistemological Category." In T. P. Flint (ed.), *Christian Philosophy*. Notre Dame: University of Notre Dame Press, 1990, 200-226.

White, R. "Fifteen Years of Calvin Studies in French (1965-1980)." *Journal of Religious History* 12 (1982): 140-161.

Whitley, B., and I. Frieze. "Children's Causal Attributions for Success and Failure in Achievement Settings: A Meta-Analysis." *Journal of Educational Psychology* 77 (1985): 608-616.

___. "Measuring Causal Attributions for Success and Failure: A Meta-Analysis of the Effects of Question-Wording Style." *Basic and Applied Social Psychology* 7 (1986): 35-51.

Willie, C. V. "Getting a Handle on Institutional Sin." *The Witness* 64 (March 1981): 17-18.

Wills, T. A. "Downward Comparison Principles in Social Psychology." *Psychological Bulletin* 90 (1981): 245-271.

___. "Similarity and Self-Esteem in Downward Comparison." In J. Suls and T. Wills (eds.), *Social Comparison: Contemporary Theory and Research*. Hillsdale, NJ: Erlbaum, 1991, 51-78.

Wolters, A. "Dutch Neo-Calvinism: Worldview, Philosophy and Rationality." In H. Hart (ed.), *Rationality in the Calvinian Tradition*. Lanham, MD: University Press of America, 1983, 113-131.

Wolterstorff, N. "The Assurance of Faith." *Faith and Philosophy* 7 (October 1990): 396-417.

___. "Can Belief in God Be Rational if It Has No Foundations?" In A. Plantinga and N. Wolterstorff (eds.), *Faith and Rationality*. Notre Dame: University of Notre Dame Press, 1983, 135-186.

___. "Evidence, Entitled Belief, and the Gospels." *Faith and Philosophy* 6 (1989): 429-459.

___. "Introduction." In H. Hart (ed.), *Rationality in the Calvinian Tradition*. Lanham, MD: University Press of America, 1983, v-vii.

___. "Introduction." In A. Plantinga and N. Wolterstorff (eds.), *Faith and Rationality*. Notre Dame: University of Notre Dame Press, 1983, 1-15.

___. "Locke's Philosophy of Religion." In V. Chappell (ed.), *The Cambridge Companion to Locke*. New York: Cambridge University Press, 1994, 172-194.

___. "The Migration of the Theistic Arguments: From Natural Theology to Evidentialist Apologetics." In R. Audi and W. J. Wainwright (eds.), *Rationality, Religious Belief, and Moral Commitment*. Ithaca, NY: Cornell University Press, 1986, 38-81.

___. "On Christian Learning." In P. A. Marshall, S. Griffioen, and R. J. Mouw (eds.), *Stained Glass: Worldviews and Social Sciences*. Lanham, MD: University Press of America, 1989, 56-80.

___. "Thomas Reid on Rationality." In H. Hart (ed.), *Rationality in the Calvinian Tradition*. Lanham, MD: University Press of America, 1983, 43-69.

___. "What Reformed Epistemology Is Not." *Perspectives* 7, no. 9 (1992): 14-16.

Wood, J. V., and K. L. Taylor. "Serving Self-Relevant Goals through Social Comparison." In J. Suls and T. Wills (eds.), *Social Comparison: Contemporary Theory and Research*. Hillsdale, NJ: Erlbaum, 1991, 23-49.

Zebrowitz-McArthur, L. "Person Perception in Cross-Cultural Perspective." In M. H. Bond (ed.). *The Cross-Cultural Challenge to Social Psychology*. Newbury Park, CA: Sage, 1988, 245-263.

Zemek, G. J. "Aiming the Mind: A Key to Godly Living." *Grace Theological Journal* 5 (1984): 205-227.

Zucker, G. S., and B. Weiner. "Conservatism and Perceptions of Poverty: An Attributional Analysis," *Journal of Applied Social Psychology* 23 (1993): 925-942.

Index

About the Author

Stephen K. Moroney graduated magna cum laude with his bachelor's degree in psychology from Duke University. His first master's degree is in clinical psychology from Wheaton College Graduate School, where he was a President's Scholar. His second master's is in New Testament and theology from Gordon-Conwell Theological Seminary, where he was a Byington Fellow. Dr. Moroney served as a graduate research and teaching assistant while earning his Ph.D. in theology and ethics from Duke University.

Dr. Moroney is associate professor of theology at Malone College, where he has been recognized with the college-wide distinguished faculty award for teaching. He lives in Canton, Ohio, with his wife, Sue, and two daughters, Grace and Joy.